Writing Baseball
THE SOUTHERN ILLINOIS UNIVERSITY PRESS SERIES

THE
BEST
SEAT IN
BASEBALL,
BUT
YOU HAVE TO
STAND!

The Best Seat in
BASEBALL,
But You Have to
STAND!

The Game as
Umpires See It

Lee Gutkind

With a Foreword by Eric Rolfe Greenberg

Southern Illinois University Press
Carbondale and Edwardsville

Preface copyright © 1999 by Lee Gutkind
First published 1975 by The Dial Press. Copyright © 1975 Lee Gutkind
Foreword copyright ©1999 by the Board of Trustees, Southern Illinois University
Printed in the United States of America
02 01 00 99   4 3 2 1

Library of Congress Cataloging-in-Publication Data

Gutkind, Lee.
The best seat in baseball, but you have to stand! : the game as umpires see it / Lee
Gutkind ; foreword by Eric Rolfe Greenberg.
p. cm. — (Writing baseball)
Originally published: New York : Dial Press, 1975. With new foreword.
1. Baseball—Umpiring—United States. 2. Baseball umpires—United States. I.
Title. II. Series.

GV876.G8	1999
796.357'3—dc21	98-27610
ISBN 0-8093-2195-5 (paper)	CIP

The paper used in this publication meets the minimum requirements of American
National Standard for Information Sciences—Permanence of Paper for Printed
Library Materials, ANSI Z39.48-1984. ∞

Writing Baseball Series Editor: Richard Peterson

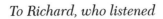

To Richard, who listened

CONTENTS

FOREWORD

Eric Rolfe Greenberg

I'm an umpire, too: West Side Little League, New York, New York. It is something of a cultural aberration that umpires exist at all on Manhattan's Upper West Side, a bastion of left-liberal social democracy ("communitarians" would be the current term of art and politics). The very idea of a single individual entrusted with authority not only to make arbitrary decisions but also to enforce them without immediate opportunity for appeal goes against the local grain. One might expect instead a committee reflecting the ethnicity and social lifestyles of the surrounding community, openly discussing each event on the field and voting on the decision only after all voices had been heard.

But no, we have umpires. It seems the game needs them.

Those of us who choose to umpire generally enjoy it, save when an early spring wind whips off the Hudson or an urban heat wave bakes the summer cement. Arguments in the West Side Little League are rare and generally civil. We soon discover that we can control the game far more easily than any coach or player. A wide strike zone encourages hitters to swing; swinging, they are likely to put the ball in play; fielders get to field, runners to run. The league rules say, "When in doubt, call it a strike." Thus do we try to avoid endless bases on balls and the torpor that overcomes hitters, runners, and fielders when walk follows upon walk. We felt a kinship in October 1997 with National League umpire Eric Gregg, whose generous interpretation of the strike zone allowed Livan Hernandez the widest latitude as Hernandez gained a postseason victory on the way to the Florida Marlins' world championship.

Eric Gregg was twenty-one years old and working in the Class AAA Pacific Coast League in 1974, the year Lee Gutkind chronicled the professional and personal lives of a big-league umpiring crew and turned it into *The Best Seat in Baseball, But You Have to Stand!* It is a book which, like Jim Bouton's contemporaneous *Ball Four*, challenged the sentimental notions and "gee-whiz" styles that had characterized baseball books from antediluvian days up to that time. Like Bouton's book, *The Best Seat in Baseball* was seen by its subjects as a betrayal of trust. But if Bouton's book was disillusioning, Gutkind's is downright disturbing, even frightening. To understand why this is so, we must go back the quarter century to when the book was written, and from that vantage point look back even further—not at umpiring, which had changed very little, but instead at sportswriting, which was in the midst of a revolution.

The Danton of this revolution was Dick Young of the *New York Daily News*, the same Dick Young whose early-season column (cited by Gutkind in the first chapter of his book) sets the mood for a "very difficult year." It was Young, in the late 1940s, who had brought his readers off the field and into the postgame clubhouse; it was Young who realized, in a radio and television age, that newspapers ran helplessly behind the new media in covering the on-field action but had an inestimable advantage in reporting the currents that flowed through the dugouts, clubhouses, and front offices of baseball. As commonly happens in revolutions, a younger generation exceeded the passions of its teachers; within twenty years, a self-dubbed band of "chipmunks," New York-based beat writers and their out-of-town kin, had so far escaped the old boundaries that they were writing about wife-swapping arrangements among Yankee pitchers. (One of these "chipmunks" was Leonard Schechter, Bouton's coauthor on *Ball Four*.)

And so Lee Gutkind, in a green silk shirt, a pair of linen pants, and a Pierre Cardin jacket with "a sharp plaid of blues, greens, yellows, and reds over an off-white background," walked into the umpires' dressing room at Shea Stadium in May 1974 to find four men whose work uniforms, navy blue suits over white shirts, were not all that different from their street clothes. That Gutkind was an astonishing and foreign figure to Nick Colosi, Doug Harvey, Harry Wendelstedt, and Art Williams is obvious; that the umpiring crew was equally astonishing and foreign to Gutkind provides a subtle subtext to his book.

What were the expectations on either side of this divide? The umpires assumed that Gutkind wanted to write about *umpiring*—the skills and competencies that the crew displayed on the field. They must have imagined a primer for professionals or interested amateurs, filled out with certain personality features to give the work some human interest. But Gutkind, heir to the chipmunk ethos, cared little about the technical aspects of umpiring, which in any case were open to study by any fan in the ballpark. His interest was the men in the group and, in turn, the group in the wider community. Given the times, it was inevitable that Art Williams would become Gutkind's focus.

Williams was the first black umpire in National League history and, in 1974, the only black umpire in the major leagues. (Emmett Ashford, who had broken the color barrier in the American League, had retired in 1973.) That phrase itself, "the first black," today has the flavor of a history book, which is natural since the 1970s were a different time with regard to race.

Gutkind's chronicle of Williams's tribulations has a particular resonance in the late 1990s when affirmative action programs are under wide attack. According to Gutkind, "Williams was in the major leagues [in 1974] because he was black . . . The National League office had very little choice in the matter. The government had demanded that there be a black umpire in the National League before the end of the 1972 season and the league had complied by picking the best of a small and relatively inexperienced crop."

To the extent that *The Best Seat in Baseball* has a story line, the Williams chronicle provides it. Gutkind introduces him as "the man the National League owners and coaches had last year called the worst umpire in the league . . . Nor were there racial overtones in this judgement, as far as Harvey could make out. Pure and simple, Williams was not a very good umpire . . ." What follows is a dramatic arc: Williams's professional insufficiencies continue, despite the best efforts of his mentors Harvey and Wendelstedt, and ultimately threaten his employment; long-simmering tensions explode in a bitter confrontation; purified by the heat of the exchange, Williams finally puts his lessons to work on the field. By season's end Harvey admits, "He's showin' me something," to which Wendelstedt replies, "I mean to tell ya." Music up and over.

Instruction manuals (which is what the umpiring crew assumed Gutkind was writing) need no dramatic arc, but other books do, and it is that arc which makes *The Best Seat in Baseball* a compelling read twenty-five years after its original publication, leading the reader to contemplate what remains the same and what has changed. Umpires remain an indelible part of the game, yet somehow at a vital remove from its core. Fans may be attuned to certain personal idiosyncracies— Frank Pulli's right-handed jab of a strike call, the now-retired Dutch

Rennart's foghorn voice—but umpires are still considered to be doing their best when they are least noticed. They are most noticed, of course, when in a classic jaw-to-jaw confrontation with a player or a manager insisting he's been robbed. Those who wince at the ethnic insults the subjects throw at one another or think them archaic need only eavesdrop at a local construction site to know they are still common coin.

What has changed? First and foremost, the pay structure: Umpires, like players, have benefited from baseball's revenue growth, and veteran umpires now earn six-figure salaries with solid benefit packages and additional pay for postseason assignments, which are rotated among tenured crew members. More subtly, umpires have changed their styles of play-calling, and Doug Harvey, a central character in *The Best Seat in Baseball*, was a primary innovator. Prior to Harvey, umpires were taught to "call it quick," to see the play and quickly make the call. It was Harvey who introduced and perfected a different style now widely practiced, a more deliberative approach that involved *making sure*—sure that a fielder held onto the ball after a tag or force, sure that a runner touched a base, sure that a pitch caught or missed a corner of the plate. The delay is hardly noticeable, less than half a second, and in Harvey's judgment (and in that of his imitators) very much worth the reward of an assuredly correct call.

In the corrosive climax of Gutkind's book, when Harvey and Wendelstedt confront Williams for his hesitancies and the permissive license he has granted to the players, Harvey's great demand is for respect—respect not for himself alone but for all umpires. In the years that followed the publication of *The Best Seat in Baseball*, Harvey won and maintained that respect. A thirteen-year veteran in 1974, he continued for another two decades, regarded as the best ball-and-strike umpire in baseball, whom the players—how's this for respect?—nicknamed "God."

Harry Wendelstedt has his measure of respect as well: The only member of Harvey's crew still actively umpiring in the big leagues, he also runs baseball's foremost umpiring school. Nick Colosi retired in 1982 after a fifteen-year career. And Art Williams, earning a reprieve from Fred Fleig, the National League's supervisor of umpires who effectively put Williams on probation in mid-1974, completed three more seasons in the big leagues, retiring after the 1977 season.

The race issue so dominates the book that the reader may miss the fascinating story that lies alongside the racial theme. That story does not lack for mythic elements: A small, dedicated band travels through hostile territory carrying the law's authority. Their isolation is nearly total: They have their own hotels, their own restaurants, their own cabdrivers, their own company (and only that). They are never at home. Because men cannot live without law, they are respected by those they police, but men also despise controlling authority, and so they are hated. It is a frontier setting: Circuit judges, Texas Rangers, even *The Seven Samurai* come to mind. The band can live with the hatred so long as they have the respect.

In the aftermath of the book's publication, the umpires were furious with Gutkind, feeling that the book did not treat them with respect. Gutkind, in his new preface printed here, argues the opposite. It seems to be a case of mutual naiveté. The umpires did not understand that a reporter's business is to write what he sees and hears, and the reporter did not understand the umpires' ignorance of the writer's trade. The cultural clash continues, as obvious as the contrast between the umpires' blue suits and the writer's plaid jacket.

PREFACE:
WILL THE REAL MEN IN BLUE
PLEASE STAND UP?

The September 1996 incident in Toronto in which Baltimore Oriole second baseman Roberto Alomar spit in the face of umpire John Hirschbeck brought back vivid memories of the season I spent with National League baseball umpires researching *The Best Seat in Baseball, But You Have to Stand!*

During that year, I attended the majority of the games that the crew about which I wrote (Doug Harvey, Harry Wendelstedt, Art Williams, and Nick Colosi) officiated, plus games involving other National League umpire crews, minor league games, and World Series and All Star games. Because of the nonfraternization practice, I had little to do with the players; I literally immersed myself in the umpire's narrow world. Umpires tended to avoid the players, which meant that they also avoided the limelight in the cities they visited, staying in smaller hotels and dining at restaurants that players normally did not frequent.

I had access to the umpires' locker room in most ballparks in the National League. We often traveled together, dined—and sometimes partied. Their candor about the game, the players, and the pressures under which they worked was enlightening. In our many conversations, they insisted—repeatedly—that somebody (Me!) had to capture the drama of the major league umpire experience for the world to witness and therefore to understand. These were compassionate and engaging men, mostly, with a sincere reverence for a game in which they were always right—even when they were dead wrong. But this is also what bothered me about the umpires: their inability to accept the limitations of their situation. The men I spent time with—Wendelstedt and Harvey especially—rejected any form of criticism. They refused to contemplate the notion that the very nature of their position attracted resentment, disagreement, and controversy. It was acceptable to criticize the president of the United States, players, and celebrities, but on or off the field, disagreement with umpires was not allowed. "Don't ever let them call you horseshit" is how Doug Harvey explained it to rookie umpire Art Williams. The umpires were so convinced of their own righteousness that their jokes and barbs concerning ethnicity and race (Art Williams was the first African American umpire in the National League) were supposed to be presumed harmless. Much of their humor was self-deprecating, which allegedly illustrated their magnanimity. Because I understood how sensitive they were—and because I loved the game with great passion—I can honestly say that I made every effort to present the umpires in a positive light. I portrayed them as real people, honorable, hard-working, and dedicated, but with warts and flaws like the rest of us. But they didn't want to be compared with real people; they wanted to be umpires—on a plateau above most everyone else.

Since this book was first published, Harvey and Wendelstedt have never once communicated with me. Wendelstedt even denied the fact that I had traveled with him and his crew, though Harvey and Williams signed statements attesting to the fact that I was with them regularly. I gather that the umpires compare me to Benedict Arnold—or Jim Bouton (*Ball Four*). I regret their response. My book introduced the "villains in blue" to the general public in ways that made them real, three-dimensional people, with whom fans might empathize. The fact is that the umpires are the only real people remaining in the game, while most every player, manager, and owner has an agent, a publicist, an inflated salary, and a personal agenda. The umpires are the common folk, like the rest of us fans: the guys charged with the thankless and impossible task of invoking order.

Which brings me back to 1996 and Roberto Alomar and John Hirschbeck. In the end, both men comported themselves well enough. Hirschbeck basically walked away from the incident, while Alomar apologized to Hirschbeck and donated money to a foundation devoted to research into the disease which was to later kill Hirschbeck's young son. Generally, however, the umpires, as a group, reacted with poor judgment, displaying a complete lack of understanding of what their positions signified.

Instead of seizing the moment and becoming role models, the umpires acted out, calling press conferences, whining and complaining, and threatening to strike if Alomar was permitted to participate in the playoffs and the World Series. (He was given a five-game suspension to be served at the beginning of the following season.) Eventually, the umpires backed down, as everyone (except the umps) suspected they would from the very beginning. I am not alibiing for Alomar, whose action was inexcusable. But the umpires could have displayed character and humility—become icons of a game badly in need of order and dignity. Instead, they behaved as badly as players, which to umpires is the ultimate criticism.

Umpires walk a difficult line. They want to engender sympathy and understanding on the one hand, but they also elevate themselves to an untouchable plateau on the other. They can't have it both ways. Umpires needn't be frightened of revealing themselves as real people with egos and insecurities like everyone else. By acknowledging the complications caused by living in the shadow of the players and by having to cross the line 162 times every year from perfection to fallibility, fans will discover, as did I while writing *The Best Seat in Baseball, But You Have to Stand!*, a new and exciting dimension to the game.

L.G.
1999

THE

BEST

SEAT IN

BASEBALL,

BUT

YOU HAVE TO

STAND!

The Beginning of a Difficult Year

The 1974 feud between umpires and major league baseball's players, coaches, and managers began in April, in one of the coldest springs in baseball history. The *Farmer's Almanac* had called for a subpar season, a cold and rainy summer, and its prediction seemed to be coming true. Games in Montreal were being snowed out one after another and the doors to stadiums in Chicago and New York were virtually frozen shut. Temperatures tumbled into the thirties and forties in most major league towns in the eastern portion of the United States, and rain and wind delayed and sometimes ruined many ball games, prompting some managers to consider issuing wetsuits to outfielders and flippers to runners trying to steal second base. Then a Canadian Airlines strike lasting two weeks forced players and umpires trying to get into Montreal to fly into Burlington or Rutland; they had to Greyhound back and forth from Vermont to Montreal.

Even worse than the weather, however, was the unsettling way in which the season was progressing. The teams that were supposed to be winning were either losing or at least not winning nearly enough. Thus, no matter how cold it was in the cities, the tempers of managers, players, sportswriters, and fans were hot enough to melt glaciers. For umpires such a situation signaled the beginning of a very difficult year.

In the National League East the Pittsburgh Pirates, favored to come back from their mediocre 1973 season and their shock over the death of superstar outfielder Roberto Clemente, were, with each game they played, sinking deeper into the quicksand of the cellar, while the New York Mets, "The Mighty Mites," the 1973 National League champions, were ineptly tumbling and buffooning right behind. By mid-April both teams had managed to win only three of thirteen games. The Philadelphia Phillies, on the other hand, a team of youngsters, a team without a superstar, a team whose fans under forty could hardly remember the last time they had played well, were momentarily in first place one full month after the season had started, while Chicago, Montreal, and St. Louis trampolined back and forth behind.

Many people thought that Los Angeles had already won the National League West. By mid-May the Dodgers were eight games in front of their closest rivals, playing at a near .700 clip. Pitcher Tommy John had eight wins and two losses and Jimmy Wynn, a reject from the Houston Astros, had already blasted fourteen home runs. What was so frustrating, however, was that three of the five remaining western division teams were also doing well—mostly against their lowly eastern division counterparts. Cincinnati had won six of every ten ball games they played, a record good enough to lead the league most other years, while Atlanta had won twelve games in a row. In all, four of the six western division teams had a higher winning percentage than the league leaders in the east. At one point, only one of the six eastern division teams was playing better than .500 ball.

Early in the season Ray Kroc, the MacDonald's hamburger hustler who had recently purchased the San Diego Padres, openly chided his team over the home stadium's public address system for its bush-league ballplaying. Steve Blass, the 1971 Pittsburgh Pirate World Series hero, twice a runner-up for the Cy Young Award which honors the finest pitcher in the league, was, at thirty-two-years old, optioned to the Charleston Charlies of the AAA International League for his inability to get the ball over the plate. Judge Roy Hofheinz, the mastermind behind the Houston Astrodome and the originator of the idea of dome-topped stadiums, announced that his hometown attendance had so far fallen 300,000 below last year's. The Astros were one million dollars behind in revenue, just two months after the start of the season.

By the end of the eighth week, it was clear to all who cared to look that this was going to be a topsy-turvy, dazzlingly different, furious, frenetic, exhilarating, excruciating baseball year.

There always have been and always will be feuds between players and teams and umpires in baseball, for the umpires are the policemen of the ballpark, the enforcers on the field, and on any one play, especially when it is comparatively close or controversial, an umpire will never please more than 50 percent of his constituency. Often he will please less. This particular year, however, the feud started earlier than usual, perhaps in part because of the weather, but more so because of the unorthodox and unpredictable way in which the teams in the National League were playing.

For what happens when a team—especially a team familiar with the bright lights and flush of victory—begins to lose ball games with an alarming rate of consistency? If a player were to blame his teammates or coaches, he would make a number of instant enemies and risk being relieved of his position in the starting lineup or his personally polished seat on the bench. And a manager or general manager publicly admitting his own mistakes is, in effect, submitting his own personal resignation. There are only two feasible solutions. First, a team can blame the umpires for unfair and inadequate rulings. Second, the players can blame Providence, "Lady Luck," for issuing a continuing series of unfortunate setbacks.

Luck, of course, is illusionary. Luck has no face or name or color or uniform. It cannot be pinned down. So the players, managers, fans and the press—most *particularly* the members of the press, who must cast their lot with their home teams and whose readership usually increases or decreases according to the play and the standings of their teams—will, more often than not, select the umpires at whom to level criticism. This makes good copy because every living, breathing baseball fan knows he is supposed to hate the umpires. Umpires are at best necessary evils.

Criticizing an umpire won't unnecessarily embarrass a home team or cause a reporter's sources to be stopped up by moping, vengeful players insulted by negative public exposure. Reporters are heartless in this way. Although their copy may be inflammatory, may break down the discipline of the next ball game following publication of their vitriolic comments or spark a near riot in the stands, they will keep writing these stories as long as grist is available for their daily mill. Although, for obvious reasons, documentation to justify criticism of umpires is almost impossible to obtain, reporters will continue writing their stories whenever a mere whiff of information is available—all season if their team continues to lose—or until their team begins to win. Umpires are sportswriters' and sportscasters' best friends because the *men* in blue are perfect material for an avalanche of attacks.

The first all-out attack on umpires came in the pages of the *New York Daily News* and was written by Dick Young, a veteran reporter known for his ability to conjure up controversial news when none is available at deadline time. The game in question was one in which the New York Mets played the Cubs in Chicago. It was officiated by chief Doug Harvey and his crew of Harry Wendelstedt, Nick Colosi, and Art Williams.

Dave Schneck, a twenty-five-year-old outfielder playing his first full season with the Mets, hit a hard fly ball to deep center field which momentarily seemed to get by pursuing Cub center fielder Rick Monday. At the last minute, though, Monday dove at the ball, landed on his shoulder, somersaulted twice, then came up holding the ball triumphantly, his glove hand high. Second base umpire Nick Colosi, who had followed the ball into center field behind Monday, signaled a clean catch. It was then a simple matter for Monday to lob the ball to Don Kessinger at second base and double up the Met runner, who, never imagining that the ball would be caught, was just then sliding harmlessly into third base. Monday, however, had injured his shoulder on the play. He received a standing ovation when he trotted from the field. None of the Mets—including manager Yogi Berra—complained about the call.

Two innings later Colosi, who had been bothered by a sore back since the end of last season, switched positions with Art Williams at third.

In the *Daily News* the next day, Young ripped Colosi for not going out far enough on the play to see that Monday had actually trapped the ball. Young pointed out that since Colosi had a sore back, he couldn't possibly have run fast or far enough out into center field to be in a position to call the play accurately. Young, on the other hand, had watched the instant replay on the monitor in the press box. It was clear, Young claimed, that Monday had trapped the ball.

In the same column, Young quoted Met shortstop Bud Harrelson as saying that three Met losses in April alone could be positively attributed to poor officiating. Young also pointed out that umpires, most particularly at Shea Stadium, were stealing dozens of baseballs each year.

Harvey, Wendelstedt, Colosi, and Williams took the criticism without public squawking. For one thing, no reporter offered them the opportunity of either denying or confirming Young's or Harrelson's claims. For another, while not oblivious to criticism, after having endured so much so often, they were intelligent and controlled enough to limit their complaints to friends and associates.

Colosi, whose back problems were not a reportorial illusion, admitted, at least to himself, that his reflexes and his speed were somewhat hampered, but he didn't think it had affected his game. Ailing as he was, he was still quicker than some of the older or fatter umpires in the league. He had seen it right: he was convinced that Monday had caught the ball legitimately. Even if he had been incorrect, Colosi knew that the call was honest and impartial. He didn't care whether the Mets won or lost. He was just trying to do his job. As to the videotape replay, Colosi knew he had been closer to the play than the camera had; moreover, he had been there at eye-level and at an angle that a camera couldn't possibily reproduce. Even so, the camera was merely telling the truth—impartially—just as he was. But, considering their different positions, why couldn't it be the camera that was wrong this time?

Privately, Doug Harvey was worried. He had been in baseball for eighteen years, long enough to know that the tone of Young's column and the bitterness of Harrelson's words might signal the beginning of a dispute that could easily build and rage all season —or at least as long as the Mets were losing. Judging from their shoddy play, it looked like a season-long dilemma. Harvey hadn't the slightest idea which three games Harrelson was referring to. Certainly the three couldn't have been umpired by his crew, but now, if past experience served as any kind of guideline, he, Wendelstedt, Colosi, and Williams could very well be made scapegoats for any generalized dissatisfaction either the Mets or the other teams harbored for the league's umpires. As the targets of the first public attack—especially from a man as influential as Young and from a city as media-conscious as New York—his crew might possibly become the targets of other writers from other towns and of other teams. To say the least, it wasn't a particularly pleasing prospect.

No one could tell what Art Williams thought of the situation, for he was characteristically quiet and somewhat aloof through the whole affair.

But the remaining member of the crew, Harry Wendelstedt, seemed completely unconcerned by the controversy caused by Harrelson's and Young's charges. When asked to comment on the situation, Wendelstedt stated:

"Harrelson is a chickenshit shortstop and Young is a corruptible cocksucker. I couldn't care less about any goddamn horse-ass crap they might have said."

MAY 1974

STANDING OF
THE NATIONAL LEAGUE TEAMS

Eastern Division

	W.	L.	Pct.	G.B.
St. Louis	13	9	.591	—
Montreal	9	7	.563	1
Philadelphia	10	11	.476	2½
Chicago	7	11	.389	4
New York	8	13	.381	4½
Pittsburgh	6	12	.333	5

Western Division

	W.	L.	Pct.	G.B.
Los Angeles	17	6	.739	—
Houston	14	10	.583	3½
Cincinnati	10	9	.526	5
Atlanta	11	12	.478	6
San Francisco	11	12	.478	6
San Diego	10	14	.417	7½

Hot
Foot
Harry

First base umpire Harry Wendelstedt felt the pain only a microsecond after he saw the ball and realized what was going to happen. The low line drive, hit from a Ron Bryant fastball by Met catcher Jerry Grote, shot off the bat like a streaking meteorite and collided with Wendelstedt's left big toe with a bone-jarring thump. Biting his lip and holding his breath, Wendelstedt waited momentarily for the fire to clear from his eyes, then threw his arm out to the left, signaling foul. Air whistled quietly through his teeth as he watched Grote, who had started running, slowly retreat down the line, pick up his bat, look up at Wendelstedt, and grin.

"That hurtcha, Harry?" asked first base coach Roy McMillan, with mock sympathy. "Did that hurtcha or did that hurtcha, Harry?" McMillan elongated each word as if he were talking to a baby. "You sure your poor little foot is still down there, Harry? Coulda been burned right off, you wouldn't have known the difference," McMillan chuckled.

"C'mon Harry," said Giant first baseman Dave Kingman, smiling and thumping his mitt with his fist, "we know it's killing you. Why don't you admit it? We ain't going to laugh."

"Not me, I'm not going to laugh," said McMillan, grinning as if this were the happiest day of his year.

"Why don't you just take time out and scream, Harry?" said Kingman.

"C'mon, Harry," said McMillan, "don't be such a big, bad umpire. We know it hurts so much you want to scream. C'mon, scream!"

Wendelstedt stared silently past his tormentors, down toward the batter's box and forced out a tight grin, worthy of a bad joke. He was still dizzy with pain. He felt as if his foot had been nailed with a large rusty spike into the reddish-brown dirt of Shea Stadium and, at the same time, as if his toe had been jammed up into his knee, but there was no way he was going to admit it, no way Harry Wendelstedt would give those rats the satisfaction of knowing he had been hurt.

Thankfully, Bryant's next pitch was a ball.

Wendelstedt gradually shifted his weight to his right foot and tried to wiggle the toes on his left. They were hot and stiff, felt sticky and wet. He shut his eyes hard to force away the pain. Then, making it seem as if it were an afterthought, he forced himself to look up and check his position. He was fifteen feet behind the base and straddling the foul line. Just about where the skin of the infield meets the outfield grass. Just right. If there was a man on first, Wendelstedt would have to move in closer to watch for pick-off plays, but as it was, with the bases empty, the umpire had more leeway to follow a ball down the right field foul line. Art Williams, his partner on third, straddled the left field line, about twenty-five feet behind the base. With plenty of time to move laterally up and down the line before a play might reach third, Williams could afford to be more centrally located. Unlike American League umpires, who positioned themselves down the line in foul territory, the National League umpires on first and third stood directly in line with home plate, one foot on the fair side of the line, the other foot foul, belt buckles marking the middle.

There are other differences between the umpiring styles of the two leagues. For one thing, with men on base, the second base umpire in the National League stands on the infield grass, while the American League umpire stands behind the base on the shallow part of the outfield. Although the National League position increases the danger for an umpire, by putting him closer to the batter where he can easily be hit by a line shot, Wendelstedt felt it enabled him to call a play more accurately, especially on a double-play ball or an attempted steal. The National League umpire is always on the inside of the throw or the inside of the base, facing the infielders' gloves and the direction of the play, while the American League umpire makes his calls from behind the player's backs. Thus, with minimum shifting, the National League umpire is always in a better position to see the play more clearly. On the other hand, he is further away from the outfield and has a longer run to make when judging whether a ball has been caught or trapped. There is good and bad in both systems, Wendelstedt admitted, but he mostly disliked the idea that the American League umpire has to move forward and into the play. Sometimes, when the play is very close, the umpire could easily and inadvertently inch into the baseline, a perfect target for a streaking runner and his high-flying spikes. This would rarely happen to a National League umpire covering second base correctly. No matter how far forward he moves, it is nearly impossible to be in the way of the runner.

Wendelstedt placed his hands on his knees in a crouch while Bryant dipped, wound, and side-armed a curve that Grote hit behind him foul on the screen. The organist at Shea followed the ball up the screen with a high-pitched twitter, then accompanied it down again with a low, elongated yawn.

The bat boy caught the ball falling from the rim of the screen, ran it into the Met dugout, and dropped it into the heavy, brown cowhide ball bag. Plate umpire Doug Harvey threw out another, which Bryant rubbed up in the palms of his hands.

The next pitch Grote hit slow on the ground to the left of second, where it was scooped up by shortstop Chris Speier. As Speier threw and Grote ran to beat it, Wendelstedt hobbled to what the umpires call the "first base slot" at about a forty-five degree angle, and approximately two feet behind and to the right of the bag. Grote could hustle, but the ball smacked into Kingman's mitt more than a tenth of a second before Grote's spikes touched the canvas. Wendelstedt hesitated briefly, checking to see if Kingman's foot was on the base and whether he held the ball. Then, in a single motion, he raised his arm up, balled his fingers into a fist, and screamed, "You're out!"

Grote, short and chunky, trotted back down the line. "I got you this time, didn't I Harry?" he said as he passed Wendelstedt. "C'mon, Harry, you gotta admit it," he smiled.

Wendelstedt, 230 pounds, six foot three, with a chest like a bulldozer's bumper and a hard, square, combat-helmet head, turned, and stared down and through the little catcher. Grote, not particularly known for his bravery or backbone, shrugged, turned, and trotted away. He threw his batting helmet into the dirt, a habit of professional baseball players, who presumably blame the batting helmet or the dirt for their own inability to get on base. Then Grote clattered down the concrete steps into the dugout and sank onto the wooden bench. "I got him this time," he said to no one in particular. "This time I got that fucker good."

The fine for throwing a batting helmet unnecessarily hard or in response to an umpire's decision is a hundred dollars. Wendelstedt watched Grote carefully, then shrugged, deciding he didn't have just cause for such an action; then he turned away. A good umpire tries to enforce the rules but at the same time allow some leeway. No use starting a rhubarb and delaying a game when it isn't absolutely necessary, umpires reason. Of course, umpires do strictly enforce rules on a team taking too many liberties. Two years before, when Wendelstedt worked with Al Barlick (now retired) and his crew, the Met third base coaches developed the habit of straying out of the coaching box and strolling far up and down the line. The rule keeping coaches inside their chalked box was made so they couldn't steal the opposing catcher's sign. Umpires usually overlooked the rule when coaches stood only a step or two from their box, particularly during later innings when the chalk might be partially rubbed away. (One of the many dirty tricks Leo Durocher originated during his stormy managerial career was to have his players drag their spikes when they walked over the coaching box, until the chalk line disappeared.) But that year the Mets were *really* taking unfair advantage. One day, after three unheeded warnings, Barlick took action. He stopped the game and called out the groundskeepers to rechalk the line. Each time part of the line was rubbed away he'd stop the game and call the groundskeepers to fill it back in. Each time a Met coach stepped as much as an inch over the line he'd stop the game, walk over slowly, ever so slowly, and order them back in. It got downright annoying, but Barlick kept it up, game after game, until he made his point. For the rest of the season the Mets called that crew "Barlick's Enforcers."

Sometimes players want to win by playing ball and other times they try to win by playing games. In either case, an umpire will oblige.

Not wanting to sacrifice his strength for what he might achieve on the mound, Met pitcher Tom Seaver, the next batter, struck out on three straight pitches, two of which were over his head, ending the inning. Seaver was one of the primary reasons the Mets weren't winning this year. He pitched well enough on most occasions for five or six innings, but then seemed to lose his consistency. His curves hung too often and his fastballs weren't as low and zippy as they once used to be. With a record of two and five, Seaver had given up more home-run balls this season than all of the other Met pitchers combined. It was too bad, thought Wendelstedt, for Seaver was the only active Met that could be at all compared to a human being. He never bitched, never cried, never begged, never complained. Wendelstedt would rather work behind the plate with Seaver pitching than anyone else in baseball. On an off day, Seaver was twice as good as most pitchers in the league.

As the Giants rolled in and the Mets scattered out, second base umpire Nick Colosi, small, slender, and at 47 slightly balding, born in Sicily, walked over to Wendelstedt. The little bit of sun the umpires had seen during their last swing west had added a golden, healthy-looking hue to Colosi's normally dark complexion. "You all right, Harry?" he asked, his speech a mixture of New York and Italian inflection.

"Hell no, Nick," Wendelstedt was able to grin.

"Maybe you ought to say something."

"Yeah, sure, and give those creeps the satisfaction of knowing I'm hurt? No way, Nick, no way."

"But if you're hurt . . ."

"So, I'm hurt. But what happened to you in Chicago, Nick, with the Mets? Tell me that. You were hurt, too, you know. Look what the hell Dick Young did to you."

" 'Course, I wasn't particularly honest about that at first," said Colosi, smiling a sheepish little boy's smile.

"You told them you had the shits, didn't you, you bastard," Wendelstedt laughed.

"Shits, hell! When the press called down to see why I had

switched from second to third base I said I had a 'gastronomical infection.' That way I could be closer to the bathroom, just in case."

"You're devious, Nick. You're goddamn devious. That's what everybody is always saying about you."

"Till old 'Straight Arrow' found out about it," said Colosi, motioning over to Harvey behind home plate. "He said, 'You better tell the truth. Sure as hell somebody is going to catch you. It's too dumb a lie to tell.' "

"He was right," Wendelstedt nodded.

"I know he was right. Thank God Young didn't pick it up. He would have crucified me. Worse. I just didn't want them to know about my back."

"So I'm saying the same thing about my foot, Nick. They find out I'm hurt, they beef every time I make a call."

"But if you're really hurt . . ." Colosi objected.

"No way, Nick. I'd rather lose a gallon of blood than admit it to those bastards."

It was the top half of the fourth inning and a batter was finally coming out of the dugout and strolling to the plate. Trying not to limp noticeably, Wendelstedt walked quickly back behind first base and straddled the line in position. No way, he said to himself again. He wasn't that kind of man, he wasn't the kind of umpire who showed weakness, the kind who showed fallibility. Square-faced and mean-looking, with a pair of heavy, ropelike lips, Harry Wendelstedt cut the figure of a Marine drill sergeant. Thirty pounds too heavy, he was still as straight, solid, and forthright as the Hall of Justice. (At a tavern the evening before Wendelstedt was told by a female patron that he looked like a German baker. He told her she looked like a stale loaf of bread.) To Wendelstedt, being an umpire in the major leagues required something more of a man, required the strength and fortitude of a man's man, one who showed no pain, no partiality, no fear, and no rage. In his own mind he believed that there wasn't, nor would there ever be, a woman capable of doing the job of an umpire—certainly not Bernice Gera, the witch who under the guise of "Bernie Gera" had tried to infiltrate the school for umpires he owned with Al Somers. Not his wife Cheryl, not his own mother. No woman!

He had told that to Gera when she had called him at his home in Daytona Beach, Florida, to complain about her rejection by the Al Somers school. "You're a liar, Mrs. Gera," he said flatly, "because you tried to get into our school under false pretenses, and umpires can never be liars. If you lie and cheat off the field, then you'll lie and cheat on the field. I have no use for your kind, no use for any person who lies to me, or for any woman who tries to break into a man's game."

Gera eventually made it into baseball, first at school through the Umpire Development Program, financed and operated by the major leagues. Then she had, through court action, landed a job in the New York-Pennsylvania Class A League. But, unable to take the abuse umpires receive from players and fans, she had quit, walked off the field, after the first game of a double-header on her first day of professional baseball. Wendelstedt found more than a little satisfaction in that. Not long after, it was discovered that she, her husband, and her attorney had packed their bags and checked out of the hotel even before the first game had started. She never had had any intention of staying in baseball, Wendelstedt and others realized. He looked forward to the day he would meet her face to face.

The Giants went ahead in their half of the fourth inning with a home run by outfielder Bobby Bonds, and Wendelstedt was now wishing that both Seaver and Bryant would throw perfect games the rest of the day. He could feel his toe ballooning up in his black ripple-soled oxfords. Icy pain climbed slowly up his ankle and thigh like mid-winter frost. In the bottom half of the sixth inning, Harrelson, the Met shortstop, hit four line drive fouls down the right field line on four consecutive pitches, all close enough for Wendelstedt to follow till the ball touched ground. He also made two calls at the base. By the end of that inning he could have cried, but he didn't, and he knew he wouldn't.

"You still hurtin', Harry?" asked a smiling Dave Kingman as he walked off the field. "C'mon, Harry, you gotta admit that liner back in the third inning stung."

"Shake it up," growled Wendelstedt, turning his back on Kingman and walking down the line. "Let's get a batter up there, let's get some fielders out here, let's get this game going, let's get moving. Now!"

No way, Wendelstedt said to himself, no way. He had been

injured plenty of times before. In the minor leagues he had gotten a broken collarbone and a broken elbow from errant foul balls. Three of his toes had been broken in three successive seasons and each toenail on each foot had been either smashed or completely stripped away at least once in his career—despite the heavy steel-toed shoes he wore behind home plate. And since when was he different from any other umpire? Jocko Conlan, the recently retired National League veteran, had had three broken collarbones and two broken elbows in his career. Larry Napp, still active in the American League, had once been struck with three successive pitches—one in the mask, two in the groin. He had to be carried off the field in a stretcher. And how about twelve-year National League veteran Bill Williams? He had been smashed in the mouth by a flying catcher's mask. During the winter his teeth began to rot and fall out, one by one.

People think all that protective equipment safeguards an umpire against injury. Well, maybe it did a little, Wendelstedt admitted. But still. A good fastball crosses the plate at a little more than 95 miles per hour. Are steel-toed shoes and a padded chest protector going to significantly deaden the pain of a ball thrown at that velocity? Maybe a little. And when a ball thrown at that speed comes off the bat, it's going twice as fast, maybe more. And can steel face masks prevent an umpire from suffering from excruciating headaches—or worse? Umpires have had their teeth shattered, jaws crushed, and cheeks ripped when steel bars in their masks broke and embedded in their flesh. The umpire behind the plate doesn't have a catcher's mitt to protect him, and the umpires on the bases don't wear any protective equipment at all. Each year, on close plays at second and especially third, Wendelstedt could expect to be slashed two or three times by the spikes of base runners.

Sure, he'd been hurt plenty of times before, but he wouldn't admit it then and he couldn't admit it now. Not unless he was cold-cocked unconscious. Especially not to the Mets or the Giants and not, most especially, to give satisfaction to that little sissy Grote. Colosi and Harvey could go for pills and medical advice to the trainers, but Wendelstedt wouldn't. Not that he resented it. Harvey had been bothered by some indeterminable illness since the beginning of the season, and Colosi had hurt his back last year and never had it properly taken care of. But Wendelstedt resolved to keep his silence.

In a confidential poll taken at the end of last season by Fred Fleig, secretary of the National League and second man to National League President Chub Feeney, Wendelstedt had been rated the second best umpire in the league by the managers, coaches, and owners of each National League team—excluding the San Francisco Giants, who had claimed that Wendelstedt was the worst umpire ever to officiate in the league. They said he was detrimental to baseball. Fleig, Feeney, Wendelstedt, and most of the other umpires in the league realized that the Giants' hatred of Wendelstedt stemmed back to two particular calls Wendelstedt had made against the team a few years ago which might well have cost them a pennant. Wendelstedt knew the calls were fair, but the Giants' resentment of him had remained kindled over the past few seasons. The Giants would be very happy and suddenly very troublesome if they were to find out he had been even slightly injured.

Aside from being the second best umpire in the league, he was also the second biggest (Lee Weyer is six foot four and 240 pounds), the strongest, and the meanest. (In fact, he and Weyer had once planned to go into professional wrestling during the off season as the "W Brothers," but Fred Fleig had refused to grant them permission.) Wendelstedt, now thirty-six, had only been twenty-five years old when he entered the majors, the first young umpire to make it into the big leagues. He had done it by being strict and snarly and icily efficient. He took no abuse and asked for no sympathy and he wasn't about to change his policies now.

No way, he said to himself, over and over again, as he shifted his weight from foot to foot, trying to balance himself on his heels and lift his toes off the ground; no way was he going to give those rats any satisfaction. What would it accomplish anyway? What would it prove?

When one of the players got hurt, his teammates would gather around offering sympathetic advice, and his trainer and manager would jack-rabbit out of the dugout ready with first aid and soothing consolation. Even the fans would murmur in sympathetic suspense and the play-by-play sportscaster in the radio booth would speak of the injured player in reverent tones. But should an umpire show he is hurt, just once, no matter how serious the injury, the fans would cheer and the sportscaster would pause for a commercial.

Worse, the players would never forget it. For the rest of the year they would blame whatever call that might go against them on the ump's injury, attributing their own inability to get on base to the umpire's inability to move fast enough to see the play accurately. Because of his injury. It had happened before, a hundred times before to other umps, but it wasn't going to happen to him.

At the stretch during the seventh inning, Wendelstedt watched Colosi walk around the field. He was standing very straight, moving his chin up and down like a pigeon pecking at its food, and swiveling his hips tentatively back and forth. Back must be bothering him again, Wendelstedt thought, and then he smiled, remembering.

In his hotel room in Houston one afternoon before a game last year, Colosi had stood in the bathroom shaving. Inadvertently, he had inhaled some shaving cream up his nose and it made him sneeze. He sneezed again a little bit harder, rested, then sneezed a third time harder still. The fourth time he sneezed so hard he stamped his foot and his head came down almost to his knee in the ricochet. Colosi froze right there, his leg up and poised in stomping position, his head almost resting on his knee. He couldn't move. A muscle had gotten pulled or tangled up with another muscle, he didn't know exactly, but either way he was stuck there, balancing himself on one foot, his body folded almost double.

God knows how long it took him to realize he wouldn't be able to straighten up in the very near future, but after a while Colosi looked at his watch, and decided to get to the phone by crawling. He inched his way out of the bathroom, stopping periodically to breathe and to moan, and by the time he reached the phone to call for help, an hour and a half had passed. The worst hour and a half of his life, he said later. Wendelstedt had eventually gotten into Colosi's room and lifted him onto the bed and a doctor was later able to straighten him up and get him into good enough shape for that night. But that sneeze had been the beginning of a long and torturous year of pain and anxiety, of fear that people would find out, fear that he might be forced to quit the game temporarily. Now once in a while there was a relapse, and Colosi would have to go scrambling from trainer to trainer for pain pills and muscle relaxers, but as the season progressed, his back seemed to be steadily improving.

Wendelstedt, standing behind first base, leaning his hands on his knees, continued smiling as he began thinking back to the first time he and Nick had officiated together. They had first met at the Al Somers Umpire School back in 1959. Nick was then a floor captain—something like an assistant maitre d'—at the Copacabana night club in New York; he also did some part-time umpiring during the day in sandlot ball for extra money. At the time, Wendelstedt was a first-year science teacher at a junior high school in Baltimore. They had gotten along well together in umpire school, mostly because Nick was so interesting to listen to as he talked about all the stars he knew from the Copa—people like Sinatra, Gable, Jayne Mansfield, and Ethel Merman. Both men had enrolled in the six-week course at Daytona Beach, Florida, with a great deal of apprehension. Neither had any idea of committing himself to a life-long career in baseball; that came later. Then it was just a question of becoming more skilled in a profession which had frequently provided them both with moonlight money.

Still and all, as the weeks went by, they grew more excited. Long before graduating they had sent away for their mail order, bargain-basement, "official" umpire's uniforms: the dark blue pants and jacket and the pale blue short-sleeved shirt. They had already purchased and modeled, in the privacy of their rooms, second hand catcher's masks and shin guards, steel-toed and steel-tongued coal miner's shoes, as well as umpire balloons and inside protectors. All they needed was a job to go with the accoutrements, no easy matter considering the competition.

Somers selected a dozen of his best students from the more than eighty graduates of his school each year to work major league spring training games in Florida; the best men would be offered jobs by the minor league organizations needing officials. Colosi, who was thirty-two at the time, and Wendelstedt, twenty-four, were teamed together. Their first scheduled game was between the Detroit Tigers and the New York Yankees. A New Yorker since arriving in the U.S. thirty years before, Colosi was especially excited to be working, officiating, on the same field where his boyhood heroes like Mickey Mantle and Whitey Ford of the Yankees, and Al Kaline and Harvey Kuenn of the Tigers would be playing.

The two young umpires had arrived at the ballpark early, dressed quickly in their tight-fitting uniforms, modeled them for each other, then stripped and folded the pants, jackets, and shirts neatly so as not to wrinkle the newly pressed cuffs and creases ahead of time. They rubbed up the balls, spit an extra shine on their new black shoes, and took turns going to the bathroom. But when the time came to dress and get out on the field, Colosi couldn't get off the toilet.

"I can't do it, Harry. I got the shits. I got them bad. Every time I get up, I get so scared I gotta sit back down again. I'm tellin' you, I just can't do it. Mickey Mantle, Whitey Ford, Al Kaline. Al Somers is in the stands. I'm telling you, I just can't do it."

"C'mon Nick, you're thirty-two years old," Wendelstedt said.

"Every time I get up I feel like I'm going to burst. You do it without me."

"How in the hell can I umpire a game by myself?"

"Tell them I went home."

"Jesus, Nick, Sinatra, Charles Boyer, Lauren Bacall—all those big stars are your friends. With those credentials, you sure don't have to worry about meeting Harvey Kuenn. Besides, you won't meet him. All you have to do is call him safe or out."

Colosi shook his head and sighed, then lifted himself slowly and sheepishly, pulled up his pants, and hobbled outside. His temporary fright had affected Wendelstedt positively, however. Doubly confident now that he had detected and cured Colosi's weakness, he swaggered out onto the field, walked quickly and soberly to the plate, and yelled "Play ball!"

On the first pitch to lead-off batter Harvey Kuenn, Wendelstedt leaned down low, peered over the catcher's shoulder, set his cleats solidly into the dirt to brace himself—then split his new, blue, mail-order umpire's pants. To this day he could not remember whether he first heard the sickening rip or the wild cheering of the three thousand or so Floridians as they saw the rip. The first picture in his scrapbook, clipped from a local paper later that evening, is of those pants and his underwear glaring white in the bright sun, as he leaned over to call a pitch. Under it, the caption reads: "Official Opening."

When the Mets scored two in the bottom half of the ninth, the game moved into extra innings; Wendelstedt felt as if his whole left leg was going to fall off, it was throbbing so hard. He kept blinking his eyes, continually attempting to redirect his concentration on the game, only the game, not on the players talking it up from the field; not on the hollering from the dugout; not on the first base coach clap-clapping his hands to induce a rally; not on the middle-aged fan with the potbelly who took off some of his clothes and streaked through the box seats behind home plate and caused a delay in the game. Wendelstedt didn't want to know about the fight that erupted between the Shea Stadium security guards and the long-haired dirtball hippie behind him in the right field stands; he didn't want to think about anything except the game and his wish that it would be over with, somehow, some way, and soon!

An umpire's prayers are hardly ever answered, but this time, for some unexplained reason, Providence was on the side of the men in blue. Seaver served up the fattest, prettiest, birthday-cake ball Wendelstedt had ever seen and Bobby Bonds hit it a mile, maybe two miles, and out of the park.

Mercifully, the game ended quickly after that. The Giants went down in order and the Mets, after putting two men on with only one out, trudged with heads hanging into their locker room after pinch hitter Ed Kranepool hit into a game-ending double play.

"You're out!" Wendelstedt cried, swinging his fist up and down sharply. Then he sighed and slumped, and hobbled slowly off the field. He entered the shadowed concrete tunnel through the visiting team's dugout and walked quietly and inconspicuously behind the clattering spikes of the victorious Giants, listening as they joked and whooped. He was very tired now, both from the ten inning, three hour and fifteen minute contest, and, more so, from fighting the pain. His whole body ached and felt sticky. The Giants turned into their dressing room and Wendelstedt continued up the concrete canal, illuminated only by two shadeless, teardrop-shaped bulbs. He entered the umpires' room silently and winked at Harvey, Colosi, and Williams, who were waiting for him. He sunk down into a chair, took off his hat, then his shoe and his blood-soaked sock. And finally, after six and a half innings and almost two and a quarter hours of painful baseball, big, bad Harry Wendelstedt leaned back in his chair and howled.

Hurry Up and Wait

The man rated best umpire in the National League opened his sticky eyes slowly, forced his way through the jungle of blankets and pillows on top of him, and rolled out of bed. He hobbled over to the window and looked through the glass at the sky. The clouds were ugly, big and black and bristly, like ragged pads of Brillo. As he stared into the polluted panorama of the Manhattan skyline, he tried to mumble a few expletives, but could only bring to the surface of his mouth a couple of dry, hacking coughs. Still on unsteady legs, he made his way into the bathroom and turned on the water in the tub, adjusting the hot and cold faucets to a soothing lukewarm. Then, flipping up the shower knob, waiting briefly till the spraying water crackled against the curtain, he stepped inside.

The water attacked his face like strong wind, washing the grit of sleep from his eyes and awakening his still-drowsy limbs. He rubbed his face vigorously with both hands, then ran a forefinger over the red line that lashed to the right down his thigh where a German Shepherd had bitten him last winter while he was vacationing with his family in Mexico.

Even with the scar, though, Doug Harvey was a handsome man, tall and slim save for the small paunch that had collected over the years at his stomach. His face was sharply sculpted and slender. And the circles under his eyes were well obscured by the beginnings of a golden suntan which, at the same time, beautifully accentuated his wavy silver hair. Even his teeth were white and perfectly straight, or at least the open and completely boyish way he smiled made it seem so. As he traveled from city to city along the National League circuit, many women—particularly airline hostesses, who seemed to find him especially attractive—told him he should have been a movie star instead of an umpire. He liked that, and usually would say in reply, "Well, thank you darlin', but I believe I'll just stay here instead of goin' to Hollywood. That way I can enjoy myself just sittin' and lookin' at you." In fact, those were the very words he had once recited to one especially pretty girl he met a little more than eight years ago, a girl with blonde hair, blue eyes, and dime-sized dimples; she had eventually become his second wife.

The water ran down his face for an indeterminate length of time before he washed, rinsed, and stepped out springily, shut off the shower and toweled himself down hard. After shaving and brushing his teeth, he moved into the other room, pulled on a pair of dark maroon trousers and a shiny black silk shirt with white buttons, and stepped into a pair of burgundy-and-white patent tasseled loafers. He was feeling better now, much better than he had felt in days, but still not like the Doug Harvey of the past, not as good as he had felt last season or during the early part of the winter when he had been able to rest with his family.

For one thing, his feet and his legs were aching all the time and it was terribly difficult for him to run without grimacing. He didn't think it had influenced his speed or his reflexes on the field, but it certainly was affecting his stamina. After every game he was so damn tired he could hardly gather the energy to shower and dress and make it back to his hotel room. He slept a hell of a lot these days, too. And he couldn't drink anymore: liquor put him to sleep. Worse, he was jumpy and irritable at times—not the perfect disposition for any umpire, let alone the chief of a major league crew.

When the German Shepherd had ripped open his thigh in Mexico, the one nurse in the little town where they had been staying had panicked and injected him with a ten times normal dose of penicillin to kill the infection. By the time he had reached the nearest hospital, seventy-five miles away, the penicillin had indeed dealt with the infection, but it was also taking its toll on Harvey's body. Constant waves of nausea and pain kept passing over him; he was in and out of a coma for days. He recovered slowly over the next few weeks there; after traveling home, he remained on heavy medication and in relative vegetation for the remainder of the winter. To make matters worse, the bed rest, along with the medication, had bloated him by twenty pounds. He felt like a dumpling. But what were perhaps the worst two weeks of that winter came when the medication was cut off. Harvey underwent a torturous period of withdrawal. He felt he could now understand something of the agony in which drug addicts were forced to live day after day.

He had visited doctors and endured a number of physical examinations over the past few weeks, but all gave him a perfect bill of health ("considering the circumstances"). Or was it a bill of goods? After sixteen years of professional baseball, twelve of them in the major leagues, he knew himself well enough to know when something was out of whack. At forty-four, in his first year as a crew chief and the first in which he had been rated best official in the National League, he didn't want anything to alter his reputation, his feeling of satisfaction, or his ever-increasing sense of accomplishment. After all, he was at the top of his profession, one of the *lucky forty-eight* who comprised the umpire roster of the major leagues.

So until he discovered the reason he was feeling this way, or until he was feeling better, he would keep the information to himself. His crew, especially Colosi and Williams, had enough problems, and this wasn't the best time for their chief to show weakness. Besides, any hint that Doug Harvey wasn't in top form would be detrimental to the high degree of control he exercised on the field. For precisely that reason, most umpires keep long-standing illnesses to themselves, whenever possible, during the course of a season, then deal with them surreptitiously during the winter.

Harvey closed the door to his room, walked down the hall, and pushed the button for the elevator. He found himself thinking of his wife. Her face emerged as in a mirage, then her long legs, curled on the grass in the sun, bronzed and slender. He hadn't seen her for six weeks and didn't expect to see her for another two. Last season, he had managed to visit his family at home a total of eight days out of seven months. *Visit* was certainly the right word: it was as if he had to reintroduce himself to his children each successive time he came home. ("I'm your daddy." "Daddy who?")

If there had been a phone in the elevator, Harvey would have called his wife—just to talk—all the way from the thirty-sixth to the first floor. He was feeling that lonely.

Harvey, Wendelstedt, and Williams gathered approximately two hours before game time in the lobby of their New York headquarters, The City Squire Motor Inn, and walked two blocks up the street. Colosi, home in the Bronx with his family, would meet them at the ballpark. The sun had taken a sabbatical that week in New York and each day had been cold and windy, as gray as the pavement on 49th Street and Seventh Avenue where the umpires descended into the dungeon of the subway station. Two trains later, they emerged across from Shea Stadium. A cold rain had started somewhere between 53rd Street and Shea and now, as they walked under the loop of seats and concessions around the playing area, it began coming down with dogged persistence.

Almost the first crew of umpires to work in Shea Stadium when it opened in 1964 had discovered the subway as the most reliable and efficient way of traveling to and from the ballpark. The umpires could surely afford other ways of transportation, if they so desired, for in addition to their salary, spread out over a period of seven months, they receive $47.50 in expenses for each day of the baseball season. They are also issued an air travel card by their respective leagues to use through the season. Umpires use their own money to visit their families during an off day or to detour to another town to visit friends. Except in serious emergencies, they will not travel on a chartered team plane or on a commercial flight with players. In fact, they will go out of their way to avoid being with players. Umpires will usually stay in the same city for no more than three days, then move in the opposite direction of the two teams with whom they have just worked. On the average, umpires will travel approximately 100,000 air miles each year.

Harvey's crew took a taxi to Shea only when they were leaving town directly after the ball game and needed someone to carry and coordinate their personal baggage. Otherwise, no matter how uncomfortable, they remained loyal to the New York City subway system. Many substantial taxi fares and long waits in traffic had been wasted in the past by umpires involved in needless experimentation, searching for *the better way.*

In other towns the situation is different. In Houston, a motel courtesy wagon transports umpires back and forth to the Astrodome every night. In Chicago, Willie Rooks, an ancient black taxi driver with steel-gray hair, has been chauffeurring both American and National League umpires for the past twenty-five years. In Pittsburgh, Joe Petraglia, a boilermaker by profession and an "umpire freak" by choice, does the driving. In St. Louis, a mortician, enamored of umpires for some unexplained reason, often sends his hearse and uniformed driver to provide the necessary transportation. In Philadelphia, a long-time friend of umpires lends his wife's car.

Perhaps because of their size or the stiff, almost surly way in which they carry themselves, the umpires were recognized by the guards at Shea and passed through without having to show their identification. The three men walked down a narrow corridor, then turned down a long concrete tunnel, passed the visiting team's locker room, periodically nodding or mumbling a friendly word or two to a player or coach lounging with a cigarette or talking to a reporter in the passageway. The visiting team's headquarters are usually located near the umpires' room in each ballpark, while the home team remains isolated on the opposite side of the field.

Umpires and players try to maintain silence or a polite facade of peace when they run into each other off the field, but usually umpires go out of their way to give players a wide berth. Mostly they don't like the players, can't quite forgive the heartache the players give them most days out on the field. Infinitely more important, though, is that the press and the public can and will justifiably question an umpire's integrity if he is seen often enough with the people about whom he is supposed to be so impartial.

"What happens if I blow a play?" explains Lee Weyer, twelve-year National League veteran. "I make a mistake and call it wrong, and it may turn out that a player I was seen with the night before is safe when he should have been out. What are people going to think? Whatever they think it's not going to be good, and they'd be right for thinking that way."

The league officers do not publicly demand that umpires maintain their distance from ballplayers, but it is an unwritten and strictly enforced rule that they do. This is far from a sacrifice for most major league umpires, however: "The players are all creeps," says Dick Stello of Tom Gorman's crew. "Who the hell wants to spend any time with them anyway?"

"They're punks," says Billy Williams, second man on Gorman's crew. "The players are crudballs. I don't say I dislike all players, but by and large, if they had batting averages as big as their egos, they'd be superstars, each and every one of them."

Umpires have very little in common with players, usually. Umpires don't care who wins ball games, who gets the hits, or who strikes out whom. They're not concerned with the recipient of the Cy Young Award, the home-run crown, or the Most Valuable Player title. Umpires are concerned only with league attendance, for the league pays their salaries, ranging from $15,500 for a first-year official for the seven-month season, to $35,000 for a twenty-three-year veteran like Tom Gorman; only with keeping the game under control, getting it started and moving it along smoothly and swiftly; only with their own continued impartiality and ability to concentrate completely from the first pitch to the last.

Pipes painted a pale military green splay down from the ceiling like the legs of a grasshopper. Cream-colored paint only barely covers the high, concrete block walls. There are four doorless cubbyholes the size of telephone booths, with uniforms hung neatly in each of them and half-empty, open suitcases covering the floor. Running through the center of the room is a rectangular, brown plywood table with a gray metal folding chair at each side and a collection of athletic socks and underwear rolled like large, puffy balls of cotton on top in the middle. A 19-inch black and white television flickers silently in the corner near a doorway that leads to a room with toilets, sinks, and showers. From front to back, both rooms are carpeted like the sidewalks of New York—in gray, drab concrete.

Although spartan compared to the conditions in the New York Mets' club dining room two floors above, such facilities signify a vast improvement from the way it used to be for umpires not too many years ago. Some umpires still remember having to dress in their hotel rooms and walk through the crowds wearing their hated blue uniforms before and after the game—a particularly bad experience after the game, when some fans always want blood. Some umpires still remember the rooms with no toilets, when they had to urinate in sewers or invade the visiting team's locker room to ask a player's permission to move their bowels. Such conditions still exist in many minor league ballparks, especially in the South. After spending anywhere from five to fifteen years in the minor leagues, most umpires never forget dressing with the cockroaches and the stench, and they thank their lucky stars for the facilities, no matter how meager, that are provided in the majors. An orderly is also assigned to each umpires' room in the major leagues to run errands, bring the food, provided free of charge, from the refreshment stands and cafeterias, clean the room, and oversee the laundering and shipping of uniforms, underclothes, and equipment. Some orderlies are better than others, but their presence makes the time before the game easier and more pleasant. Each umpire tips the orderly three dollars per man per game.

Harvey, Wendelstedt, and Williams troop into the room somberly, slowly peel off and hang up their street clothes, then sink gingerly into cold metal folding chairs. Leaning forward, Harvey gropes blindly under a pile of clothes in his equipment case, eventually emerging with a metal foil pouch of Red-Foxx chewing tobacco; he stuffs two fingers full into his mouth. Still leaning forward, he moves the dry tobacco back and forth from cheek to cheek, soaking it in saliva; then, when it has gained the necessary gummy consistency, he tucks the soggy wad back into the far corner of his mouth. He hooks a wastebasket with his foot, drags it beside his chair and hawkers into it. Then he leans back; now he can relax.

For a while they sit in their white jockey shorts and T shirts, their feet up on the table, watching the silent television flutter. "I guess somebody should turn up the sound," said Wendelstedt, pulling his left foot onto his right knee to examine his wounded toe. His toenail had been smashed and partially stripped and a blue blood pocket had swelled up under the remainder of the nail, but he guessed he would live through the season. Another smash in the same toe, though, wouldn't help his cause any.

"Yeah, somebody sure should turn that television sound up," said Harvey, chewing intently.

"So what's wrong with you?" asked Wendelstedt. "I'm a wounded man."

"Me?" said Harvey, slightly smiling. "I'm the Chief."

"And chiefs don't do menial labor, I suppose?"

"You suppose right. We give the orders. You underlings do the job."

"You hear that, Art?" said Wendelstedt. "Underlings are supposed to do the menial labor. Can you beat that?"

"I hear it," said Williams, his eyes half-closed, seemingly oblivious.

"All I get is abuse around here," said Wendelstedt, shaking his head and pursing his lips. Wendelstedt had an absolutely infallible way of feigning righteous indignation. He would make his face go red and his cheeks puff out as if he were going to burst, then he would shake his head gravely and emphatically back and forth. He never smiled after faking his anger. A stranger could never tell whether he was joking or telling the truth.

"Abuse," Williams mumbled.

"Well, somebody ought to turn up the sound on that damn TV," Wendelstedt said.

"*The Untouchables* going to be on soon," Williams added.

"You really like that show, Art?" asked Harvey.

"Always good to see a bunch of white motherfuckers killing each other off."

"Goddamn lack of respect," said Wendelstedt.

"Art, you been so quiet tonight I didn't know you were around," Harvey said.

"I always know when he's around," Wendelstedt said. "Every time he walks into the room, it gets *spooky.*"

Williams sat up, suddenly laughing, and turned to Harvey. "You hear that, Chief?" He pointed at Wendelstedt. "You gonna let him talk to me that way?"

Harvey spat into the basket and shrugged. "What can you expect from a goddamn Nazi racist pig? A person with a name like *Wendelstedt* don't know any better."

"All them Africans like *The Untouchables,*" Wendelstedt continued, "cause they like the sight of blood."

"It's part of their past," said Harvey. "They got the voodoo in them. You got the voodoo in you, don't you, Art?"

"Still in me," said Williams, "so you better watch out. I got plenty of curses conjured up for you." He ran his fingers through his black springy hair, neatly cut into a well modified Afro, smiled, and played idly with a patch of gray about the size of a domino. A former minor league pitcher whose career was cut short by a sore arm, Williams had rich, dark brown skin, broad shoulders and a wide chest, somewhat softened now from inactivity. All around he was a good twenty pounds overweight, although he still looked much younger than his forty-three years.

Harvey rolled his head over to the side, spat with deadly accuracy into the basket, then closed his eyes. Only during the past few weeks had he felt completely comfortable joking with Williams this way. In fact, the joking had turned into fun for all four of the lonely men. Harvey knew that the by-play was a safety valve, more so for Art than anyone else, although it helped them all get by and kept them from each other's throats, something which is a constant danger when four men work together day after day for seven straight months.

Along with his appointment as chief this year, Harvey had been assigned the difficult problem of dealing with Williams, the man the National League owners and coaches had last year called the worst umpire in the league. Number twenty-four. Nor were there racial overtones in this judgment, as far as Harvey could make out. Pure and simple, Williams was not a very good umpire and Harvey and Wendelstedt, the two best in the league, had been teamed specifically to work with Williams and help him improve.

For sure, Williams had the talent and the desire to become a good major league umpire, but he lacked the confidence and experience the normal six or eight years of major league ball gives an ump. Williams was in the major leagues today because he was black, not because he had learned enough to be justifiably promoted, according to Harvey's sources. The National League office had very little choice in the matter. The government had demanded that there be a black umpire in the National League before the end of the 1972 season and the league had complied by picking the best of a small and relatively inexperienced crop. It was the league's own fault. Not until after the government's verdict did professional baseball begin an active and wholehearted recruiting drive to attract black prospects. And even that move had so far been a failure. The number of black officials in minor league baseball could be counted on the fingers of both hands.

As early as spring training Wendelstedt and Harvey had fashioned a set of rough signals to help guide Williams during the coming season. If he was calling pitches too high or low, lacking consistency, Wendelstedt would rock back and forth on his heels. If the game wasn't moving as fast or as smoothly as it might, Wendelstedt would tip his hat. If Williams took too much back-talk from players disputing his calls, Wendelstedt would dig his shoe into the dirt. Not that Williams needed instruction all of the time, but if and when he did, the signals had been established.

Harvey and Wendelstedt, discussing the problem at the beginning of the season, were well aware of the pressure under which Art worked each game and of their responsibility, partially at least, to help ease it. Williams was the first black umpire in the National League and only the second black umpire in the history of major league baseball. The recent racial difficulties of superstar Hank Aaron, who had been threatened and verbally attacked by people resenting his bettering Babe Ruth's home-run record, was a perfect and frightening example of the problems Williams might well be forced to confront.

"By the end of this season he should be all right," Harvey said, "but we've got to keep the kid loose while we're teaching him."

"One way to keep him loose is to start by hitting him where it hurts," said Wendelstedt, "right at his color. Then we hit ourselves back twice as hard. We leave ourselves open for him to hit us, too, which will teach him to strike back at others as well. We can't let him take abuse from players, managers, fans, or even other umpires. He's got to learn to stand up under pressure."

"I think he'll be a good umpire in another year or two," said Harvey. "He's got the size, he's got the natural instincts. I think he can be damn good, but we gotta keep him loose. We build up his confidence off the field, it will affect his confidence on the field. That's half the battle of being a good umpire, isn't it? I mean, the first thing is, you have to be right. The second thing is, you have to know you're right. Art is usually right, the problem is he doesn't always know it."

Now, two months later, Williams had progressed, but he was still far from the kind of umpire a major leaguer ought to be, Harvey realized. A good deal of work and training was still going to be needed. Williams's problem was less a question of knowing the plays and calls and more a question of experience, and confidence. He just wasn't sharp or consistent enough in making his calls. Worse, he backed down under the pressure of belligerent players and intimidating managers. For an umpire interested in establishing respect, this was not good.

Harvey leaned his head back and raised his eyes, trying unsuccessfully to listen through the floor above for the patter of rain. "You oughta use some of that voodoo on this weather," he said to Williams. "If the rain stops or even lets up for two and a half, three hours, we'll get in this game."

"Ain't a bad idea," said Williams, propping up his calloused feet and nodding.

"I sure don't want to come back to this town any more than I can help it," said Harvey. He thought about his home in San Diego, his wife by the pool stretched out casually in a redwood chair, his children playing in the grass with their blue and red plastic toys. In the cooler part of the evening, after dinner, Joy would brush the dog, clean its ears tenderly with an alcohol-soaked cotton dabber, then run with him. She was a master breeder and was hoping to someday become a show dog judge. She moved fluidly with her dog, her two legs in constant and gentle synchronization with the dog's four as they practiced together for an upcoming show. The image faded. He had been away from his family for so long, he couldn't keep them in mind for too long at any one time.

"Gotta come back here two, three more times anyway," said Wendelstedt.

"Yeah, but listen Harry, we play this one, that's one that's been played. You know that well as I do. Besides, what else do we have to do? Game starts at what? Eight? We got to wait at least an hour, maybe more, before they'll call it because of the weather. Then we get dressed and subway back into town. By then, it's ten o'clock; not much time to do anything after that anyway."

Harvey sat up, leaned forward and spat. Then he shook his head and waved his arms. "People think we like these rainouts. Gives us a day off. They forget we have to stay here half the night while the home team tries to decide when and if the rain's going to stop. And so what happens if the game *is* called?"

"I'll tell you what happens," said Williams. "We come back here and make the game up at the end of the season. At least some umpires will have to, if not us."

Harvey nodded. " 'Stead of single games in August and September, we get double-headers. What'd we have last year? Six, seven in a row?"

"Seven," says Wendelstedt. "I remember because it was fucking ninety-five degrees out. We were in Philadelphia for four games on a Saturday and Sunday, then moved to Chicago for double-headers Monday and Tuesday, then finally, St. Louis. By that time the heat wave left Philadelphia and moved west. We probably took it with us on the plane. Wherever we went, it was hot. Damn, six, seven hours in the sun, seven days running. I wouldn't want to do that any more than once a year. It was really hot."

"So were the tempers," said Williams. "Last year we had that five team race in the east and any one of those teams could have won it. Man, last year in Atlanta I thought I was going to melt out there, and those damn players were bitching about every call. Every call." Williams shook his head. "Pitcher could have heaved the ball into center field and if I wouldn't have called 'strike' he'd be on my ass in a flash."

"They're under a lot of pressure," said Harvey. "We gotta try to understand that."

"So are we under pressure," said Wendelstedt. "Who the hell are you kidding? While they're sitting in the dugout half of each inning bitching at us, we're out in the sun, wilting. We know there's plenty of money riding on each call. Damn players think we don't realize . . ."

"You don't have to tell me. They're all a bunch of crybabies," said Harvey, "especially the small change hitters."

"Like Grote," Williams said, grinning toward Wendelstedt.

"Yeah like Grote, like any of them. They hit for two, two and a quarter, lucky to be on base one out of five times and they got the nerve to bitch on every call.

"They're trying to *steal* first base," continued Wendelstedt,

" 'cause they can't get there on their own."

"The good players never complain, only the lousy ones. Mays, Aaron, Stargell, Billy Williams, they never say a word."

"Mays is working for the Mets now," said Williams, "sort of a glorified batting coach and scout. A little bit of public relations probably in there, too."

Wendelstedt shook his head. "Boy, you talk about Mays. I worked that World Series last year—the Mets and the A's—and it was pitiful to watch him. It was really awful to see the great Willy Mays tripping all over himself, couldn't catch a ball, couldn't run the goddamn bases. I was embarrassed for him."

"Man didn't know when it was time to quit," said Williams.

"Well my grandmother coulda told him. I tell ya, it was pitiful."

"He never complained though," said Harvey, "in all his years in baseball, he never gave umpires any trouble. He knew you were doing the best job possible and he was doing the best job possible. All the really good ones are like that, except maybe Cedeno in Houston."

"Cedeno's a kid," said Wendelstedt. "He'll learn he doesn't need an umpire's help to get on base. Can do it all by himself."

"I remember when Frank Robinson (who became the first black manager in baseball in 1974) was a kid in Cincinnati," said Harvey, "not too different from Cedeno. Boy, he was some hothead. One time Eddie Mathews, when he was playing for the Braves, put a particularly hard tag on Robinson when he was sliding into third base. Robinson gets up slowly, you know, sneering, acting tough, wipes the dirt from his pants, then says to Mathews, gets right up close to his face and he says, 'You better not ever tag me like that again, you bastard.'

"Eddie waits for a second and then he smiles. Got the goddamned deadliest smile I have ever seen. Smiles really big, almost apologetically. Then he punches Robinson right in the mouth, knocks him three feet behind the base, bends down right in close to Robinson's bleeding nose and says, 'How about that tag?' One of the funniest things I ever saw. The kid didn't say 'boo' for a week." Harvey shook his head chuckling, then got up to walk around. He stepped heavily, as if stamping at a bug, testing his sore legs.

Williams pointed to the silent television. "That's what we need, one of them submachine guns. No arguments in a game with Eliot Ness behind the plate."

"You don't need a submachine gun," said Harvey, "you got the Black Panthers to keep order for you."

"Least I'm pure black and beautiful," said Williams, "thank God I'm no fucking Indian half-breed." He turned to Wendelstedt. "When the old chief over there gets mad, he liable to scalp somebody."

"Bad enough working with a guy who's half fucking Indian, but when the other half is Californian, we draw two losers in one package," said Wendelstedt.

"All the goddamn hippie freaks in California come from New York and Florida anyway," said Harvey. "We native Californians are pure American perfection."

"You keep Florida out of this," said Wendelstedt.

"Those Jews down in Florida find out they got a Nazi racist pig in their homeland, they'll run your ass out of there. Remember what happened to Eichmann."

"Jesus Christ," said Wendelstedt, shaking his head, pursing his lips, blowing his face up watermelon red. "I'll tell ya, I can't take this any more. You're always insulting my nationality. You've got no moral dignity. Do I insult you because you're a half-breed Indian, red-faced bastard? I tell you I can't take this abuse much more. All I get from this crew is abuse. You'll be sorry when I quit and become a German baker."

"That's what you look like," said Harvey, "a Nazi racist German baker."

"I tell you," said Wendelstedt, "all I ever get is abuse around here."

"Damn," said Colosi, stomping his feet and shaking water from his black, rain-stained coat as he closed the door. "I been in those stands for half an hour."

"Thanks for taking my place out there," said Harvey.

"What for? No infield or batting practice to watch today," said Wendelstedt.

"I brought my boy here tonight," Colosi replied. "I stayed to talk to him. I didn't mind."

Umpires work a continuous rotation, the crew chief calling the first game of the year behind the plate, the others manning first, second, and third base in order of seniority. In this case that meant Wendelstedt, Colosi, then Williams. In addition to calling balls and strikes, the plate umpire rubs up the balls before the game, keeps score, and accepts the lineups from both team managers. From home, Harvey would move to third, Wendelstedt to home, Colosi to first, and Williams to second. The rotation continues that way through the whole year.

Since it is the easiest and the least taxing position, the third base umpire usually has the added responsibility of monitoring the field before each game. It is his job to sit in the stands during batting and infield practice of both the home and visiting team and enforce the non-fraternization rule. Simply put, players from opposing teams are not permitted to speak to one another before the game.

"It's a silly rule," says senior National League umpire, Tom Gorman. "After all, the players are talking to one another all through the game anyway. On the other hand, it just doesn't look good for the fans to see the opposing pitchers, for example, talking to each other before the game. The fans start getting some nasty ideas. This whole game is based on honesty. We don't want an idle conversation to cause suspicion.

"Actually, it's not much trouble for umpires," Gorman continues. "When the weather's nice, it's relaxing sitting out there, and when it's raining, they won't have infield practice anyway. The Spanish-speaking ballplayers break the rule more than anybody. There aren't too many people in the game who speak their language or talk about their homeland on each team. So when they see ballplayers from their own country, they take advantage of the situation. The only thing is, the league considers this a serious infraction and we have to report all known fraternization to the league office. The player will usually be fined a hundred dollars. I'm not quite sure a five-minute conversation is worth that much.

"There are a lot of things about baseball I'd like to see changed," says Gorman, fifty-five, a major league umpire for twenty-three years, with thirty-seven years in baseball. "This fraternization rule, though, is something different. I like it because the rule puts the umpire in a position to see things he isn't necessarily supposed to see.

"One time I was sitting in the stands, for instance, in Candle-stick Park in San Francisco. Only a few years ago. The Giants were playing Los Angeles. It was a good two hours before the game, and I was just sitting, enjoying the sun. There were some other people around me, so I couldn't be recognized from the field easily. Besides, we're supposed to sit out there in street clothes.

"Suddenly I see Herman Franks, who was the Giant manager at the time, stick his head out of the dugout and look around. Then he motions with his hands, all the time looking around, and suddenly I see three, four guys from the groundcrew come up behind him and start dragging out a fire hose. You know what they did? They soaked down the first and second base paths, quick as a flash, then they dragged that hose back in. Didn't take them more than two minutes, but it was lucky I was there.

"The point was, the Dodgers had Maury Wills at the time, you see. Not only could Wills steal bases, but he liked to bunt to get on. Now, in the two hours before the game, the field would dry sufficiently so that you couldn't tell it had been soaked down, but it would also be soft enough to slow Wills up by maybe half a step.

"Well, I delayed the game an hour and a half till the basepaths were completely dry. Franks was apologetic. 'Oh,' he said, 'I never considered Wills,' he said, 'I was just smoothing out the terrain a little, wanted the field to look nicer, you know? I was cleaning up.' He went around apologizing to everybody. OK, I figure, I give him the benefit of the doubt and I don't report this to the league office like I should have.

"You know what happened the next day, don't you? I'm sitting in the stands talking to a friend. It's early, couple hours before the game, and we're just sitting around, and suddenly I see Herman Franks peek out of the dugout, then motion behind him. And damn. It's that same groundscrew with the fire hose and Franks directing them. They soak down the base paths a second time. Can you figure that? Two days in a row, after I warned him. Well, you can imagine I wrote him up good.

"But that didn't bother me nearly as much as what happened a couple weeks later. Now, all through those two days with Franks soaking down the base paths, the Dodger manager, Walter Alston is indignant, bitching all over the place about how I should have called a forfeit of the game. He kept screaming about good sportsmanship. Oh, he was furious.

"So a couple of weeks later, I pull into Los Angeles, it was the Coliseum at the time—Dodger Stadium hadn't been built yet—and the Dodgers are playing the Giants. Well, I'm on third base, and it's my turn to watch for fraternization. Now I have to admit that maybe half the time umpires forget about this rule. They just don't want to go to the trouble of getting there especially early and sitting in a hard uncomfortable seat watching players and coaches beat the ball around the infield. Even the fans don't watch this. I'm as delinquent as anybody.

"It so happens I was there early that day and sitting up in the stands. Then I see Walter Alston, two 'weeks ago the indignant manager, and now he's peeking around the corner of the dugout, looking to see if any official is watching. He doesn't care if there are a few fans out there because they won't understand what he's doing anyway, but he looks around, then sort of nods his head down toward center field. You see, since managers don't know which umpire crew is coming into town for each series, it puts them at a disadvantage. They don't know what faces to look for.

"Suddenly I hear an engine start and see this goddamn big bulldozer come pulling out through the opening in the center field wall, roaring down and across the infield. You know what Alston's doing? He's hardening up the base paths, flattening them down so that his man Wills can get more traction. Also, he has the base path pressed down, but the foul line is still raised, making it almost impossible for a soft bunt to roll foul. Can you imagine the nerve?" said Gorman. "Of course, Franks and Alston weren't the first guys to pull these tricks. It happens more than I'd like to think about.

"I'll tell you, there's a lot of things to be thankful for. Baseball has given me a good life. But the most disappointing part of the game, at least for me, is the ballclubs' attitude toward it. We spend a lot of energy talking about fair play and sportsmanship, but you find out over the years that that's not what the game is all about.

"The ballclub officials spend a few days a year making and discussing the rules, then expend all their energies for the rest of the year trying to find a way around the rules. They're sissies, they'll do absolutely anything they think they can get away with to win—as long as the fans don't find out about it.

"In the end you realize that with the players, managers, coaches, and owners, it's not how you play the game, it's simply whether you win or lose that counts. That fraternization rule may sound silly to some people, but I'm all for that or any other law that helps put a stop to the people who care more about their own skins than the quality and dignity of the sport."

Harvey stuffed a second wad of tobacco in his mouth; the tobacco was the size and shape of a dying fig.

Wendelstedt grimaced. "Jesus Christ, that's a disgusting habit, chewing that seaweed. My wife says although I'm not too good looking, she gives thanks I've never allowed that saliva-soaked poison in my mouth."

"It's better than chewing gum," said Harvey.

"How do you figure?"

"There are no calories in tobacco, for one thing. For another thing, you'll never find a wad of tobacco sticking to your ass after sitting on the subway train. Chewing tobacco is hygienic."

"That logic escapes me," said Wendelstedt, shaking his head in amazement, "Talking to an Indian is like talking to a totem pole."

"You believe what you want," said Harvey. "I'll believe what I *know*."

"How many times you been spit in the face with tobacco?" asked Wendelstedt.

"Couple."

"Goddamn right, more than a couple. Plenty more. I'm telling you that stuff is a lethal weapon. I can name one guy that's got me probably a hundred times . . . Walter Alston."

"Well, that's a different story," Harvey said.

"What's so different about it?" Wendelstedt turned to Williams to explain. "You know how Alston stutters when he gets mad? Well, when he stutters, the goddamned tobacco comes out in a spray. Soaks your face.

"Herman Franks is worse than Alston, though," Wendelstedt continued. "He's a goddamn gnat catcher. When he chews tobacco, the juice rolls down his chin in a gooey sweet mess, and when it's a hot day, the gnats and flies collect there. They just stick to his chin. Sickening. Of course, Franks spits at you, too, but he does it on purpose. He's been ejected a number of times for spitting on umpires. I'm telling you, Art, one of the things you gotta learn is that we take a lot of abuse."

Said Harvey: "When Gene Mauch (Montreal Expo manager) gets mad, his veins start to pulsate in his neck until it turns all different shades of crimson. He looks like a pinball machine. Mauch's a good manager. He probably knows the rule book better than any other player or manager in baseball."

"Quit trying to change the subject," Wendelstedt interrupted. "He's trying to change the subject," he turned to Colosi, "so I won't tell you what happened to our fearless leader once in an argument with Expo coach Walt Hriniak."

"I don't care if you tell or not," said Harvey, hockering into the trash can. "It's just not true."

"It's true all right, you just don't want to admit it."

Harvey shrugged.

"The Indian squaw over there," said Wendelstedt, "is having this big discussion with Hriniak last year over a play. Hriniak was coaching first base, and he was really steaming about a call our leader over here made. Hriniak is a worse gnat catcher than Herman Franks. Sometimes he's got a beard of bees and flies around his chin, he's such a slob, and he and Harvey are hunched over first base, jawing and chawing at each other.

"Suddenly, Harvey stops midway between a sentence and tears ass toward the dugout.

"Well, I don't think much about it for a while, but the minutes pass and we had to get the game going, so I went down to see what was holding up our half-breed crew chief here, and wouldn't you know I find him in the goddamn visitor's dugout gagging over the water cooler.

" 'Aha! Aha!' I yelled. 'You finally did it. I told you that stuff was horseshit. You swallowed your chaw!' "

"Serves him right," said Colosi, laughing.

"Teach you a lesson," said Williams to Harvey.

"You think our fearless leader here, Cochise's answer to the atom bomb, would tell the truth? You think he would own up to it?" asked Wendelstedt.

"I told you what happened," said Harvey, "why do I have to repeat it again and again?"

"Because I can't believe it."

"I don't see what's so hard to believe," said Harvey, "a bee flew down my throat."

Wendelstedt dragged a box of sparkling white Spalding baseballs over to the wastebasket and pulled up his chair with a scrape. After emptying the box and removing the orange tissue paper wrapping from each of the balls, he lifted a three-pound coffee tin filled with mud down from the shelf above and poured a half cup of water into it. He scooped a dollop of mud about half the size of a level teaspoon with the index and forefinger of his right hand, spat into his left hand, rubbed his hands together, then lightly blanketed a virgin white baseball with a translucent coating of the mud. With the mud applied, he began rubbing it in hard but evenly with his thumbs and palms from one end of the ball to the other until the mud almost completely disappeared into the cowhide and the factory-new gloss had been thoroughly rubbed away. With the ball still white, but now dull in finish and with only traces of the mud remaining around the stitches, Wendelstedt threw it back into the box and picked up another. It had taken him approximately twenty seconds to properly prepare a game ball.

At the beginning of the game, umpires are given five dozen new baseballs to rub this way (eight dozen for a double-header). The balls remaining at the end of each day are counted by the home team and new balls are placed in the umpires' room to equal the required number. Ninety-five percent of the time, five dozen will be far more than enough.

Umpires, however, are not *ruining* a good game ball or sabotaging a pitcher's best efforts. The ball is mudded-up for some awfully good reasons.

First, the gloss on baseballs coming directly from the factory makes the ball too slippery, often too difficult, for a pitcher to maintain a grip. A sophisticated pitch like the knuckler, for example, is thrown only with the thumb and the tips of two fingers. As it is, the knuckler is difficult to control, but without a sure grip, it would be impossible. To control even the most elementary of pitches, however, a pitcher's body movements must be in perfect synchronization with time of release. A slippery ball could inadvertently be released too quickly. It could sail way over the catcher and harmlessly bounce into the backstop—or it could rocket directly at the batter's head.

One might think a shiny white ball would be easier to see and consequently to hit, but actually it is both dangerous and difficult for a batter. The ball, new and bright, is often swallowed by the sun during a day game or melted into the lights at night. A ball with a contrasting color rubbed into it is much easier to follow.

More often than not, a pitcher will request a new game ball because it isn't rubbed up enough. He will almost never complain if a ball gets by an umpire's watchful eye with too much dirt or with grass stains for, with any external matter attached, the ball can and usually will do some amazing tricks. Without half trying, a pitcher can make such a loaded ball dip and twist, spin or somersault; it is the umpire's responsibility, by carefully inspecting the game ball after virtually every play, to make sure a hurler doesn't get that opportunity.

A batter will obviously request a new ball if he suspects foul play or if he thinks the ball hasn't been rubbed evenly enough. The most difficult ball to hit is one with only a patch of factory gloss remaining. That patch will glint off the sun or the lights, giving the batter a distorted picture of where the ball really is. When a pitcher throws this ball, the batter will turn to the umpire and ask, "Shine ball?" If so, the umpire will throw a new ball in.

Not all mud will dull the gloss of a new baseball without significantly changing its color, not even some mud, but only a special kind of mud found in one place in the United States, a secret location on the moist banks of the Delaware River. This mud, discovered nearly a half century ago by Lena Blackburne, a former ballplayer for the St. Louis Browns, is very heavy and dark and consists of minute black particles of a substance similar to silicone. These particles remove the gloss from the ball, yet they are so translucent as to be almost invisible. Many other muds, from locations all over the world, have been experimented with by enterprising ballplayers and entrepreneurs, but the descendants of Lena Blackburne, to whom he passed down the secret location, are the only people who can successfully supply the material that can do the job without staining the ball.

Blackburne's family charges the ballclubs $150 per three-pound coffee tin, but this "super mud" is so efficient that each team only uses a container a year.

As Wendelstedt rubbed each ball, he inspected it carefully for cuts, scrapes, or sloppy workmanship at the seams. Balls of questionable quality were put to one side to be used by the home team for batting practice. He thought back to his season in the Class A Northwest League in 1963, or the year before that in the Georgia-Florida Class D League, when virtually any ball, as long as it was loosely covered with a substance resembling leather, was judged fit for play. Any of the balls he had eliminated from these ball bags in the major leagues were at least ten times better than the best of the balls used in the minors. He remembered watching many of the team owners scoop up the used balls at the end of each game and take them home where their children would use red rubber pencil erasers to rub out the grass and dirt stains and their wives would wash and scrub each ball with soap. The next day the owners would try to convince the umpires that these were the "new balls."

Back then, twelve years ago, when he first entered professional baseball, he had considered the minor league team owners the most corrupt and disgusting excuses for human beings possible. That was before he came to know the major league team owners, administrators, and managers. At Wrigley Field in Chicago, Pat Pfeiffer, the stadium announcer who seemed to have been with the Cubs for centuries, would position himself and his microphone directly beside the ball bag. When the home plate umpire wasn't looking, Pfeiffer would go through the balls, throwing out the best balls to be used when the Cubbies were at bat and the worst for when the visitors were at the plate. The ball boy, also a Cub employee, never interfered. It got so bad that the umpires had to mark each ball that was thrown out of the game with a ballpoint pen so that Pfeiffer couldn't slip them back in when the opposition was at bat.

In 1970, when Pfeiffer was moved up to the press box, the umpires were relieved, but not for long. Although he could have used the phone, Pfeiffer would visit the umpires' room before each game to check their current rotation. Each day he would ask for a free baseball for his grandchildren. ("You must be the most productive cocksucker in all of Chicago," Wendelstedt once told him.) The umpires would hand over a ball, usually, thinking it would promote good relations, much as they would give a ball to friends, once in a while, or to policemen for their children, but Pfeiffer would then take the ball directly to the club general manager. "See," he would say, "the umpires are stealing. They're giving away your new baseballs!"

Wendelstedt lifted a ball, partially split at the seam, and shook his head. This was the first year the major leagues had switched from a horsehide to a cowhide-covered baseball and none of the players were very happy about it. The ball looked and weighed the same or just about, but although neither the league administrators nor owners would admit it, the cowhide was most definitely inferior. For one thing, the cover was frequently knocked off the ball. This happened once every other game, not where the stitching was sewn in, but on the leather right around it; the leather would have been stretched and weakened during the sewing process, and that's where it would split. With the advent of the cowhide ball the major leagues had been sending the materials for stitching to Haiti to save labor costs. Since then the stitches had been far from even, often as much as an inch or inch and a half off balance. For another thing, the ball would die in the air. He had seen many well hit balls that would probably have been home runs in horsehide that suddenly just died and dropped in the wind on the field. Even the pitchers weren't too pleased. Privately, they claimed they couldn't control the ball nearly as well. But the cowhide ball provided each owner a savings of about two thousand dollars a year. And in baseball, when it's money versus a better game, the former will always win out.

Wendelstedt threw the last ball into the box, leaned back and breathed deeply. "Well, are we going to play or not?"

"It's raining like hell," said Colosi.

Harvey said, "I just called Jim Thompson, the business manager. The game's supposed to start at eight o'clock and he says they talked to the Weather Bureau and they said the rain would stop by nine."

"My son's out there," said Colosi.

"Goddamn," said Williams.

"Well, Straight Arrow, old chief," said Wendelstedt to Harvey, "deal out the cards."

By then, it was fifteen minutes before eight.

"I wish we could do something about changing that rain-out rule," said Harvey, picking up the king of diamonds Wendelstedt had just discarded and splattering a glob of briney tobacco juice into the waste basket. "Here we are, sitting and waiting for the damn rain to stop, and more than likely it's not going to stop. So the umpires have to sit and wait, the players have to sit and wait, and the fans are getting soaked to the gills. The rule says the home team has control until the game starts, then the umpires take over. I think we should have control all the way down the line."

"But the fans think it's us," said Colosi, shaking his head. "They're sitting there freezing their asses off 'cause we won't call the game. That's what they think."

"Right," said Wendelstedt, surveying his hand studiously before discarding. "This rule allows the home team too much leeway to play their silly games."

"They're not impartial like we are," said Harvey, nodding. If the home team is on a winning streak, the owners will do anything possible—put the fans and the players through hell—to get the game played. If the home team has been losing, they'll call it way before they have a right to."

"Or if the home team has been playing a lot of games lately," said Williams, "they'll call it just to give their players the rest."

"It all depends on money," said Colosi. "If they think they can get a lot of fans out for a twinight double-header the next night, they'll call a game for that reason alone."

"Everything depends on money," said Harvey, "and on winning. The home team is supposed to take the weather forecast and the condition of the grounds into equal consideration before making a decision on calling a game for rain or fog or whatever. They don't do that. They say to themselves, 'Do we have a better chance of winning today or tomorrow? Will we make more money calling the game or playing it?' That's what they want to know first."

"When the visiting team isn't coming back into town for the rest of the season, the umpires have the authority. Don't we override the home team in that instance?" asked Williams.

"That's true," Wendelstedt nodded, then turned to Harvey. "But look, Doug, you gotta be fair. You can't blame the Mets for this."

"I'm not blaming the Mets, alone," said Harvey, "every team does it. I'm just saying it's not good sportsmanship, that's all."

"The fans suffer the most," said Colosi, "and everybody blames the umpires."

Clucking his tongue, Harvey arranged some cards in his hand, then threw out the three of spades. Wendelstedt snatched it up quickly, then discarded the king of clubs. He had very big hands and hard, heavy fingers, each like the barrel of a gun.

Harvey said, "More than anything, the starting pitchers affect the decision. I remember when Koufax was pitching. The Dodgers would go out of their way to start a game. They'd wait two hours, maybe more. Otherwise Koufax, who had already heated up, would lose a turn. With Koufax in his prime, it was almost a guaranteed win for the Dodgers.

"Sandy Koufax was the best pitcher I've ever had the pleasure of seeing," said Wendelstedt. "Even better than Seaver. And Seaver is tops today."

"Walter Alston was a smart manager. He brought Koufax along real slow, didn't rush the kid. He knew that when Koufax found his control he'd be the best pitcher in baseball."

"What do you mean was a smart manager, Nick?" Wendelstedt asked. "Alston still is the best manager in baseball. One time I ran into Hank Aaron at an airport. This was a few years ago, but the Dodgers had just won the pennant the year before and Alston had been named to manage the National League All Star team. Aaron was on his way to join the team, but we got to talking about all the honors he'd had in his career. 'The most important thing to happen to me is still coming up,' he said. (He wasn't so close to Ruth's record back then.) 'The most important thing is working under Walter Alston this week,' he said, 'I respect him more than any other man in baseball.' "

Harvey said, "I was working the plate a couple of years ago on the West Coast in a game in which the Dodgers were getting clobbered. It was something like the third inning and the Dodger pitcher, Don Sutton, had already given up eight runs—three in home runs. He was really stinkin'. Finally, Alston comes out and walks up to me real slow, shaking his head back and forth, back and forth, looking really disgusted. 'I'm taking this man out,' he says to me, real gruff-like, nasty, motioning over at Sutton. 'And you want to know why?' he said. I just stared at him, didn't say a word. 'I'll tell ya why,' he said. 'Because I'm sick and tired of you umpires fucking over my pitchers.' I stood there in shock. I mean, I didn't do anything to deserve that. Sutton just didn't have it that day. On his way back from the pitcher's mound, after Sutton had left the field, Alston poked me in the ribs and winked, then walked back into the dugout."

"Now there's a man with a dry sense of humor," said Wendelstedt smiling wryly, turning his attention back to his hand.

"By the same token," said Colosi, "getting back to Koufax, the home team would call the game *against* Koufax, too. One time in Pittsburgh, I think it was my first year in the league, the game was supposed to start at two o'clock and Koufax was supposed to be the starting pitcher. Well, it had rained through the whole night before, so at ten-thirty the next morning they called the game. By noon the sun was out, and it turned out to be a beautiful day, but it was too late then. The Pirates thought they were real slick, calling the game so early, but they ended up looking like idiots."

"The artificial surfaces have made the whole proposition of calling the games because of bad weather more difficult," said Harvey. "Used to be if the game was stopped because of rain for a long enough time, all we had to do was walk out and take a look at the field. If the infield was too muddy or the outfield was submerged in ten feet of water, our decision was easy. Now the whole situation is different. Those automatic rollers can get a tarp over the infield three times faster than a bunch of men could—even when they worked like hell. And the grounds crew has got those machines now that suck up water riding all around the outfield during the rain. I forget what you call them."

"Game Savers," said Wendelstedt.

"Something like that," said Harvey. "So anywhere with artificial surfaces—and most National League clubs have them these days—the field is going to be fit to play on. The way the rule book reads, you gotta wait an hour every time the game is stopped because of rain. Then you gotta determine if the field's in good condition—which it always is. So the decision comes down to whether you think the rain is going to stop or it isn't. The only way to know that is to wait and find out."

"And if we get the game going again, and it starts raining again, then we got to wait another hour," said Colosi, "before we can call it."

"That's about right unless we have reason to think it won't clear up. Good reason," said Wendelstedt.

"As I say," said Harvey, "we should try to get the rule changed or clarified."

"And how we going to do that?" said Wendelstedt. "It's the most ridiculous thing I've ever heard of. There are forty-eight umpires in charge of enforcing all the rules in baseball and there's not one damn umpire on the major league Rules Committee. You tell me if that makes sense."

"We gotta do something about that," said Colosi. "This winter an umpire better be on it."

"The owners want to control the committee. They like to design the rules with loopholes so they won't have to abide by them. That's real sportsmanship," said Harvey, shaking his head and frowning.

"You talk about sportsmanship," said Wendelstedt. "Last year after the last game of the World Series, I ran into Chub Feeney down in the dressing room. Now here we got the president of the goddamn National League at the end of a successful season. Right? Me? I'm real happy, 'cause I'm going home to see my wife and kid. 'Well, Chub,' I say, 'hope you have a real great winter.'

" 'Great winter? Great winter?' he says. " 'How the fuck can I have a great winter when the Mets lost the World Series? They were my team!'

" 'Well thanks a lot, sports fan,' I told him, and walked on out. You call that sportsmanship from the president of the National League? He jumped all over me."

"Gin," said Harvey, smiling broadly and plopping a card face down on the discard pile.

"Damn, I told you there's no sportsmanship around here. I'm telling a story and while my back is turned, suddenly the old Indian squaw over here gins. I don't get no justice."

When the phone rang, Wendelstedt moved over beside Williams

at the television, watching Met announcer Ralph Kiner doing an elongated pregame show to fill in the network time. "Look at that dumb bastard," Williams said, shaking his head. "He keeps trying to get people to say things they don't mean."

"No different than any other sportscaster," said Wendelstedt.

"I been listening," said Williams. "He gets an older ballplayer or a former ballplayer on like Willie Mays, and he tries to get Mays to say that the major leagues are bringing ballplayers up too early. He keeps hinting around at this so Mays will say it. Then he goes to a commercial and when they come back afterwards, Mays is gone and Dave Schneck, a rookie, is there in his place. Then Kiner tells Schneck there's a better crop of young ballplayers in the majors than ever before. He's a two-faced bastard."

"One thing about Kiner," said Wendelstedt, "he'll give you a nickel for a dime anytime. That's the kind of guy he is. Only guy worst than Kiner that's been associated with baseball is Leo Durocher."

"Remember that old joke," said Harvey, hanging up the phone.

" 'Call me anything,' " Wendelstedt nodded, " 'call me *motherfucker,* but don't call me Durocher.' "

"What's the definition of a Durocher?"

"A Durocher," said Wendelstedt, "is the lowest form of living matter."

"Goddamn, it's nine-fifteen," said Colosi, "I wish to hell I hadn't brought my kid out here. What's the story on the game?"

"They're going to wait another fifteen minutes."

The game was postponed officially at 9:45 PM, precisely three and a half hours after the umpires had entered Shea Stadium and two hours after most of the fans had arrived. Colosi dressed quickly and left to pick up his son while the remaining three men slipped unnoticed out of the stadium and into the crowd. Then they stood in the subway train silently, jangling and bouncing the forty-five minutes back to their side of town.

Willie Rooks's Shirt

Whenever the sun made a brief, albeit frosty, appearance over Wrigley Field that bleary spring, almost everyone in the sparse, spartan crowd pulled himself out of his hunching cocoon of wool and fur to pay homage with a standing ovation. During the three games Doug Harvey and his crew officiated in Chicago on the tenth, eleventh, and twelfth of May, the temperature never once went over forty-seven degrees and the wind coming off the choppy waters of Lake Michigan blew at no less than 30 miles per hour.

Even though Harvey, Wendelstedt, Colosi, and Williams layered themselves with four-ply long-johns, black turtleneck sweaters, and canvas windbreakers for the weekend contests between the Cubbies and the Mets, they still returned from the field after each nine-inning set, stiff and brittle-boned, blue from the tips of their fingers to the tops of their toes.

Despite the discomfort, however, Chicago has always been if not a home away from home for umpires, at least one of their very favorite cities.

"Old man Wrigley doesn't want to install lights in his ballpark," explains Colosi, "so we don't have to work night games. This means we have our evenings to ourselves. 'Most everywhere, ninety percent of our games, except those played on Sunday, are at night, but here, we can go to a show, have a good dinner, live a more normal life."

"As normal as possible," said Wendelstedt, "considering this is the mugging capital of the world. Why, I wouldn't go across the street at night in Chicago without taking a cab."

"That's all right with me," said Willie Rooks, who sat stolidly behind the wheel of his green and white taxi, twisting and turning his body while his 1972 Checker wove through the lanes of buses and homeward-bound cars on Madison Street. "I'll take you anywhere you want to go. I ain't afraid of nuthin' 'round here."

"You mean," said Wendelstedt, "there ain't nuthin' 'round here you ain't afraid of."

"Shit," chuckled Rooks, hastily applying his brakes for a red light, "I'se fearless."

"Yeah, fearless. One time I asked Willie to take me to the graveyard, but he wouldn't do it. How's that for fearless?"

"I ain't goin' to the graveyard but once," said Rooks. "And when that day come, I'se stayin'."

Harvey, who had been watching the road, braced himself against the dashboard while the three men in the back crashed against the front seat, then bounced back into their chairs. "Well anyway, you *drive* fearlessly," said Harvey. "Goddamn it Willie, don't you ever watch where you're going? You almost hit a goddamn bus."

"He watch the girls," said Williams, shaking his head. "He watch his passengers. He watch his fingernails."

"If he has any time left," said Colosi, "then he'll watch where he's driving."

"I been at this so long," said Rooks, turning to address Colosi, Wendelstedt, and Williams, "I can smell my way through this here city."

"The way you drive," said Wendelstedt, "you must have a chronic bad cold."

"Goddamn it, Willie, would you watch the goddamn traffic!" Laughing, Harvey grabbed Rooks by the shoulders and turned him around, facing front.

Willie Rooks is an easy-going, smiling man who knows every ballplayer, every reporter, every bookmaker and policeman in town. Almost everyone, anyway. Anyone he didn't know, he had always figured, weren't hardly worth knowing. His life had been both satisfying and successful since he purchased his first cab more than twenty-five years ago and began to prowl the streets of Chicago the necessary sixteen, sometimes twenty hours a day to make his living. With his savings, Rooks had sent his youngest son to maritime school, and the child had done the father proud, becoming the first black to captain a federally-owned freighter, carrying government cargo from one end of the Mississippi to the other.

A handsome old man, Rooks is brown and shiny-skinned, somewhat paunchy, with closely-cropped, gray-white hair clinging to the back of his head. When Willie Rooks is asked his age by friends or regular passengers, each time he tells them truthfully, "sixty-two, eighty-five, ninety, forty-seven," depending on the way he feels that particular day.

As to how long Rooks has been transporting umpires back and forth from hotels to their respective ballparks, or to the airport to catch a departing plane, he actually cannot remember. He vaguely recalls that soon after he purchased his cab he picked up a group of big, joking men at the airport late one night. He got along so well with them that by the time they had reached their destination, he had agreed to chauffeur them around the city for as long as they wanted. Each time that crew returned, they called up the Rooks Cab Company and subsequently more crews began to phone. After a few years there wasn't an umpire in either league who didn't ride with Willie Rooks and there wasn't a taxi driver in all of Chicago who transported umpires except for Willie Rooks.

When umpires first started riding with Rooks he offered a cut-rate deal, since they had only about seven dollars a day to spend for transportation, food, and lodgings and their highest salary back then was no more than eight thousand dollars. Rooks is no stranger to hardship, but he vividly remembers the umps and the way they struggled to make ends meet. He remembers that they would stuff themselves with the hot dogs, Cokes, and packaged miniature pies provided after each ballgame, thus eliminating the need to waste money on dinner that evening or on lunch the following day. At least Rooks's job was steady then. At least he didn't have to worry about earning and saving enough money in seven months, to stretch out for an entire year. But as the umpires grew more prosperous, eventually striking for and gaining salary hikes and increased expense accounts, so too did Willie Rooks's prosperity grow. Now he received much more from umpires than from regular fares and, as gasoline prices and operating expenses increased, so too did the contributions of the men in blue. Just yesterday, Harvey and Wendelstedt had decided to pay Rooks sixteen dollars for each trip back and forth to Wrigley. And Rooks had never had to ask. Not once. Other umpires weren't so generous, but all were fair and scrupulously honest.

"I went down to George's last night after dinner," Harvey said. "That's the place old Jocko used to take us to. Jocko Conlan (former National League umpire) knew how to find the nice places and the good people in every city."

"Was Annette Sax still there?" asked Colosi.

"She'll always be there. Did you know she used to sing for Al Capone? Capone used to send his limousine over for her on nights he had parties. She's a grandmother with three grandchildren now and although George has moved his club a couple of times, Annette has sung for that man for forty straight years. That's really something. I really admire that. Before he retired, Jocko used to take me there, and as soon as he walked in, Annette would stop whatever she was singing and drag him up on stage. Jocko was the best tenor I ever heard. They called him the singing ump. I'm tellin' ya, no man could sing prettier. The place is really run down now, ya know, and her voice is a little scratchy, but it still makes me feel pretty good to go there, just to know she's still around singing those oldies. She knows every song that's ever been written."

"That's what I like about this city, and that's what I like about baseball," said Wendelstedt. "The tradition. Especially here in Chicago where the ballpark is still real old time. At Wrigley, you can smell the hot dogs, popcorn, and peanuts. And you can imagine that the same dirt you're standing on, give or take a layer or two, was occupied by guys like Gabby Hartnett, Cy Young, Babe Ruth. That's really somethin' when you stop to think about it."

"Of course, old isn't necessarily good," Colosi said.

"You better believe it," said Wendelstedt. "You remember the old Houston ballfield? You remember what happened when it rained?"

"The water spread like a rug over the outfield grass," said Harvey. "And it laid there all day. I remember coming to Houston my first year in the league. That was 1962. I had come from the minors to the majors, but when I got to Houston and saw what those poor guys had to play on, I thought I had been demoted again."

"It rained so much the water never had time to evaporate and the outfield was a swamp." Wendelstedt shook his head. "The ground was always so muddy and wet, it choked the power mowers. The grass grew up to our ankles and they couldn't cut it. And you know what lived under those nice high blades of beautiful grass?"

"Snakes," said Harvey. "I used to watch outfielders go after a fly ball, then suddenly scream and run in the other direction as the hitter rounded the bases. You found out later that the fielder had stepped on a snake. It was ridiculous."

"And how about those mosquitoes?" said Wendelstedt. "In the afternoon they came in like dive bombers the size of your fist, but at night they sent in the heavy artillery. They were smart to build the Astrodome. They knew that if they didn't get their team inside somewhere, the city would never sustain and support a major league franchise."

"You can't say that about all or even most of these so-called stadium engineers," said Harvey. "For the most part, the men who choose the sights and do the designing of these 'masterpieces,' are the laziest, dumbest sons o' bitches I ever heard of. You take Shea Stadium."

"You take Shea Stadium. That place is worse than a backyard in a tenement."

"They built the damn park too fast, without much forethought," said Harvey. "They made it mostly out of cement and put a thick layer of clay below it. Consequently, the outfield was covered with six inches of water throughout the season and none of the fans, players, or even the engineers could figure out why. I coulda told them there wasn't any drainage, but it took 'em years to figure that out. Two years ago they had to chop up all the cement and replace the clay with granite. So, some stupid engineer cost the taxpayers a fortune."

"Shea is pretty bad all right," said Wendelstedt, "but the worst ballpark is Candlestick Park in San Francisco. That place is cold and windy, you never know where a ball's going to land; it's just beyond belief. The engineers commissioned to pick a sight for Candlestick musta thought they'd been told to pick a sight for a memorial to Boris Karloff or Lon Chaney, 'cause there ain't no more despicable place in America, that's for sure. I tell ya, they had to be drunk to pick that place. Candlestick Park is the 'monsoon bowl of the world.' It's unfair to the fans, unfair to the players, unfair to everybody. You'll never see good baseball played out there. Why do you think the San Francisco Giants have never won a championship?"

Rooks pulled up at the curb in front of the gray, dusty, circus-like edifice of Wrigley and watched silently while the umpires trooped out. Then he took his cab around the corner and pulled it into his reserved "no parking" slot. He had decided to stay and watch the game today rather than attempt to cruise the city. It was too cold and raw and windy for an old man to care about drumming up a few dollars' business. Maybe a few years ago, but not now. Besides, he liked to spend as much time as possible talking to the umpires, and perhaps even better than that, listening while they talked. Those boys had been all over everywhere, from Candlestick to the Astrodome to Yankee Stadium, from one end of the country, from one end of the world, in fact, to the other. And he hadn't been many places at all. It was his hope someday to attend a World Series, although, to his sadness and chagrin, he was damn well certain that the Cubs would never be in it.

Upon arrival in Chicago, Harvey was notified by telegram that his crew would be required to measure and confirm the dimensions of the field and bullpen pitching mounds at Wrigley. This is a complicated and rather painstaking task performed by umpires in each ballpark twice a year.

Umpires must insure that the pitching mound is comprised of an eighteen foot in diameter circle, the center of which must measure fifty-nine feet from the back of home plate; that the front edge of the rubber must be eighteen inches behind the center of the mound, thus establishing a distance of sixty feet, six inches, from the front edge of the rubber (pitchers plant their spikes and push off against the rubber) where the pitcher begins his motion, to the point where the catcher receives the ball at the back of home plate. But the most difficult and time-consuming part of the entire process is the confirmation of the pitcher's slope: this includes the height above home plate at which the pitcher is permitted to throw, as well as the length and uniformity of the slope of the mound.

To check this, umpires, assisted by the groundscrew, (they call the head groundskeeper in Chicago Dick the Prick) hammer one stake into the ground at a point six inches in front of the rubber and a second stake six feet in front of the rubber both in line with home plate. Then they tie strings to the bottom and top of the stakes and stretch both strings from one stake to another across the mound. Finally they step back and survey the mound, trying to decide if it is uniformly sloped from one inch to ten inches within a five foot by six inch distance. They will measure this many different times and in many different ways before granting their approval.

Doug Harvey explains: "Actually, we're pretty sure no one is going to tamper with the field mound. Whatever its height or condition, right or wrong—and the groundskeepers work hard to keep it right—it's going to equally affect both the home and visiting pitchers. We don't even have to be too concerned with the mound in the home team bullpen, but you better believe we're especially careful when we examine the mound in the visiting team's bullpen. What the home team has been known to do is sometimes raise or lower or otherwise tamper with the height or the uniformity of the slope just to ruin the rhythm and the timing of the pitchers warming up there. And you know, the funny thing is, when we do find something wrong, you can't believe how the goddamn coaches and players argue with you. We don't accuse them of anything, we just tell them that they better get the groundscrew to straighten it out before the game and to keep it that way. But they actually believe that when we find something like this, we should ignore it, not make any waves. Can you imagine? They expect us to compromise our principles—even jeopardize our jobs in their behalf!"

Aside from officiating each game and measuring pitching mounds, umpires are obliged to follow up each ejection of a player, coach, or manager both with a personal phone call to league president Chub Feeney, within twelve hours after the game and, subsequently, with a written report of the ejection outlining the reasons for such drastic action. Such a system eliminates the possibility of an umpire being vindictive to a player or a team. It also enables league officials to be informed immediately in case a game is protested in response to the ejection.

Players, managers, and coaches are ejected for many good reasons—for unnecessarily delaying a game by doggedly and uselessly disputing a call or for yelling at an umpire mercilessly during a game and ruining his concentration. Colosi had ejected a groundskeeper earlier that year for incessantly rapping with a hammer on a Plexiglas screen. "I warned him ten times," explained Colosi. "You have to try to warn the players, tell them they're gone if they don't stop doing what they're doing. Most of the time, they listen. Sometimes they don't and then you've got to give them the thumb. You can't let people step on you in this game or you won't be up in the big time for long."

"More often than not," says veteran Tom Gorman, "you're throwing people out because they're using vulgar language. Any man who calls me something I wouldn't call him is going to be in trouble. This is not to say that we all don't swear once in a while —but sometimes there's reason, and sometimes they do it just to be nasty. For example, if anybody comes down on my family, my mother, they get the thumb. Right away. Instantly. I can't stand looking at them, they're no damn good. Get out of here. On the other hand, some guys can't seem to put together a sentence without swearing. You take Gene Mauch, manager of the Montreal Expos. Every other word he says is *fuck*. 'Fuck this, fuck that.' He probably says fuck when he goes to church and makes his confession. If I threw him out for every time he swore in a week, he'd spend the rest of his life in the locker room. Why, he's the vulgarest man alive. You see, we take this into consideration. He doesn't necessarily mean anything by it."

What happens if you throw a man out and he won't leave? Or if, after throwing him out one day, he cusses you out the next? What happens if, no matter how often you try, you can't seem to discipline the player, manager, or coach successfully?

"Well," says Gorman, "the league is supposed to take it from there. They have the option of suspending a man or fining him, after they talk to you and read your report. The problem is, the league is very hesitant about taking positive action. The president doesn't want to get the owners mad at him. After all, the owners pay his salary and if he suspends a player or a manager for a few days, he's not going to have so many friends come reappointment time."

Gorman, a thick-necked man with a scarlet Irish face and heavy, sagging jowls, hesitated for a moment, then smiled.

"One time, right before Chub Feeney took over for Warren Giles as president of the National League, I was having trouble with Johnny Logan, shortstop for what used to be the Milwaukee Braves. I threw him out one day for swearing at me. Next day, he swore at me again and I threw him out again. Logan just didn't seem to care.

"That night I called up Warren Giles and told him I needed some help with Logan, couldn't control the son of a bitch."

" 'I'll see what I can do,' Giles said. I got the distinct impression he didn't care one hoot about my problem.

"Next day I saw Logan on the street and I told him he better watch his mouth or he was gonna end up fined or suspended. 'I ain't gonna let you play another ball game,' I warned.

" 'Yeah, sure,' Logan says, 'go take a walk. Don't bother me.'

"Next night, same thing happened. Logan cussed me out, called me every name in the book and I ejected him. Later, I called up Giles and Giles was as disinterested as ever.

" 'Ok, ok,' he says, 'so Logan swore at you a little. Doesn't mean I need to take drastic action. Give the guy a break. Ain't you got any compassion?' he says. 'So what if he called you a few bad names?'

" 'Called me bad names?' I said to Giles. 'Called me bad names? It's you he says is *horseshit.*'

" 'What did he call me?' Giles all of a sudden went crazy. I thought he was going to have a heart attack.

" 'He called you *horseshit,*' I said.

"Next day, Logan was fined $250."

"Warren Giles," says thirty-year veteran National League umpire Al Barlick, now retired and working as a part-time consultant on umpires for the National League. "Warren Giles," he says again, sadly shaking his head. He is a large man, with a belly as big as a beach ball, a gravelly, trombone-like voice, and salt-and-pepper hair cut in a military flat top.

"Every time I hear his name, it gets me upset. He was the worst excuse for a league president I've ever seen," says Barlick who, periodically through his career, was troubled by a weak heart.

"In 1956, when my heart first went bad, the league office, then in Cincinnati, sent my league physical to my personal doctor. I had been just recently hospitalized and Fred Fleig figured the physical I had taken at the beginning of the season might help the doctor diagnose my problem. It was nice of Fleig. Fleig has always been nice to umpires. He's always been a man we could trust. Chub Feeney is a good guy, too. He doesn't understand as much about umpires as he should, but he's fair and decent and honest. He keeps his word. But Warren Giles . . .

"Earlier that spring," says Barlick, "when I first took the physical, I called up Giles and asked him about the results. He said it didn't look good. That's all he ever said. 'It didn't look good.' I coulda told him that myself.

"When my doctor read the physical report from the league, he looked up at me in astonishment. 'Jesus Christ!' he yelled. You know what that physical said? It said I had high blood pressure, sugar diabetes, and emphysema, but Giles never once said a word about it. He decided not to tell me, I figure, because he didn't want to pay an extra umpire's salary all season while I was in the hospital. I guess he was just hoping I would last out the year.

"In 1963, when the league changed the rule on the balk, and the sportswriters were taking potshots at us for calling the balk on pitchers so often, I tried to get Giles to back us up, to defend us, to tell the writers and the fans that we were just doing our job. You think he would? Hell, no! He made the balk rule, but he wanted us to enforce it without him getting involved. He wasn't interested in backing us up by saying one word.

"One day I got really fed up. I called my crew into the umpires' room and told them I was going home, quitting. I'll tell ya, that was the longest plane ride I ever took, but I had my satisfaction. Giles called me at home every day for two weeks, but I refused to talk to him on the phone, I was so pissed off. He wouldn't give us any support on a rule he made up himself. He didn't even have the guts to point out to the writers and fans that the umpires don't make the rules, they only enforce them.

"Warren Giles," says Al Barlick again, shaking his head and

staring at the ground. "Warren Giles was the nearest thing to nothing I've ever seen."

Abandoning the umpire's shirt and cap he usually wore during the work day week, Willie Rooks went to church early that Sunday morning, wearing his new, gray tweed sports jacket, a red shirt, charcoal pants, white tie, and brown and white shoes. At 11:30 AM, after services, he drove to the Pick Congress Hotel to meet the umpires, load their baggage, and transport them to the ballpark in plenty of time for the two o'clock game. At Wrigley, the police permitted Rooks to pull right up on the sidewalk to unload the umpires' suitcases and store them safely in the ticket office. After parking, Rooks joined Colosi, Wendelstedt, Williams, and Harvey in the umpires' room, talking, laughing, and sipping cups of black coffee until the game started. Then he selected a place to watch the game from any vacant seat in the house. And there were plenty of them, as cold as it was this spring. Near the end of the game, Rooks reloaded his taxi and waited on the sidewalk, engine running, for the umpires to emerge from the ticket office, carrying disguised bottles of Budweiser in brown paper sacks. With any break in the traffic, Willie Rooks would have the umpires at the airport within forty-five minutes, concluding an enjoyable and profitable day.

Wendelstedt leaned forward over the front seat and lifted the lapel of Willie Rooks's jacket. "You know, Willie, I've seen that shirt you got on before."

"That a very popular style," said Rooks.

"It's got a funny kind of weave in it, something like linen, except it's even nicer. Looks nice with your white tie."

"I got it at Chase's. You ever heard of Chase's? Goddamn best men's store in the goddamn city. Paid a pretty penny, too, I don't mind tellin' ya."

"I used to have a shirt just like that," said Wendelstedt. "I remember the weave. I like the way it looks. I think I bought it in New York, three, four years ago, sometime after I got married."

"Went down to Chase's and told the man I wanted something really smart to go with this new tweed jacket. You like this jacket, Harry?"

Wendelstedt nodded disinterestedly. "Looks good."

" 'Price is no object,' I tell the man," said Rooks. "What a man put on his back, got to make him look good and feel good, 'specially on Sunday."

Wendelstedt, still leaning forward, lifted some of the slack material of the shirt and ran his thumb and forefinger up and down its surface. "That even feels familiar, goddamn it. What the hell did I do with that shirt?" he turned to Harvey.

"You think I'm your goddamn valet? I'm a crew chief."

In the back, Colosi covered his mouth with his palm, and Williams turned to smile out the window. Rooks gritted his teeth, seriously attempting to concentrate on the road. Then he said: "That man show me white shirts, gray shirts, silks and plaids to try on, but I tell him I ain't going to fool around. I can't exactly describe the shirt I want, I tell him, but soon as I see it, I'll know."

"I can't remember what I did with that damn shirt," said Wendelstedt, frowning. "You remember the shirt I'm talking about, Nick?"

"I got my own wardrobe to worry about," Colosi said gruffly.

"There was this one blue shirt I liked a lot that he show me," Rooks continued, "with a special knit. He call it cable knit. But I tell him, no, I need something to wear with a tie. Then he brings out this here shirt I got on and I know right away this is what I want. I try it on and it fit just right. Fit like it was made for me. Never once ask the price. I don't care what I pay for a shirt, long as it feels good on my back," said Rooks. "A shirt got to look good and feel good for a man to be happy, is what I always say."

Wendelstedt shook his head, leaned back in his seat, locked his eyes in a half-shut position, then meditated for thirty seconds. Suddenly he jumped forward, grabbed Rooks, and lifted the collar of the fancy red shirt. "Goddamn it, Willie, that's my goddamn shirt! That's my laundry mark! Since when is your name *Wendelstedt?*"

Wendelstedt folded his arms, shook his head, and flushed his cheeks, then looked around at his friends for any sign of interest or recognition, but Harvey was reading a newspaper, Colosi was studying his fingernails, and Williams was staring at a particularly nice-looking statue of a Civil War hero to his right out the window. "Can you imagine the goddamn abuse I have to take? Can you imagine the nerve?" Wendelstedt mumbled to no one in particular. "My own crew turning against me, stealing my favorite shirt and giving it to a lying goddamn black bastard cab driver. I'll tell ya, that's really something, really something. All I ever get is abuse around here."

Wendelstedt leaned back, lifted an amber bottle, and took a deep swallow of beer. His big, blunt face seemed to light up when he drank beer. He always liked two or three bottles, especially after a tiring game, and he disposed of them fast, like water. After studying the traffic for a while and concentrating rather distantly on receding passersby, he said: "Remember that time the Mafia was after you, Willie?"

"Hot dog, I sure do." Rooks glowed, shook his head, then chuckled.

"Wait a minute, Willie, you claim to be fearless," said Harvey. "You didn't let them dagos bother you, did you?"

"In this town, when The Organization after you, all bravery cancelled out," says Rooks.

"This was two years ago when I was traveling with Lee Weyer," said Wendelstedt. "And you know Weyer; he'll do anything for a practical joke. Anyway, I go with Weyer into this novelty store down the street from the hotel and we buy a string of firecrackers and some of those decals you put on the rear window of your car that make it look like you've been sprayed with machine gun fire. Then we go back to the hotel and I call up Willie and tell him to come early to pick us up before the game, tell him I want to buy him a cup of coffee before the other guys get there."

"That's all you got to tell Willie. He'll do anything as long as somebody else will pay for it," said Harvey. "Of course, he didn't charge us anything for wearing your shirt."

"Except the shirt," said Williams.

"Yeah, we had to promise to give him the shirt."

Wendelstedt sneered, shook his head, and continued: "Weyer waits in the lobby till he sees Willie pull up and walk into the coffee shop. Then he sneaks out, pastes the decals on Willie's rear window and walks, cool as a cucumber, back into the lobby and meets us in the coffee shop.

"Meanwhile, there was this gang war going on in Chicago at the time, see, spread all across the front pages of the newspaper—everyone was discussing it—and Willie and I were sitting and talking, and I'm giving old Willie all the gory details about the five people killed so far. Really laying it on, telling about how their skin was all shredded by machine gun bullets and how police had to search whole city blocks to find the remains of the victims. Willie, you know, he's not much for reading the newspapers, so he's just listening to all this stuff open-mouthed. Thinks the whole thing is fascinating. Keeps saying to me, 'Is that right? Is that right? Right here in Chicago? Well, goddamn! Hot dog! Waddya know!'

"Then Weyer sits down, orders a cup of coffee, and joins in the conversation. I'll tell ya, Weyer's really slick, calm and quiet, although you know he's just bustin' up inside, thinkin' about what he's going to do to poor old Willie.

" 'The funny thing about these shootings,' Weyer says, 'I was just talkin' to this cop and he was tellin' me that each and every one of these murders took place in a cab. Only when the victim was in a cab.'

" 'No shit,' Willie says. Already you can see his whole face turnin' purple.

" 'That's what this cop told me. The victims were all killed in cabs between the hours of noon and one o'clock.'

" 'What time is it?' I say to Weyer.

" 'Quarter to twelve.'

" 'Goddamn!' said Willie. Man, that was the first time I ever saw a black man go completely flush."

"Well," Willie turned, remembering, "I got to thinkin' how them victims coulda just as easily been in my cab, as anyone else's. Besides, them boys, Wendelstedt and Weyer, were really convincing. Sure enough, they could fool the Pope."

"Anybody could fool the Pope," said Colosi.

"Pope goes the weasel," said Williams, laughing.

"After a few minutes talking, we tell Willie we want to go for a ride through the city," Wendelstedt continued. "It was really pretty that day; the flowers were blooming in all the parks."

"That's one of the main reasons I like this town," said Harvey. "The parks are just beautiful; spread out along the banks of the lake are flowers of a hundred different colors. Rainbows of petals. In other cities the downtown area is dreary and dirty, but in

Chicago it's pretty and sweet all the way from the hotel to the ballpark. Reminds me of home."

"Nothin' reminds me of home more than women," said Williams, "and this town is chock full of them black beauties. I'm having breakfast this morning over at the Harrison Hotel across from the Pick and these four sisters come in and sit down beside me. One of the waitresses right away tells them who I am and before I know it, they're all gathered around, asking me questions and gettin' my autograph. But this one—Williams paused to simulate the curves of her body with his outstretched hands—this one, named Violet, I swear, she was endowed with everything imaginable in a woman. I swear, she was beautiful. She ask me what I'm doing tonight, whether I dig the good wine, the sweet weed, or the sets."

"What the hell is sets?" asked Wendelstedt.

"You don't know the lingo, you out of the picture," said Willie Rooks from the front of the cab.

"I tell her I got a wife and grown children at home, and besides I gotta leave town today, but man, I was sorely tempted. Really tempted.

"Know what she said? 'Brother, that ain't got nothing to do with what we could get together right now.' Man, was I tempted. Lucky my heart is pure," he laughed.

"So we get into Willie's cab," Wendelstedt continued, raising his voice momentarily to regain the floor, "and Weyer starts telling Willie where to go. Turn here, turn there, you know. In the course of the ride, Weyer also mentions that every one of these killings happened on Washington Boulevard. He just sort of throws that out casually. Meanwhile, I could see old Willie up there in the front seat sweating; his hands are shaking slightly and he's puffing on his cigar so hard it looks like a volcano.

"Just then Weyer says, 'Turn here!' And before Willie knows what's happening or thinks about resisting, we're driving down Washington Boulevard."

"Goddamn," said Williams, laughing, "old Willie musta shrunk three feet down in his seat."

"What I don't understand," said Harvey, "is why Willie didn't see the decals on the back of his cab."

"Shit. You ever know Willie to look in his rear view mirror?"

"Too many things happening in front of me," said Rooks "to worry about what going on behind."

"Anyway, here we are driving down Washington Boulevard between noon and one o'clock in a taxi, and you can sure guess what Weyer did next. What I'm tellin' you is the absolute truth."

"It's true," said Rooks, "I almost died through it, it's so true."

"Weyer waits for a time when we're going real slow and there's not much traffic around, then he takes out his string of firecrackers, rolls down the window, lights the crackers and throws them outa the car. You should have heard those explosions. It sounded so real, I thought I could hear the ricochet of the bullets.

"Well, Willie goes crazy. He pulls halfway to the side of the road, slams on the brakes and turns around. What's he see? There's me and Weyer slumped on the seat, our eyes all bugged out, and we're looking so fucking dead it's sickening. And there's poor old Willie Rooks, who's turned almost albino by this time. Willie looks down at me, my tongue is hanging out. He looks at Weyer, he's got his eyes closed and his mouth all contorted up like some deranged killer. Then he looks up and sees the machine gun bullet holes through the rear window. 'Mutha Fuck,' he said. Real long and drawn out, 'Mutha Fuck.' The next second he was gone. In my whole life, I never saw an old man jump so high or run so fast. We caught him hiding—no, he was cowering—behind a building nearly two blocks away."

"That Weyer is a real bastard," said Harvey, smiling. "You guys really had old Willie going."

"Worst thing I ever done to anybody in my whole life," said Wendelstedt.

"I don't know about that," said Rooks. "You got me that time good, but you got me worst before. When they together, I wouldn't trust Weyer and Wendelstedt far as I could spit."

"I wish they were still together," said Harvey. "They deserve each other."

"Hey, Willie," said Wendelstedt, smiling broadly, "you remember when Pete Roselle called you?"

Late one night last spring, while transferring planes in Chicago for a game on the West Coast the following day, Wendelstedt and Weyer wanted to phone Rooks from the airport. When they looked up his number, they discovered that Willie had taken out a full-page ad in the Yellow Pages for Rooks Cab Company. "Go Anywhere. Anytime." It was two in the morning when they woke him up.

"This is Pete Roselle, commissioner of the National Football League calling," Weyer had said. "I'd like to speak to Mr. Rooks personally."

"This is Mr. Rooks," Willie had said, groggily.

"Mr. Rooks? This is Pete Roselle. I've got thirty National Football League officials stranded here at the airport, and I want to get them downtown to a hotel, and there are no taxis out here right now. We've got a convention to go to tomorrow and I want them to get some sleep. Now, can you send some of your men out here to pick them up?"

"My men? What do you mean, 'Some of my men'?"

"Some of your drivers."

"I ain't got but one man," Rooks had said, "and that's me. And I'm sleepin'."

"You only have one taxi?"

"How many taxis one man need?" Willie had asked.

"Then what the hell you got a full-page ad in the goddamn Yellow Pages for?" Weyer had replied in a furious tone of voice.

"Cause ads is cheaper than automobiles," Willie had answered firmly.

A few minutes after Wendelstedt finished the story, Rooks pulled into O'Hare airport and chugged up the drive, passing each terminal slowly until he stopped at the blue and white American Airlines sign. Each man shook hands with Rooks somberly, then they picked up their cases and walked inside. In seconds they were gone, blurred first by the thick glass of the sliding doors that lead into the terminal, then swallowed by clusters of scurrying travelers.

Rooks folded the money they had given him into a much larger wad of ones and fives that he pulled from his pocket, then climbed slowly into his green and white Checker. He looked at his watch and mumbled. If he hurried, he could make it back home in time for a cold beer before dinner. He started his car and pulled down the drive, kicking gravel and burning rubber as he shot onto the expressway.

The Battle of the Burning Cigars

Harry Wendelstedt neither knew nor cared whether Willie Rooks had recognized Lee Weyer's voice that night at the Chicago airport more than a year ago. It didn't matter; the success or failure of the joke they had pulled on Willie Rooks had nothing to do with the purpose of it. What mattered, pure and simple, was that Rooks had permitted the umpires to have some fun at his expense; for whatever reason, Rooks had been willing to serve as a diversion then, and on many other long, lonely nights and boring, listless afternoons that the umpires endured on the road. Certainly there was no harm done, playing an innocent prank, and yes, the stories the umpires told about their exploits with Rooks were usually embellished more with each subsequent version. But that didn't really matter much either. Along with Harvey's appreciation of Chicago's flowers, Williams's harmless infatuation with Chicago's women, and Colosi's enjoyment of normally-scheduled evening meals here, Willie Rooks had humanized this city for Harry Wendelstedt as he had for many other umpires. And Wendelstedt appreciated that more than anything.

For umpires, most cities are bloodless, juiceless, odorless, and stainproof, like artificial turf. While ballparks have their share of characters, most lack character. By eating out night after night, food, even in those cities with good restaurants, begins to taste the same. All hotel rooms, luxurious or lowly, still have four blank walls, tired pillows, unfriendly beds, repetitious TV.

Sometimes Wendelstedt felt as if he were following Perry Mason reruns around the country, not baseball teams. Sometimes he felt that reading one more local newspaper, taking one more walk around a strange block, watching one more boring soap opera, making one more whirl through a bleak lobby, or listening to one more dripping faucet would drive him batty.

There were, of course, friends you made, bouncing back and forth from town to town, season after season. There were special people, old, young, freaky, or ordinary, everyday people. Wendelstedt thought back ten years to one lonely night, and to the beginning of a very memorable friendship with one old man, now dead.

Wendelstedt had been a raw rookie then, in the first month of his first year of major league ball. The night in question he worked a game in Los Angeles and had had a rough time behind the plate; he had been involved in two controversial calls and was eventually forced to eject Dodger Manager Walter Alston. It was his first ejection in the major leagues and Wendelstedt cursed Providence for making it Alston.

He was the junior man of a crew comprised of Shag Crawford, Ed Vargo, and Doug Harvey. After the game Harvey went to meet his wife, who was visiting from San Diego; Crawford and Vargo were planning to dine with friends. All alone, tired, and somewhat deflated in spirit and confidence, Wendelstedt wandered into the Hollywood Roosevelt Cinegrill, across the street from Graumann's Chinese Theatre. He sat down at the bar next to an old man with bristly gray hair, who was wearing an old-fashioned, double-breasted, pin-striped gray suit.

For a while, Wendelstedt sat and stared into the mirror behind the bar, sipping Scotch, and regretting every minute he had ever spent in baseball. He had worked four years before being called up to the majors—an unusually brief apprenticeship before reaching the top of his profession—but still, he had worked damn hard. Now here he was, all alone, perhaps the most hated man in Los Angeles at that moment. It just didn't seem fair.

Wendelstedt watched the band assemble on stage for their next set, then watched as the bandleader in a shiny black tuxedo approached the microphone to announce that the next half hour of music would be dedicated to Sam Messenheimer, the composer of scores for many movies, most especially the *Wizard of Oz*.

The music soothed Wendelstedt; old music almost always delighted him. And the music tonight brought back memories of an old movie house near Baltimore and the Sunday afternoon when his parents had taken him to see the *Wizard of Oz*. The memory was pleasant but it also made him homesick. He had come so far and traveled so fast since that lazy, hometown, suburban Sunday years ago; it was a long way from the rage and ridicule he had so recently confronted on the field. He ordered another Scotch and turned to the old man beside him. "Boy, that's pretty music," Wendelstedt said.

"I like it," said the old man, wrinkling his sun-bronzed leathery cheeks in a smile. "It sure beats rock and roll."

"I like all music," said Wendelstedt, "but tonight this just fits my mood; it reminds me of old and pleasant times."

"Same way I feel," said the man, nodding. "I remember a lot of pleasant moments, listening to this stuff."

"Yeah," said Wendelstedt. "I had a bad day today, but this makes me feel a lot better."

"Sorry to hear that. Me? I had a wonderful day. I went to the ball game."

Wendelstedt grimaced, but remained silent. He began to turn away, but the old man continued speaking.

"Of course, when I go to the baseball game, I don't care who wins or loses; I don't have any favorite players. Me, I got a thing I like to do, never met anybody else but me who liked to do it, but I get a real kick out of watching the umpires. I go to as many baseball games as I possibly can, but all I ever care about is watching the umps."

"What the hell for?" asked Wendelstedt, incredulously.

"I don't know. Oh, I guess I do. I'm fascinated with anonymity, the people behind the big plays and the big names. For example, everybody remembers Judy Garland from the *Wizard of Oz,* but who knows Sam Messenheimer? Nobody." His smiled faded momentarily to sadness, but then he shrugged and said: "Listen, did you see the game?"

Wendelstedt nodded.

"The most exciting parts of the game were two controversial

plays at the plate and an argument over the second play between Walter Alston and the umpire. Right? Now that game wouldn't have been worth anything without that argument. I mean, it was a boring game until the rhubarb made it exciting, and the umpire made the rhubarb. I mean, he didn't start it, but without the umpire, there wouldn't have been an argument. The ump was a young fella named Harry Wendelstedt, a big guy, but still, we wouldn't know him in a thousand years if he came here. And you wouldn't know this guy Messenheimer, either. But without Messenheimer's music for Judy Garland to sing, without Wendelstedt for Walter Alston to dispute with, without them, where would we be? It would be an awfully dull life."

"You're putting me on," said Wendelstedt angrily, his large hand rolling into a sledge of fist. "I had a bad time tonight and I'm just not up to being put on."

"What the hell are you talking about?" said the man, who was suddenly getting angry too. "You know, I'm under a lot of strain tonight myself and I don't need no young punk to make it worse. You started talking to me first, I didn't speak to you."

"If you weren't such a goddamn old geezer, I'd punch you right in the mouth," Wendelstedt nearly yelled. "I don't like being put on." A number of people had turned to listen to the argument, but at that moment he didn't really care. For an instant he felt as if he were confronting Walter Alston all over again, jawing at home plate.

"What the hell are you talking about?" the old man repeated, lifting himself from his bar stool and curling his fists. "I may not be your age, but I'll fight you any time you're ready."

Wendelstedt almost laughed at the frail old man. Why, Doug Harvey could knock him cold with a splat of tobacco juice, he thought. "You know exactly what I'm talking about," he said, "I'm Harry Wendelstedt."

"No!" The old man peered intently through the dark at Wendelstedt's face.

"That's right."

"No."

"I'm telling you."

"And you know who I am?" said the old man.

"I suppose you're Sam Messenheimer," said Wendelstedt sarcastically.

"Right."

"No."

"I'm telling you."

Immediately, they whipped out their wallets and exchanged driver's licenses. Both men had to read each other's identification two or three times to believe what had happened.

From then on, there would be two tickets waiting for Sam Messenheimer at the Los Angeles Dodgers' press gate whenever Wendelstedt or any of the other umpires to whom he introduced Messenheimer came into town. Messenheimer often returned the courtesy by inviting umpires for bourbon and music at his tiny apartment in North Hollywood, which was crammed with records and scores of original music in every corner and cubbyhole of each shabby room. Although the *Wizard of Oz* and other Messenheimer hit songs had brought fame and fortune to many people, the old man lived modestly on a few remaining royalties and social security payments. Without the umpires, he couldn't have afforded to go to so many ball games, nor would he have had so many good friends.

"Hey, Doug," said Wendelstedt to Harvey, as the four umpires sat in an airport, sipping coffee, waiting to catch a plane. "You know who I was thinking about the other day? Sam Messenheimer."

"Old Sam. Goddamn, I miss that old cockroach. How long has he been dead?"

"Couple years. I ever tell you how I found out about his death?"

Harvey shook his head.

"The year before last," said Wendelstedt, "I had been in L.A. two, three times without seeing him. You know, he'd come down to the dressing room after the game, or he'd meet us at the Cinegrill. Anyway, I called him up one day, and there was no answer. Finally the operator clicked on and told me the phone had been disconnected."

"He was always so damn nice to umpires," said Harvey. "You know, you're away from home twenty-nine out of thirty days a month, and it was comforting to know that there would always be a friendly face and some real good music waiting for you when you hit L.A. without your having to sit in a bar. He was probably one of the few real fans umpires have had."

"An umpire can count his fans on his thumbs," said Colosi. "I get cards once in a while on my birthday. People wish me a happy birthday, then they say they hope it's my last."

"So the operator tells me that his phone is disconnected and that all calls are being taken by another number. I call there, of course, ask for Sam, and this guy on the other end, sounds like a kid, maybe twenty-five or thirty, tells me matter-of-factly that he's Sam's son and Sam's dead. Been dead a couple months. Well, you know I suspected something like that, with his telephone disconnected and all, and not seeing Sam around that season, but still, you know? I felt like somebody had dropped a ton of shit on me."

"Sure."

"So I offered my condolences and hung up. I was in shock. He was an old man, but still, you're always sad and suprised when somebody you really like dies without warning."

"Anyway, I got myself together and the next day I called back, introduced myself again, and asked the kid if I could have a picture of his father. Do you know what he said?

"He said, 'That's the stupidest sentimental thing I ever heard.' "

"Damn," said Harvey.

"I said to this kid, you know how Sam's closets and shelves were stuffed with all those old compositions and records? I said, 'Do you have any of his old music you might be willing to give away? Just so I could have something as a keepsake. He was really a good friend to me.'

" 'I threw all that shit away,' he says."

"No!"

" 'And listen,' he says, 'don't bother me about my father any more. I couldn't stand that old bastard.'

"I'm telling you, that's what he told me. I tell you, if I woulda known where to find him, I woulda gone out and beat that kid's young ass. You ever hear anything like that before? That goddamn punk bastard," Wendelstedt said, raising his voice and frowning, "I woulda ripped into that guy like a grizzly bear after a pig."

"Sam was part of our family, Harry, he was one of us. He was as much an umpire in spirit as you or me."

"Don't you think I know that? Why do you think I was so mad?"

"You know, it's surprising when you think back," said Harvey, "it's surprising how many good people you meet, traveling the way we do. I mean, it seems so lonely almost all the time. We've got so many hours to waste every single day; the traveling and the motels are such a drudge. Then you look back and consider how many fine people like Sam we've run into, really nice, downhome, decent people."

"And some famous people, too," said Colosi. "Remember when Ernest Borgnine came to visit in the dressing room?"

"And Milton Berle?" said Harvey. "There's a sharp guy who's always been friendly to umpires."

"It gets you sick when you find somebody fucking over people like Sam," said Wendelstedt.

"There're good people all over," said Harvey, "if you only take the time to look for them. We've got our own little family, you know, in every town.

"Will you ever forget Shag's (Umpire Shag Crawford) birthday party in Pittsburgh?" asked Wendelstedt.

"Oh shit," said Harvey, resting his head on the cushioned back of his chair and lifting his eyes.

They were all there that night—all the friends Harvey and Shag and Wendelstedt had made over the years in Pittsburgh. Billy Conn, the former heavyweight fighter, one of the few men who had ever knocked down Joe Louis; Joey Divens, Conn's good friend and part-time bodyguard; and Bobby Conroy, the policeman who had guarded the umpires' room at Forbes Field, and then at Three Rivers Stadium. Good old guys.

Someone, maybe Conn or Divens, had brought Shag a big box of dollar cigars, so thick and long and juicy they looked like foot-long hotdogs. They met at Coyne's Shamrock Bar in the Oakland section of Pittsburgh after the game, an old Irish café and a longtime umpire hangout, with pool tables and murals of Billy Conn and other great fighters handpainted on the walls. Harvey lost track of the time after a while, from swilling boilermakers (whiskey with beer chasers). With so many men puffing on those long fat cigars, one after another, the whole place began to look like a steamroom, wrapped in a gauze of smoke.

"I was half-finished my fourth or fifth cigar," said Harvey, "and it was finally getting to me, making me nauseous, what with the whiskey and beer I had consumed and everyone else's smoke. But I couldn't find an ashtray and I didn't want to throw it on the floor and waste it. So I had to find something to put it out on. I looked all over the place till I found just the right receptacle."

"My arm," Wendelstedt nodded toward Colosi. "That son of a bitch Harvey dug the hot coal of that cigar right into my arm, twisted it around a few times, and put it out in my burning flesh. I think he drilled halfway down to the bone. I'll tell ya, I never felt more pain in my whole life."

"But do you think for one minute that Big Bad Harry Wendelstedt would admit that it hurt?" asked Harvey.

"No way," said Wendelstedt. "You think I want to give you the satisfaction of knowing you've inflicted pain on me?"

"But you did the next best thing," said Harvey, nodding and laughing.

"Goddamn right. I did the only thing a man like me could do," he said, extending his arms and slightly bowing toward his comrades. "I put my cigar out on Billy Conn's arm."

"And do you think that bad guy would show pain?" Harvey laughed. "No way. He just smiled that goddamn, steely-eyed grin of his—he's the meanest, roughest-looking son of a bitch I've ever seen—then turned and put his cigar out on Shag's bare arm. Then Shag put his cigar out on Joey Divens's arm. And Joe put his cigar out on Bobby Conroy's arm."

Wendelstedt grinned. "Before you know it, we're all staggering around the room, lighting our cigars, puffing till the ends are red hot, then dowsing them on somebody's bare flesh. We were burning holes all over everybody's goddamn body."

Wendelstedt, Harvey, Colosi, and Williams were all laughing so hard now they were shaking.

"The funny thing was," whooped Wendelstedt, his cheeks gleaming like polished red automobile fenders, "it hurt like hell. It hurt worse than anything I ever felt in my whole life—I still got six or seven burn scars on my arms and legs—but not one of us would admit to it. Not one of us would relent and show the slightest pain. Everyone in that goddamn bar was cooking everyone else's flesh, but not one person had the guts to admit that it hurt. I sneaked up to Shag, right behind him, and shoved that burning cigar right through his pants, almost up his ass. And he laughs. He looks at me with his eyes absolutely livid with anger, but all he can do is laugh. Laugh! Then he sinks his goddamned hot coal deep into the back of my neck. I'm tellin' you, I coulda killed him. But what do I do? I laugh!

"We're all screwed up drunk and we're all in excruciating pain, but all we can do is look at each other and laugh like stupid hyenas. It was the craziest thing I've ever been a part of in my whole life."

Wendelstedt whipped out a handkerchief and blew. It sounded like a foghorn. "Of course, old prim and proper Indian squaw Harvey didn't want to have anything to do with us. He had started the whole thing, but then at some point I realized he wasn't joining in the fun. I looked around and found him hiding in a corner of the room pretending he didn't know us. Anybody got near him, he'd stick up his goddamn white, lily-livered, chicken-ass hands and say, 'Not me, fellas, not me, count me out of this.'"

"Well, listen, Harry," said Harvey, "I was wearing this white turtleneck ski sweater my wife had just spent half her life knitting for me. What the hell was she going to say if I came home two weeks after she sent it to me wearing something that resembled Swiss cheese?"

Wendelstedt shrugged.

"You got me pretty good in spite of my protests," said Harvey.

Wendelstedt turned, regarding Colosi and Williams with contemptuous scorn. Colosi was coughing and Williams was pounding him on the back and, at the same time, wiping the tears from his eyes on the sleeve of his shirt. "Look at those idiots," said Wendelstedt. "They don't even know what the hell they're laughing at."

"You guys are out of your minds," said Colosi. "That's what we're laughing at."

"I couldn't do that again in a thousand years," said Harvey. "My old bones ache right now just from thinking about it. 'Course, back then we were younger."

"We had this giant birthday cake," said Wendelstedt, "biggest damn birthday cake I've ever seen, sitting on the bar. It said

'Happy Birthday, Shag, You Faggot' or something off-color like that. Anyway, Shag was getting pretty damn angry at old Straight Arrow here for not participating in the fun. So he went up to that cake, scooped a handful of rosettes and blossoms and stuff off the top, mushed this all up into a ball and hurled it across the room."

"Splat," said Harvey. "Right on the back of my head."

"That started a whole new activity," said Wendelstedt. "Suddenly everybody was tossing birthday cake balls at everybody else. Splat, splat, goop."

"At everybody else, like hell!" Harvey objected, poking his chest with his thumb. "At me. I felt like a garbage dump for a bakery shop. I had 'Happy Birthday, Shag,' splattered under my armpit and rosettes sticking out of both my ears."

"You looked pretty bad, I admit."

"That's about the last thing I remember of that whole night," said Harvey. " 'Most everything else seems to have faded away. I've got some other vague recollections, but they never did jive together. I remember trying to wipe my sweater, digging the cake and icing out, but every time I got it halfway presentable, somebody would hit me with another glob of cake.

"I remember hearing sirens and a few minutes later feeling myself being loaded on a stretcher, at least I assumed it was a stretcher. I felt myself being picked up and I felt the air on my face when we got outside. I remember opening my eyes just for a second and seeing myself being dumped into a Pittsburgh police paddy wagon. I remember trembling a little bit, sort of scared about what was going to happen to me and my career. Then I completely blacked out.

"Next thing I know it's morning, or pretty close to morning, 'cause I can hear the chirping birds. I was in a bed. I knew that because I could feel the softness of the mattress against my legs and back, but you see, I was afraid to open my eyes. I figured I'd open my eyes and I'd be in the goddamn drunk tank. I didn't want to face that possibility just yet.

"Lying there, I imagined my whole career down the drain. After all my years in the minors and all my work to make myself into a good major league umpire, now I was going to have to call up Warren Giles and ask him to bail me out of jail. I didn't relish that thought. Christ, I don't mind tellin' you I was damn scared.

"I didn't know how I could face my wife, I didn't know what I would say to my kids, I couldn't even imagine looking a ballplayer straight in the eye.

"Eventually I screwed up my courage and opened my eyes. I looked to my left and I looked to my right. I saw my suitcase, my traveling alarm clock, my picture of my wife. Can you imagine? Joey or Bobby or one of those guys got the Pittsburgh police to take me home in a paddy wagon, undress me, and tuck me into bed!

"That was really something. Can you imagine what the desk clerk thought when he saw the cops carrying me in? I never got drunk like that again and I never will. It's just not worth the trouble.

"I've got too much good in my life to jeopardize. What I've earned with hard work and dedication—my family, my career— deserves to be protected. This kind of happiness is too fragile to squander."

Women in Blue

From the moment the wheels of the American Airlines 747 touched the ground and skidded across the runway at Lindbergh Field, the San Diego airport, to the moment he would have to climb aboard the PSA shuttle for the short jaunt to Los Angeles the following afternoon, Doug Harvey had a little more than a day and a half to spend with his family. And, after falling exhaustedly into his bed for almost six hours of sleep, that short, precious time had already diminished. Yet, those few hours remaining to reacquaint himself with his children and to talk with and hold his wife Joy, was worth far more than the extra expenditures, the airport inconveniences, and the hectic hustle of a chaotic schedule.

"It's like celebrating a hundred honeymoons," Doug Harvey said. "When I leave home after being with my family for a while I always find myself thinking, 'It can never be any better than it was this time.' But it always is. Each time I'm home with my wife and children through the season is more joyful than the one before it. It's hard to explain. I don't think I can explain it. I mean, I love them very much. Maybe I love them more because I'm away from them so often than I would if I were home. I don't know the reason for my feelings, I only know what I feel.

"You get used to being away as often as we are, you get used to it enough so that you don't complain, but that doesn't mean you enjoy it. For seven months, I'm miserable inside. You talk to ballplayers and coaches, you know? They tell you, 'Man, we're on this ten-day road trip, and I don't know if I can stand it another day away from home.' Do they realize who they're talking to? Ballplayers are the most insensitive people alive.

"When I was younger, I did plenty of things I'm not particularly proud of. An umpire has a thousand chances to fool around with women, the places we go, the kind of people we meet, but you gotta learn to resist temptation, you gotta keep trying to think about what you've got waiting for you at home. I don't deny that I flirt with a waitress or a stewardess once in a while, that's only natural. But day-to-day, I work as hard on my loyalty to my family as I do on my concentration on the ballfield. I don't think I could bear to lose either baseball or my family life."

"No one can deny that people in baseball cheat on their wives," says Harry Wendelstedt. "I see it every day. And just because the players and the coaches are about a million times more guilty than umpires doesn't mean I'm justifying my own kind. I mean, I can't see any reason for players to cheat—they're not away often enough to justify it, compared to us—except that most players are immature kids who still think it's worth a gold medal to tell the guys you just kissed a girl's fanny. You can understand more easily if an umpire gets involved in a 'situation,' however, with us being away for so long a time, but players? It's hard to believe what goes on.

"Coaches and managers are worse. When it comes to loyalty to family, wife, and home, Alvin Dark, who's managing the Oakland A's, is the biggest two-faced bastard in baseball.

"You meet Alvin Dark in public or listen to him talk on radio or TV," Wendelstedt continues, "you think he's the most religious, God-fearing, pious man in America. He's always quoting the Bible. He loses a game, he gives you a Bible quotation. He wins, he comes up with a Bible quotation. On the outside, he looks and sounds like a happily married man. The fans probably think he's a second Billy Graham. What they don't know is, he's the most foul-mouthed fucker on the field you'd ever want to meet. Not a clean word comes out of his mouth in a month.

"What really gets me, though, what really irritates me, is that between the times he was quoting the Bible and going to church with his family each Sunday, he was also having an affair with an airline stewardess twenty years younger than him. What do you think of that, Oral Roberts?

"And can you imagine—when Dark finally decided to end the affair, he announced it to the newspapers. He confesses he's done wrong, says he's overcome with remorse and embarrassment, and publicly asks God and his family for forgiveness. What a two-faced joke. Who does he think he is? Who does he think he's kidding? I'll tell ya, he may be fooling some of the people some of the time, but he ain't for one minute fooling the Lord."

Harvey says: "Plenty of umpires, especially in the minor leagues, have had serious marital troubles. They still do. A guy is umping in the Texas League or the Southern League, for example, and his family lives in Boston or Maine. Why, he's lucky to see his wife and kids once during the season. They don't make money enough to jump back and forth around the country on off days. A guy in the high minor leagues gets seven hundred dollars a month for seven months and out of that they gotta pay some of their own expenses. And when most of the umpires who are in the majors today were in the minor leagues, we got two hundred and fifty or three hundred dollars a month to start. No way we could live and see our families on that. Even with the money we get now, it's hard as hell to maintain contact and control of a family and to function as a working member. Look at Lee Weyer. He just got divorced two years ago. Terry Tata is divorced and remarried. Stan Landes (a former umpire) was divorced three times. Maybe Stello, Wendelstedt, and Sudol have the answer. They didn't get married until they established themselves in big-time ball. They and their wives were older and more mature."

"The idea of marriage," says eighteen-year veteran Eddie Sudol, "never once crossed my mind. Since high school, thirty-two years ago, baseball has been my life. I wasn't the kind of man that could have both a woman and a mistress, so I chose the latter. I worked my way up to the high minor leagues as a player and, in six or seven years, when I realized I wasn't ever going to get to the majors, I started to umpire. I was always traveling. In the winter I worked South American ball. Puerto Rican League sometimes. I never had a home. I never had any furniture. I never had more clothes than I could stuff in a couple of suitcases. There just weren't any women that were particularly attracted to that way of life."

"For as long as I can remember, I've been alone," says thirty-seven-year-old Dick Stello. "I was in an orphanage till I was twelve and then I was sent to live with foster parents on a small farm in rural Massachusetts. Even today, I still remember how to milk cows. The people who owned the farm were very nice to me; they were French and I stayed with them for five or six years. I even bought a home for them in Florida a couple of years ago so that they could take it easy in their later years and I could see them more often.

"But still, through the years, I've become quite comfortable with the idea of being alone. I guess I realized that this was my lot, the kind of life I had been born into. Very early, I became set in my ways. You know, this is the first year in all my thirteen years in baseball I haven't worn a jacket and tie to the ballpark? It's not easy to break old habits when you're alone, no matter how trivial.

"There was one girl I was sort of interested in, but I swear, I could never get to first base with her. Every time I took her out, she kept wanting to talk about other umpires, Harry Wendelstedt especially. Couple of months later I introduced Harry to Cheryl and they were married within a year."

Dick Stello's wife is involved in an occupation that forces her to travel the country even more than the average umpire. Lillian Stello, a burlesque queen better known as Chesty Gabor, is billed as having a seventy-six inch bust. Consequently, she is most frequently in demand.

"Both of us are mature people," says Stello. "We have our own careers and, during the season, go our separate ways, but we both thought it would be damn nice to have somebody to be loyal to, you know? When you're all alone it sometimes gets to be a terrible burden not having somebody to rely on. She wanted to get married first. And me? I don't know. I did it three months ago and so far it's working out. Before getting into baseball, I used to be a night-club comedian, so I know a little bit about show business. In the winter I might travel with Lillian as her manager.

"The only thing I don't like about being married is that now, every time I go into a new town, there's always some horny sportswriter who knows about my wife's measurements, and who wants to get a few laughs by taking a potshot at me in a column. There was a kid last month in Pittsburgh who wrote something like 'Now that Stello's married to a stripper, he won't have any trouble locating the strike zone, or calling a pitch up around the letters.'

"I had to call that kid down from the press box and really give him hell. I scared him half to death. You know, the press can criticize me for my umpiring all they want. That's their job. But I can't understand why they got to get into a guy's personal life. I can criticize a reporter's writing, but what reason would I have to come down on his wife?"

Says Doug Harvey: "Most people don't seem to realize that an umpire has a personal life. They never think of us as having a heart beneath our shirt and sex between our legs. To the fans, we're just anonymous men in blue, necessary evils, machinelike—cold, calculating, and gruff. I only wish that all the players and all the fans would have a chance to meet my children and my Joy. They'd be pleasantly surprised."

She sits by the pool behind her home, which is tucked like a book on a shelf into a hillside in the suburb of Mission Hills, overlooking San Diego, California. The sun coming off the water is dazzling, but the humidity is comfortable. A cool breeze strokes her cheeks and lazily lifts and flutters strands of her silver blonde hair. She stretches her legs over the lip of the pool, dangling her toes in water, wraps a few strands of hair around her forefinger, and looks up at the sky.

One of the rules of their marriage is that they savor each moment they have together. When Doug Harvey returns home for those few days during the baseball season, there will be no unsettling surprises waiting for him when he walks through the garage and in the side door. The problems of domestic life are brought to her husband's attention on each of the three nights a week he phones. They also write long and involved letters to each other once a day into which they slip clippings on interesting subjects spotted in newspapers and magazines. Most recently, Joy Harvey had received an article on the evolution of the hot dog from her husband in Philadelphia. Before that there was a piece from San

Francisco on the lack of direction and accomplishment in the grape pickers movement, headed by Cesar Chavez. On the days her husband phones, they speak for a long time, almost as much as if the family had gathered around the dinner table for an evening meal. They spend approximately two hundred dollars each month on long distance telephone calls, but Joy considers the expense more necessary than going to movies or going out to dinner or the other entertainments she and her children do without when Doug is on the road. "My husband is home, whether he's home or not," Joy says, smiling.

Closing her eyes to the sun, Joy mentally ticked off some of the things she wanted to tell her husband when he phoned that afternoon. She wanted him to know about eleven-year-old Todd's recent visit to the doctor and his new high-protein diet; about the arrival of the new reclining chair for their bedroom that they had received as part of their winnings from a recent appearance on the TV game show, *Hollywood Squares;* about the visit of the real estate agent who had told her that the house they had purchased for $28,000 three years ago was now worth $56,000 on the open market. All the news was good, but the latter was especially pleasing since both Doug and Joy well remembered the hard times of their first five years together when Doug was umpiring minor league ball.

Joy remembered cleaning the apartments of other tenants in the building in which they lived in El Centro, California, for extra money. She remembered that first Christmas when they had agreed to buy each other only new bedroom slippers and how she had smoothed out the green wrapping paper from the slippers she had bought for her husband, cut it into the shape of a Christmas tree and pasted it on the living room wall. She remembered the jewel box Harv bought her in violation of their sworn agreement, how they laughed when she calmly tried to explain to her husband that she had no jewels. And how she had cried after they had laughed. His salary was $350 a month for seven months that year, out of which came $150 per month rent, and all of Harvey's traveling expenses in the Class C California League. They mostly ate potatoes and macaroni for seven dollars a week. For entertainment each Saturday night, they alternated between a drive-in movie that charged a dollar a car and a miniature golf course near their apartment where they played for forty cents apiece. To prolong the fun, they played each hole twice.

And yet, despite the difficulties and the discomforts, despite the loneliness, their marriage had not only endured, but prospered. An elder in her church, she sees the importance and value of trust and faith in God. She talks about the tenets of their marriage as fluidly and reverently as if she were reciting from the New Testament. "In our house, we believe in commitment. In our house, we believe in goals. To us, promise is belief. We have taken our oath together with that understanding. When somebody puts that kind of burden on you, you must live up to it. There is no other choice.

"We've established ground rules for living, for raising our children, even for arguments. We don't 'grab-bag'—don't bring up items from the past that've been bothering us; we don't shout; we don't bring our families into it. This may sound like an overly structured way of living, but with our kind of life, it's what we need.

"Doug has very definite ideas about raising children. He wants our two boys, Scott, eight, and Todd, eleven, to be tough and he wants them to be self-reliant. 'When you're man enough to whip me,' he tells the boys, 'then you can do what you want. Until that time, you do what I say.' "

"I came home after one long road trip," says Harvey, "only to discover that Todd, who was eight at the time, was getting beat up by all the older boys in the neighborhood. He's a tough little guy, but he can't handle kids twenty pounds heavier than he is, so I got out the gloves and gave him a few boxing lessons. By the time I returned again, he had whipped every kid on the street. A boy's got to learn how to take care of himself. At least my boys do, I'll tell you that."

"When I first met Doug he was very hostile to women," said thirty-seven-year-old Joy Harvey. "I don't know whether many people know it or not, or can imagine a man as handsome as him losing the allegiance of a woman, but his first wife was very unfaithful, and he was scared to death of involvement for a long time. I know that for his own well-being the vows we made eleven years ago will have to stick."

("On the day my divorce was finalized," says Harvey, "I went home to gather up the last of my personal belongings. I like music.

Old time stuff. Dorsey, Benny Goodman, Glenn Miller. I had a thousand records with every song and sound you can think of. I walked into the house. My wife wasn't there, so I went into the kitchen. There, I discovered the fragments and the black dust from all those records that my wife had shattered and ground into the linoleum floor with the heel of her shoe.")

"I don't lead a sad or a lonely life," says Joy Harvey, smiling broadly, a light imprint of crowsfeet tugging at the corners of her eyes. "I lead a different life than most people, that's all. It's hard. Some of the wives in the many neighborhoods we've lived—we've moved fifteen times in eleven years—resent me, think of me as a young divorcée, just looking, just hoping to get the opportunity to play around with one of their husbands. Some of our acquaintances even expect us to fool around, Doug and me, since we're away from each other so often. It's funny the logic some people use.

"I used to complain quite a bit," she says, "but I honestly never think of Doug's work now. I've learned to cope, to accept what he is and what I have to be. I play racquet ball, I play golf, I read a book a day, I involve myself in the workings of the church, I manage a house and care for the children, and I have gotten quite interested in Chinese calligraphy. I wish we had more friends and I wish we could go out socially more often. I wish we didn't have to be so careful about the friends we can afford to have; some of the other umpires would resent it, knowing we have friends involved in baseball. We see some of the players and people who are part of the administration for the San Diego Padres socially. Some of the umpires would say that we are kowtowing to management, ingratiating ourselves, so we have to be careful. There are also some people, nice people in fact, who just don't seem to want to understand the seriousness of the game of baseball and Doug's absolute commitment to it. I remember one Sunday afternoon, Doug and I met a doctor and his wife out on the golf course.

" 'I never thought I'd meet a blind son of a bitch,' the doctor said.

" 'I never thought I'd meet a bloody human butcher,' Doug told him in reply.

"But all in all, I think to myself, as long as Doug is happy, then I'll be happy. I knew what I was getting into when I married him and it's too late for me to back down from my commitment now. As long as he's happy in his work, then on those few months that he doesn't work, the time we have together will be ever so memorable and sweet. Not many women can say that, you see. Many women are with their husbands every night, and have very few pleasant moments to total as the sum of their lives.

"I remember," says Joy Harvey, "that first year we were married. During the winter Doug got a job as a security guard in San Diego for a dollar-thirty-five an hour, and we scrimped and saved so that by the end of that winter we had enough money to drive up to San Francisco for a night and a day. The first place we went was Candlestick Park. In all his years in baseball, Doug had never, up to that time, been in a major league stadium, so we went that morning and asked if we could go in and look around."

Joy saw her husband's eyes sparkle, his whole face beam, as they walked up higher and higher into the stands. In a few minutes they were all the way to the top and they sat there for a while, perfectly silent, listening to the wind roar through their ears, peering down at the seats below. Then Doug said it. As corny and silly as it was. He sounded just like a little boy making a totally improbable plan.

"It came right out of a grade B movie," says Joy Harvey, shaking her head at the past, "but I knew for all he was worth, Doug meant it to come true. 'Some day,' he said, 'I'm going to umpire in this stadium. I promise you that, Joy, some day I will.'

"I didn't laugh then and I can't laugh now. How can anyone laugh at something said with such sincerity of emotion? And now that Doug has attained it, how could I do anything but go along with that dream? How could I ruin it by complaining? How could I show dissatisfaction? How could I fail to recognize that I have married an extraordinary man? How many men in this world have fulfilled their highest dreams? I am not the happiest woman in the world, but I'm far from unhappy. How could I be unhappy and love a man who is what he has always wanted to be?"

She sighs. She stands and reaches into a basket on a table beside her redwood lounge chair and lifts out an ink stone, a slanted slab of what looks to be onyx, with a deep, wide groove pressed into it, almost like an impression made by a serving spoon in clay. The ink comes in a hard, wide stick, and she grinds the ink into the ink stone with a circular motion, like a pharmacist preparing a prescription. As she grinds the ink around and around, the sun shimmers on the pale blue water, the breeze caresses her cheeks, and she looks both tranquil and comfortable, yet involved and alert. This process of inkmaking is called "centering the universe" in the ancient Chinese religion. She repeats to herself the words of her calligraphy instructor, with whom she spends many evenings:

"The prudent man makes his own ink, the lazy man hires someone to make the ink, the worthless man will buy the ink and paint a worthless print."

Joy Harvey grinds and grinds, pouring the ink mixed with water into tiny paint pots resembling miniature porcelain tea cups. She places the container of yellow ink high above the pool on a shelf, since the yellow ink is almost pure arsenic and Joy doesn't want to chance spilling it. There are three cats and one dog around the house who might very well lick some of it up.

The brush is held awkwardly between the index finger, the forefinger, and the thumb, straight up and down, at all times perpendicular to the rice paper matted on felt. She dips the dagger-like point of the thick, wide brush into the paint pot, flipping her wrist slightly and quickly with each stroke. A shaft of bamboo takes form, nodule by nodule, slanting beside an already-inked orange blossom. As she paints, the golden glow of the sun becomes more intense and the shadows of the passing day fall like silhouettes over the vegetable garden and sink into the water, dancing on the floor of the pool.

At one point, she steps back from the painting and watches it carefully as the sun dries it. She stands perfectly still for a long while, the brush still frozen awkwardly between her fingers. Then she goes into the kitchen and emerges with a solution of freshly brewed tea. With a clean brush, she wipes the tea in long even strokes across the rice paper. Now the yellow bamboo shaft and the orange blossoms and the rice paper acquire a pale, rather aged tinge. Finally, she lifts another brush, dips the point into black ink and signs her name. She works for half an hour on a perfect signature, a series of characters that have taken her a full year of study to master. The Chinese characters she has selected for herself have a meaning. They symbolize peaceful joy.

One hundred and fifty miles south of San Diego, in Bakersfield,

California, where, just outside of town, onions, watermelons, and grapes ripen in sun-drenched, sandy fields and migrant farmers sit on stoops of trailers or in aluminum lawn chairs fronting ramshackle barracks, another woman, a broad-backed, red-haired, black woman with a seemingly ever-present smile, is also waiting, skittishly, by the telephone.

Her name is Shirley Williams and, up until the time her husband was promoted to the major leagues, she had worked her whole adult life as a registered nurse in a nearby hospital. Now she spent a goodly portion of her waking hours attempting to bridge the generation gap between her four children, the youngest son, Scotty, eleven, her oldest son Art Jr., twenty, who had recently enlisted in the Navy, and her two daughters in between. On Tuesdays, Wednesdays, and Thursdays throughout the year, Shirley Williams was also director of the Bakersfield Family Planning Center where, in the evening, she counseled young girls on birth control and venereal disease, and helped direct those already past the need for counseling to the proper state or federal agency. It was not the most comfortable kind of work, but she earned much satisfaction from her many accomplishments at the Center.

Shirley Williams glanced nervously at her watch, then at the high-powered, AM-FM portable radio that sat on the table near the telephone in the living room of their seven-room home. She went into the kitchen and made herself two pieces of toast, buttered both slices lavishly, then returned to the living room to continue her vigil, glancing once more at the radio. She used the radio to listen to the games her husband umpired when he worked the West Coast. She picked up Los Angeles, San Diego, and sometimes even San Francisco—on clear, cool nights. Even though the radio announcer doing the play-by-play sometimes wouldn't mention Art's name once through the whole game, it still gave her pleasure to know that he was an integral part, an indispensable part, of the contest which she and a million or more other people up and down the California coast followed so carefully. She liked it best, of course, when Art was on television, especially when he was doing the NBC *Game of the Week* on national TV. After Art appeared on that, she often received letters from friends whom she hadn't seen in ten years and long-lost relatives who wanted to congratulate Art and her on their good fortune and great success. Usually, they would also ask for free tickets, which Art provided when possible. Her life and the life of her entire family had turned out to be very rewarding, much more than she or her husband had ever imagined possible. She only wished she didn't worry so much about Art and his progress in baseball. During the past two years, sitting home alone, listening to the games he officiated and waiting nervously by the telephone, she had gained forty pounds. She wished she could lose the weight, she knew she *should* lose the weight, but the pressure of having a man in such an important and responsible position, bore heavily on her. She finished her toast, wiped her hands on her apron, glanced at the telephone one more time, and sighed.

Shirley couldn't remember a time when she hadn't known Art Williams. They had grown up in the same neighborhood and had gone to elementary school and junior and senior high together. Everybody knew Art Williams, in fact, especially in senior high school, where he was a star on both the baseball and basketball teams, but he was just a guy to her, someone to whom she wouldn't have paid much attention except that her best friend had been his steady girl all through school.

"We were walking down the street one day," says Shirley, "my girlfriend and Art and myself, just walking and talking pleasantly enough, then I felt someone tugging on my sweater. I looked over at Art, but he was just talking calmly and staring straight up the road. We walked some more and somebody tugged on the back of my sweater again. I looked at Art real quick this time, but Art was still talking to that girl as we walked toward home. I looked all around, but there wasn't anybody else in sight, so I figured it had to be him, although he never once let on. Not once.

"A few days later I had to go to the hospital to get my tonsils taken out, and the first face I saw as I opened my eyes after the operation was Art Williams's. He came over to my house every day after basketball practice while I was recuperating and he took me out every night, to a movie or just for a walk, when I got better. We were engaged even before we got out of high school and were married the day of our graduation. It was quite a courtship."

They had both been born into large families; there were eleven in Art's and twelve in Shirley's. So when Art was drafted by the Detroit Tigers as a pitcher and sent to Idaho Falls, they left

Bakersfield with nothing more than a suitcase full of clothes and hearts full of hope. "We had nothing," said Shirley Williams, shaking her head. "We didn't have sheets or pillowcases, no furniture, towels, or even cooking utensils. We went into that town empty-handed.

"But the business manager of the Idaho Falls team was waiting for us at the bus station to help. I remember the blue and red credit card he kept in his hand as he took us from store to store buying things for us to set up housekeeping. It was a very exciting day. We came with nothing, you see. From that day forward, no matter what Art might say, I've always reminded him that baseball has given us a lot.

"We caused quite a stir in that town, however. Far as I know, we were the first black people ever to live in Idaho Falls. Could very well be the last. That was 1953 and Art was the first black athlete to be signed by the Detroit organization. I remember walking to the ballpark early in the evening or strolling downtown to buy a few things at the grocery store and having the little children in town running along behind me, yelling 'Here comes a chocolate drop. There she is.'

"But baseball has given us a lot," says Shirley Williams, nodding and glancing once more toward the white, push-button princess phone on the table near the alcove leading to the kitchen. "I won't have nobody say no different. It has lifted us out of economic difficulties and offered my family a brand new exciting life."

Tom Gorman sits contentedly in a chair in his home in Closter, New Jersey, his bare, calloused feet propped on a highly polished walnut table. With a ruddy face and white hair falling on the green pillow behind his head, Gorman looks like Santa Claus, except bigger and quite a bit meaner. One couldn't imagine a man as big and heavy-jowled as Tom Gorman cheerfully carrying a red sack, brimful of presents, and sliding down a chimney with a light thump. When you look at Tom Gorman, you see a man larger and more magnetic than many people can relate to, you see a man at the twilight of a fine career; his face is lined with age and worry, but seems chiseled for posterity in steel-gray granite.

Gorman has a voice like a deep bass drum. Even when he speaks softly, the large living room echoes.

"I remember the way Marge Faye looked when we were young, I remember it as clearly as my own name. She had the raven black hair, the pale, butter-soft complexion of the finest of the Irish lassies," says Gorman. "She had blue eyes as clear as the water. I used to walk with her from school each afternoon and carry her books. She used to come to the football and baseball games on Friday night and cheer for me. I remember it all so very well," Gorman smiles as he rocks. "It was a wonderful romance.

"After high school I pitched for a couple of years in the minor leagues in Toronto and when I was brought up to the majors by the Giants in 1939, Marge and I married. I did pretty well for the Giants in thirty-nine and all through forty, then my manager, Bill Perry, suggested that I enlist in the Army and get my military obligation over with before the trouble started. It was my bad luck that war broke out a few months after I went in and I was stuck in Tunis and Tripoli for four and a half years. So you see, Marge got used to being alone.

"Because I hadn't used my arm while in the service, I developed large calcium deposits on my throwing elbow. Recognizing this, the Giants peddled me immediately to the Boston Braves. In those days a guy pitched from the beginning until the game ended—whether he won or lost, gave up one run or ten runs, he was in for the duration most of the time. They used to shoot up my arm with novocaine, then push me out and make me pitch until I felt my arm was going to drop. I was finished. Marge knew it better than me and she told me so. But baseball was my life and I wanted to find some way of hanging on. I was even offered a $25,000 a year contract by the Mexicans at a time when they were buying many American ballplayers in an attempt to build up their own league. I was going to take it, but when the National League established a five year embargo on any player jumping to Mexico, I changed my mind. I wouldn't have done very good in Mexico anyway. I had had it; I was through.

"We decided that if I wanted to stay in baseball—and there was nothing else I would have even considered—I should go into umpiring. Back then you could be the worst umpire in the history of the game and still get a job as long as you satisfied the single most important requirement: if you had your own car, you'd be hired. I was assigned to the New England League, Class B baseball, and Marge and I moved up to Brockton, Massachusetts. Can you imagine? In 1946 I was making twenty thousand dollars a year as a major league pitcher. In 1947 I was earning one hundred eighty dollars a month for seven months as a minor league umpire. Despite this, and me on the road all the time, Marge took care of the kids and went to work to supplement our income. She never complained or shirked her responsibilies. Not once."

Gorman paused to unwrap three sticks of chewing gum and cram them into his mouth. The paper wrappers disappeared in his big fist as he continued.

"One of the people I remember most clearly during our stay in Brockton was a butcher," said Gorman. "This kid worked in one of those old-fashioned shops, with the meat hanging on hooks and dripping blood all over the place. He was a good kid, very skillful with the knife, and every time I'd come into the shop with Marge, he'd stop whatever he'd be doing to talk baseball. Wouldn't let me leave sometimes. I always had to tell him I was starving and that I wanted to go home and eat dinner, before he'd let me go. Christ, one time he offered to make me a steak right there, as long as I stayed and talked. This guy played in a sandlot baseball league in Brockton, and his dream was to become a major leaguer. That's all he ever wanted to do. I didn't hear from him for a few years after that, then suddenly his name starts turning up in the paper. This was Rocky Graziano, who eventually went on to become the middleweight boxing champion of the world.

"I stayed in the New England League two years, then moved up into the AAA International League. In 1951, when the major leagues went from three to four man umpiring crews, I was brought up. It didn't take me too long in the minors, but Marge woulda stuck with me three times longer, as long as it took, in fact. That's the kind of woman she was. Don't get the impression we had it easy in the majors, however. My first year, I only made five thousand dollars.

"My wife was a fiercely proud woman and a baseball nut. When we moved back to New York a few years later, she'd sit in the stands for every game I umped in that city and root for me. Probably the only person at Ebbets Field or the Polo Grounds that would ever cheer for an umpire. That was Marge. Whenever anyone in the stands would boo me, or in some way criticize my work on the field, she'd jump all over them, holler and scream and threaten all kinds of legal action until they'd apologize. I can just picture her, the way her eyes got all fiery when she was angry. A stranger could pretty well figure there was no percentage in disagreeing with this girl. She'd murder them.

"I remember once a newspaper reporter—Charlie Russo— wrote something about me, talking about how sloppy I was. 'Course, I never thought I was sloppy, I just never wore my clothes too well, but Russo, who wrote for a New Jersey newspaper, says, 'No matter what Tom Gorman wears, he'd look like an unmade bed.'

"Marge was furious. She called the guy every hour for three days running until he could muster up enough courage to call back. I remember hearing Marge yell at him over the phone, 'I want a retraction! I want a retraction! My husband is a good dresser. He buys fancy clothes!' "

Gorman smiled broadly, shook his head, tossed the gum wrappers into an ashtray on the opposite end of the table, then continued.

"When Leo Durocher was managing the Giants his wife Laraine (actress Laraine Day) would sit in the box seats along the third base line and, when I was in town, Marge would always join her. Now I've had my disagreements with Durocher in the past. He was a lying, despicable, cheating bastard on the field. He'd do anything to win. And I'm pretty sure he didn't have much use for me, either. I threw him out of many a ballgame, but Laraine and Marge, they always got along fine.

"One time, with Laraine and Marge watching, I'm umpiring third base and Leo, he's coaching third. We get to about the fifth inning, the Giants are up with the bases loaded and one out. Now the guy at bat hits a bloop—a Texas Leaguer—out to the outfield. Thinking initially it's going to fall in for a base hit, the guy on third streaks for home, then about halfway down the line, he changes his mind and streaks back. In the meantime, the man who was on second is thinking base hit all the way, and he's barreling head first into third.

"Well, we all come at the base together, the guy running from second, the guy returning to third, the third baseman waiting for the ball, me trying to get in there close enough for a call, the ball, and Leo, trying to squeeze in and hinder the fielder. Splat! It was the most sickening collision you've ever heard, pro football without padding. And guess who's down at the bottom? I got my leg wrapped around my neck, somebody's head under my ass, and arms and hands flailing all over my body.

"Eventually everybody starts getting up slowly from on top of me. First Durocher, then the guy who was originally on third, who limps back down the line and crosses the plate. The crowd starts to scream and then Frankie Frisch, the manager of the Pirates, comes running out, steaming. Durocher thinks that the run should count from third and that the guy coming in from second is safe. Frisch, on the other hand, is calling for a double play. Me? I don't even see the ball.

"Of course, I found all this out a few days later in the hospital. All I could see right then was this huge cloud of dust and fog that seemed to be surrounding me. I couldn't concentrate. I heard these two managers screaming bloody murder at me, but I couldn't make out what they were saying for a while. Then I finally realized what was happening—vaguely—and I recognized a phrase, somebody was yelling. 'Was he safe or out? Was he safe or out?'

" 'Who wants to know?' I yelled.

" 'Durocher,' Leo says.

" 'Then he's out,' I told him.

"Marge said later that she had never seen Leo so goddamned mad in his life. He stomped around the field and raged for half an hour. I don't believe Laraine was angry, though. According to Marge, all she did was stare at her husband, shake her head, and chuckle.

"The one thing about my wife, Marge," Gorman said, lowering his voice as if what he had to say was absolutely confidential, his smile fading from his lips, his heavy jowls somehow drooping, "the one thing about Marge was that she was never sick a day in her life. She was as strong and perky at forty-nine as she was when we dated at seventeen. Maybe that's why I was so stunned when she died two years ago. Stunned is the right word. I mean, I was numb for a long time. You expect sickness before death, especially in a woman so beautiful and strong and young. But there was never any warning. She was forty-nine-years-old and suddenly she got blood poisoning in both her kidneys. I was traveling out on the West Coast, enroute somewhere. Before I knew she was even sick, she was dead.

"Since then I've been attempting to father and mother my children from great distances. We have a live-in housekeeper, but my eldest daughter, Patty Ellen, helped finish bringing up two of the boys. Without her, I just couldn't have done it. Patty Ellen is married now and Tommy, he just graduated from Marquette University this year. Kevin is still in high school and Bryant is in junior high. I keep in as close contact as I possibly can and I'm home as often as time and schedule permits. I go out of my way to come home, so I can be with my children.

"I've been thinking of getting married again," says Gorman. "I have someone very special in mind, but I won't do it. I won't do it. Not on your life. Not until I quit umpiring. I couldn't bear to go away so often and so long from the people I love again."

Tom Gorman rocked rhythmically in a green chair in his living room at home, watching the late afternoon sun stream through the window in golden shafts of light. "There is one thing that still saddens and shocks me when I think about it. There is one thing about that whole affair that has soured me against baseball somewhat," he says.

"About an hour after I had buried Marge I got a call from the league office in San Francisco. They wanted to know when I would be back to work. You'd think they'd give a man some time to lay his wife to rest."

JUNE 1974

STANDING OF
THE NATIONAL LEAGUE TEAMS

Eastern Division			
	W.	L.	Pct.	G.B.
Philadelphia	25	22	.532	—
St. Louis	23	22	.511	1
Montreal	20	20	.500	1½
New York	20	27	.426	5
Chicago	18	25	.419	5
Pittsburgh	17	26	.395	6

Western Division			
	W.	L.	Pct.	G.B.
Los Angeles	36	14	.720	—
Cincinnati	26	19	.578	7½
Atlanta	26	22	.542	9
Houston	26	24	.520	10
San Francisco	26	25	.510	10½
San Diego	18	35	.340	19½

Overhustle

Art Williams wasn't exactly nervous before those games in which he worked behind the plate. His hands didn't tremble, his knees didn't quake, butterflies didn't dance in the pit of his stomach, light-headedness never set in. But still, there was something different going on, not within him as much as around him, nothing he could see or feel, nothing a doctor could diagnose, nothing biological that a microscope could dissect into tiny, flitting, bacteriological particles, nothing his loved ones could fathom, but all the same, there was something, a feeling, a dream, a gnawing, doubting, tickling, fog-warped, unsettling sensation.

Being a black man in a white man's world was hard; being an umpire, an official in a game of skill and chance, a lawman in a game where your every judgment could very well influence, if not decide, the fate of a man's career, the size of his paycheck, the weight of an entire team's purse—that was even more difficult. But to combine those two problems, to be the first black umpire in the National League and the only black umpire in all of the major leagues, to be a black official in a game that has been and will continue to be supported by white owners, white management, and white spectators—that was to be, at least potentially, a misfit supreme. That was to be in a position of terrible vulnerability.

Art Williams did the best he could both on and off the field and as he grew older and more experienced, he felt himself increasingly capable of dealing with what he confronted as an umpire in the major leagues. Yet there were times, most especially every fourth game when it was his turn to call the plate, that a momentary uneasiness set in. This was an umpire's most difficult and tiresome job. This was the time in which all eyes were unavoidably on him.

Early that evening in the umpires' room at Jarry Park in Montreal, Williams stripped down to his shorts, carried the boxes of new baseballs and the can of Delaware River mud into the bathroom, and sat down near the sink. Colosi, Harvey, and Wendelstedt were in the dressing room talking quietly, but Williams turned his back and concentrated on rubbing the black briny mud into the smooth white balls. Usually he listened with eagerness to the advice and the easy-going banter of his more experienced companions, but today he felt tired of baseball and didn't want to hear what anybody had to say.

He glanced up at the mirror. The whites of his eyes were yellowish this evening and his cheeks and the smooth skin above his brow seemed wrinkled and sorrowful.

Yesterday night had been an excruciatingly bad night for Williams, his worst of the year as an umpire. He had been working first base and doing what he considered to be a competent job when fleet-footed Montreal shortstop Tim Foli hit a slow ground ball to third. It looked like it would be a close play, but Williams was on it, stepping into the slot to the right and at a forty-five degree angle from first base, dropping down on one knee to watch when the ball slapped the glove and the runner's foot touched the base. The ball beat the runner by nearly half a step, and Williams jumped, whirled around, raised his right fist and yelled, "Out!"

Then, for a split second, he was confused. The fans were cheering, and his fancy movement on the out call left him somewhat off-balance. He might have lost sight of the play, he wasn't sure, but the next thing he knew, the ball was rolling on the ground. His fist, signaling out, still hung like a black hammer in air as he lifted his eyes and ran the play back on the screen of his mind. Had Foli knocked the ball out of the first baseman's glove? Interference? He thought so. "Out!" he bellowed again.

"He dropped the ball! The first baseman dropped the ball!" Foli croaked, jumping on his haunches like a frog.

"No, he's crazy!" yelled first baseman Dick Dietz, motioning at Foli. "He grabbed the ball. He grabbed it!"

"You're wrong, goddamn it!" first base coach Walt Hriniak bellowed into Williams's face, so close that Williams could taste the warm tobacco juice on his breath. "You're wrong, wrong, wrong!"

The three men crowded around the lone umpire, barking and shouting, jumping up and down like angry dogs. Williams regarded them momentarily, then blinked his eyes shut for an instant, remembering Doug Harvey's words. "I'm telling you, son, you can't let them double team you, triple team you, quadruple team you. That's what they like to do. They like to get you so damn confused you look and feel like a fool. You tell them like I always tell them: 'One man, I'll talk to one man only. I'll talk to one man or no man at all.' "

But Williams knew he had hesitated too long, losing the advantage of his authority. He stood there, paralyzed on that spot of grass and dirt, realizing that perhaps only fifteen seconds had passed, and knowing also, through experience, that too much time had gone by for him to effectively take command of the situation. With his stomach feeling as if it had sunk to his ankles, Williams swallowed and accepted the dreaded situation.

"What are you going to do?" yelled Foli. "I was safe. I had it made, goddamn it, I had it made. I was safe!"

"Out!" shouted Dietz, jumping in front of Foli.

"Safe! Safe! Safe! Safe!" Hriniak jawed, pushing Dietz out of the way.

Williams composed himself and opened his mouth, with the intention of clearing the field, when Hriniak suddenly stepped forward and bumped him. Whether accidentally or on purpose, it was hard to tell, but instinctively, without stopping to breathe deeply and gather up his frazzled nerves, Williams pushed the man back hard. "You're gone," he yelled, pointing to the dugout, "get out of here!"

"You pushed me, you . . ." Hriniak rushed forward and bumped him again. This time it was no accident, but Williams held his ground and his temper. "You're gone! You're gone! Get out! Get out!" His arm shot out once more toward the dugout.

Simultaneously, Harvey, Wendelstedt, and Expo manager Gene

Mauch reached first base and pulled the men apart, but Williams knew the damage had been done. Whatever the player or coach might do, however they acted, the umpire had to control himself and, in so doing, control the situation. It was an indisputable rule: an official maintained order with respect. He should never exercise authority physically. Besides, the argument had started at least partially because he, the umpire, had turned his back on the play. Rule number two broken: never lose sight of the situation you are judging.

After the game, when Wendelstedt and Colosi were in the shower, Harvey said to Williams, who was sitting dejectedly in his sweat-soaked blue uniform, hanging his head in disgust: "You can't ever allow yourself to become off-balance on a play. You've got to plant both feet and keep your eyes on the play until you're sure the play has concluded. You can't get overconfident, Art. It takes eight years in the major leagues to make a good umpire, Art, and you haven't been in for even two.

"I know you just made one mistake, two mistakes, but we're not supposed to make any mistakes. I know it doesn't make sense, but it's true. Umpires are human. Umpires do make mistakes. We're not supposed to make mistakes, but we do, and we suffer for it afterwards. A man who begins his career as an umpire must be perfect, then improve significantly every day after that. That's the kind of ideals we have to live up to."

Harvey walked over and put his arm on Williams's shoulder. "Why don't you take your shower," he said.

That night Williams paced his room, periodically reading and watching television, attempting again and again to compose exactly the right words to use in explaining the incident when he called League president Chub Feeney the following morning. Williams wasn't worried that Feeney would fire him. It hadn't been that bad a mistake, and Feeney was a good and fair man. But it was embarrassing to admit to anyone—especially the president of the National League—that he had broken two iron-clad and elementary umpiring rules.

Of course, Feeney wasn't the man who had hired him. Fred Fleig, the National League secretary and supervisor of umpires, was the one who had called him, after only two and a half years of minor league ball, to ask if he thought he could work in the majors. He remembered that night very well. In fact, lying there in that dark room, mounds of pillows hunched up behind his back blankly staring at a late night television show, Williams saw flashes of his past come back to him in vivid, darting images.

In 1953 Art Williams became the first black to be signed by the Detroit Tigers organization, receiving a one hundred dollar bonus, a figure that became standard for black players. Directly out of high school, he was assigned to the Tigers' Class A farm team in his home town of Bakersfield; he posted an 11–6 record. The next year he was offered a contract for AAA ball in Buffalo, New York, but the Tigers refused him enough money to bring his wife. So Williams declined the offer, and was consequently sent to the Tigers' Class A organization in Idaho Falls, Idaho. He pitched well there for the first half of the season until he hurt his arm. Despite his physical troubles, he chalked up a 9–3 record that year.

But as the only black in the entire Detroit Tiger organization, an organization that even today doesn't go out of its way to court black athletes, and coming up with a sore arm so early in his career, Williams felt his prospects for the future were significantly diminished. He turned down an offer to play A league ball in Augusta, Georgia, the following year on the advice of his father. Like all black men who grew up in the South, the elder Williams knew that Georgia was no place in 1954 for a young black who wanted an opportunity to make the big leagues. The senior Williams felt there was no way his son could spend a season in the Southern League, pitching in Alabama, Georgia, and Florida and return to his family both spiritually and physically healthy.

So instead, Williams signed that year with the Wanetka Tigers in the now defunct Class C California League and, on the advice of Tiger scout Joe Gordon, agreed to pitch a game every other day. "This is the only way you're going to prove to our management," Gordon told the young pitcher, "that your arm is strong enough for big league ball."

Whether the advice was faulty or downright cruel, Williams still isn't completely certain twenty years later. Maybe he really didn't possess what a black needed in those days to make the majors; then a black man had to be virtually twice as good a player, sheer superstar material in fact, to harbor any serious hope of ascending the major league ladder. Whatever, Williams wore out his arm while pitching as many games as possible for the next two years. He won twice as many as he lost, but never once received any indication he was being scouted and considered for advancement in the Detroit or any other pro baseball organization. He returned home at the end of the 1957 season and quietly and unobtrusively retired from the game.

He was so disappointed that he swore to his wife Shirley that he would never again involve himself in baseball. He would never watch a game, in fact, if he could help it. He tucked his memories of those years—the odor of neatsfoot oil rubbed into cowhide, the smell of sweat clinging to dry, hot dust, the crack of a bat and the slap of a ball, the thudding of a mitt, the scrape of steel spikes against concrete runways, the splat of tobacco juice against splintering dugout walls, the banter of teammates and, most especially, the roaring gratification of a crowd—he tucked those thoughts back into the deepest corners of his mind. He did so with a quiet shrug and an off-hand sheepish smile, without any sign of bitterness toward the game or the people who very well might have impeded his progress. Art Williams had always been and would always be a man who took his punches without showing anger outwardly; he was able to mask his pain with a grin.

A second child was now on the way and so Shirley was no longer able to both continue to nurse full time and care for their growing family. Williams turned to an employment where colored men almost seem to maintain a monopoly: he went to work for the Bakersfield Sanitation Department.

Today, as Williams travels in the first class sections of airplanes and hires porters to carry his baggage into fancy hotels, he often thinks of his years hefting the garbage of both the rich and poor of Bakersfield. Today, no one has to crawl into a truck and stand knee-deep in filth like you used to have to do, he reflects. There are automatic compactors and, most important, there are union contracts. It gave Art Williams more than a little satisfaction to read that the sanitation workers in San Francisco had recently been awarded a contract guaranteeing them a little less than twenty thousand dollars a year. It rather tickled him to see white faces popping up on the garbage trucks around the country as he walked the streets of National League cities. Did that mean that collecting garbage now had its own measure of dignity? Or was it merely that Old Whitey disregarded his dignity when it came to making a hefty piece of change? He pondered the question with a smile.

Williams was soon promoted to supervisor in the Bakersfield Sanitation Department, and he worked for the next twelve years overseeing anywhere from 120 to 150 men. His family grew until he had four children, and for extra cash he took a part-time job with the Bakersfield Recreation Department supervising evening activities at a playground near his home. He also started attending classes part-time at Bakersfield Junior College and began refereeing high school basketball. For seven full years he kept his peace with, and his isolation from, baseball. He wouldn't watch it on television. He refused to join his friends for the 120 mile, two and a half hour trip to Los Angeles to see the Dodgers play ball. It hurt too much to be confronted with what might have been.

But when his eldest son, Art Jr., began playing little league baseball, Williams agreed to umpire some of the games. Before he really realized what was happening to his life, Williams quickly moved up into high school and college contests. Within two years he was the most skillful and sought-after umpire in amateur baseball in the state. As a former pitcher working behind the plate, Williams could easily follow a breaking ball with his eye from the moment it left the pitcher's hand to the instant it struck the catcher's glove. Often, just by watching the motions of the pitcher, Williams could anticipate what kind of pitch to look for even before the ball was released. On the field, his sense of the game deriving from his past years enabled him to take off in the obvious direction of the play almost as soon as the batter made contact with the ball.

All of the old feelings, all of the smells and sounds, the excitement and the satisfaction of competition came back to Williams in those next few years. It was like the continuation of an old love affair for the now thirty-eight-year-old father of four children. In the winter of 1969, with his wife's reluctant blessing, Williams enrolled in the major league's Umpire Development Program and spent six weeks attending classes and learning his trade in St. Petersburg, Florida, under the direction of former AAA Class minor league umpire Barney Deary.

Even then the federal government, armed with comparatively new civil rights legislation, was beginning to poke with suspicion into the hiring practices of National and American League officials. With justification. Close to half of all the athletes playing baseball in the major leagues were members of minority groups, yet there was only one black umpire, Emmett Ashford, in the American League, and he was planning to retire the following year. The situation had changed significantly since Art Williams had been selected to break the color barrier for the Detroit Tigers in 1953, but in 1969 he was again a pioneer having to prove that a black man was at least as good as, perhaps even better than a white man. Now he was to plunge into the strange white world of law and order, of enforcing rules in a game which, two decades ago, only white men were good enough to play.

"I got a call from the National League office in San Francisco," says a major league umpire who had been working as an instructor for the Umpire Development Program in St. Petersburg that winter. "They wanted to know if there were any good black candidates and asked me to pick the best so that they could be sure he got a job. Not that these blacks mightn't have gotten jobs anyway, but there were about two hundred candidates that year for thirty or forty jobs, and they wanted to be sure a black got hired. Well, I picked Williams. He was maybe the best black candidate we had that year—maybe the best we ever had—but what I liked about him was, well, he was respectful. I mean, you could talk to him because he was respectful. Some of them coloreds are, well, uncouth."

Williams was hired by the Class D Pioneer League in Southern Florida that year for $525 a month for seven months, including expenses. Simultaneously, he relinquished his position with the Bakersfield Sanitation Department which had netted him eleven thousand dollars annually. Shirley was forced to go back to work that year and for the next four years, but Art was certain of his ability to make it into the big leagues.

He was elevated to the Class A Midwest League in 1970 and traveled for the season with another black umpire, Harold Van, who had been in baseball for a number of years and was, at the time, a National League prospect. Van, unfortunately never reached the proficiency in his calls required of major league umpires.

One evening in Appleton, Wisconsin, after a particularly difficult game, a tall, broad-shouldered, gray-haired, middle-aged man came into the umpires' room and engaged Van in a quiet conversation. Williams showered and dressed, then lingered in the passageway waiting for Van.

The stranger and Van entered the passageway some time later, stopping in front of Williams.

"What's your name, son?" the man asked gruffly.

Williams told him.

"Well, I think you did a fine job out there tonight. Just keep on hustling."

"Goddamn," said Van later, "you got yourself a fan. That man don't know what the word 'compliment' means, but he handed one out to you, sure as hell."

"Who is he?"

"Why, that's Fred Fleig, the supervisor of umpires in the National League—the man who does the hiring and firing."

"Well goddamn," said Williams.

That night he called to tell Shirley. He felt like a real giant that night.

Williams worked hard for the rest of that season, harder perhaps than at any time before in his whole life. He had a sense of deep confidence that if he could hang on and perform with a hustling, well-concentrated efficiency, he would accomplish his long-sought objective of reaching the major leagues. Many times he reflected on the silliness of the whole idea. Here he was, a thirty-eight-year-old father of four, attempting to chart a new course in life by officiating a game for boys. Often he was wrenched by the thought that he was abdicating his responsibilities as a father and husband; his wife had had to assume the role of both parents and worse, she had had to become a semi-provider. Most frightening was that Shirley's long letters communicated a constrained fear of impending financial disaster, even with both their salaries taken into account. Slowly, but ever so surely and certainly, the savings account reserve on which they had counted when Art relinquished his sanitation job was dwindling. Each month they were forced to dip into the well more than they had planned, and now the bucket was nearly scraping bottom. At that point his telephone service had been cancelled twice for non-payment of the bill.

Although his salary had increased to six hundred dollars a month for the seven months of the season with his promotion to the Midwest League, Williams had to withhold some of that money for winter financial obligations and for the obviously important traveling expenses during the season. Often during that long summer Williams would spend his nights curled and cramped in the back seat of his car, washing and shaving at local gas stations to save a few dollars to send back home. He had never had a more difficult, heart-breaking, ego-deflating year. On the other hand, he couldn't deny his happiness and satisfaction at being awarded a second chance to fulfill his boyhood dreams. He returned home at the end of that season with no fear, no dread, no second thoughts about his future. He returned home with a triumphant feeling of confidence and accomplishment.

Since major league ball clubs invite so many extra players to their spring training camps and divide their teams into two sub-teams (A and B), the American and National League offices require a number of minor league umpires to help officiate. Williams was included in this group of two dozen in January, 1971. The letter came directly from Fred Fleig.

Of course, there were two dozen of these young umpires and at most there might be two major league umpiring slots open each year; moreover, not all or even many of these men had a chance of ever being selected anyway. Some had worked spring training games four or five times in the past and had already been judged by the major league umpires with whom they worked to be too old, too slow, too fat, or too inefficient to cut it in the big leagues. Williams was the only black prospect and he had advanced quickly in his two years of professional ball.

He officiated twenty-six B team ballgames that spring while most of the major league umpires worked the A team contests, but what he remembered most of that month he spent in Arizona was his meeting with a man who was to become his confidant, a

source of strength and of knowledge when he ascended to the
major leagues.

Doug Harvey, tall, deeply tanned, white-haired, was working
the plate in a game between the Padres and the Giants, and
Williams, who had finished his game earlier in the day, was sitting
on the sidelines watching him. He liked Harvey's style, the way
he steadied himself on one knee and leaned way over the catcher's
shoulder to see the ball. Of all the umpires Williams had studied,
Harvey seemed to get closer to the plate and to be able to stay with
the pitch much longer than anyone else. This was perhaps the
most difficult part of being a successful umpire: the ability to
ignore outside influences and internal pressures and to maintain
absolute concentration on the game and only the game, including
each individual play and pitch. Williams had never seen anyone
more in control of himself and of the situation around him than
Doug Harvey. It was as if the man put himself into a deep and
totally consuming spell, as if time and space, heat, wind, and thirst
were immaterial; as if the entire universe consisted only of a bat,
a ball, a game.

Near the end of the game, however, between the eighth and
ninth inning, Harvey abruptly turned from his position behind the
plate and walked toward Williams. "You're Art Williams," he
said, offering his hand.

"Nice to know you." The two men smiled at each other and
shook hands.

"Look, I've got a problem. I just bought a house back in San
Diego and I've got to make a plane in forty-five minutes to get
back home to sign the papers and close the deal. I wonder if you
could take over for me behind the plate?"

"You want me to call the plate for you? With Willie Mays
coming up?"

"The pitches don't come in no different to Mays than anybody
else. You call your own game and it doesn't matter who's swinging."

Art Williams never forgot Doug Harvey's kindness and his
consummate skill behind the plate and when it was time to request
a crew for his first year in the majors, he told Fred Fleig it

wouldn't matter with whom he worked, as long as one of the men was Doug Harvey.

For the first five weeks of the 1971 season, Williams was elevated to the Class AA Texas League. But when veteran National League umpire Tony Vinson had a heart attack, Larry McSherry of the AAA International League was promoted to the major leagues, and Williams subsequently moved up another notch, assuming McSherry's position. He remained in the International League that year, working the playoffs, and then returning both to major league spring training and to the International League in 1972. Again he was selected to work the playoffs, an honor bestowed only on the best umpires in the league. Since this particular year the playoffs were to be held in Hawaii, as a celebration Williams was planning to take Shirley. He knew she deserved a vacation after helping to support their big family for three straight years.

The phone jangled in the small frame house in the south side of Bakersfield, California, that day, only twelve hours before Art and Shirley were scheduled to leave for Hawaii on their first vacation in four years. Shirley, then black-haired and slender, was in the kitchen. She listened until her husband picked up the phone, then cranked on the water, and began to scrub the maple syrup and pancake remains from the grimy breakfast dishes.

In a while, Art came in and stood in the doorway, watching his wife in silence, her bare black arms elbow-deep in bubbly white dishwater. He was smiling but when he spoke, he hung his head and covered part of his face with a towel. "Damn," he said softly, shaking his head. Then, when his wife did not respond, he said it again louder—"Damn!"

"What now?" asked Shirley, lifting a glittering plate from the bubbly water and running her thumb against it until it squeaked.

"That was Mr. Fleig," said Williams somberly.

Shirley turned to watch her husband. "And . . ." she said cautiously, sensing something, probably something bad, by the way her generally open and enthusiastic husband was speaking.

"Well, something has changed," said Williams, shaking his head and rubbing his face with the towel.

"What's changed?" said Shirley.

"I hate to tell you this."

"Well, you have to tell me sometime. Now what's the trouble? Is something wrong?"

"We're not going to Hawaii," said Williams softly, shaking his head again and again.

"Why? What's happened?"

"You don't want to know."

"Of course I want to know. Now tell me what's going on."

"We're not going to Hawaii," said Williams, pausing. "We're not going to Hawaii," he said again, slowly. "Because . . ." he paused. "Starting tomorrow . . ." he paused again.

"C'mon! Starting tomorrow, what?"

"Because starting tomorrow," Williams shouted, throwing the towel into the air, lifting his wife high by the waist and twirling her around the room, scattering dirty water and light silvery soap bubbles in every direction, "starting tomorrow I'll be in the major leagues!"

Art Williams suddenly found himself chuckling as he lay in his rumpled bed in the Sherbrooke Motor Hotel in Montreal watching the morning light quietly curl in through the cracks in the curtains. Thankfully, he had endured the darkness and the boredom by thinking his way through the night. He washed and shaved quickly, then looked at his watch, shrugged, and went down to the coffee shop for breakfast. He consumed an order of pancakes and two orders of sausage, washed down by four or five cups of bitter-tasting coffee. Afterwards, as he headed back to his room, he patted his stomach, wishing he hadn't eaten so much. It was becoming increasingly difficult to control his weight lately. This year alone he had picked up more than ten pounds.

Back in his room his heart beat heavily as he recited the number of the National League office to the operator. As he listened to the phone ringing, he was still attempting to conjure up an adequate explanation for yesterday's two very embarrassing and hard-to-excuse errors. Turning his back on a play and pushing a player were mistakes on the level of an electrician's testing an appliance he had forgotten to plug in. Sure, he knew that neither Fleig or Feeney would do anything drastic to him. It was the embarrassment of confessing to his absolutely inexplicable errors. The operator told Williams no one seemed to be answering.

Williams looked at his watch, thumbed through his wallet, and read the operator Feeney's home number.

"Hello?"

He heard Feeney's voice, somewhat groggy and distant.

"Chub?" Williams tried to sound cheerful. "This is Art Williams. I'm in Montreal. How are things in San Francisco?"

"Who?"

"Art Williams. I'm in Montreal with Doug Harvey's crew."

"Well, what do you want?"

Had Feeney already heard about the game? Williams couldn't quite understand the reason for Feeney's instant irritation. He took a deep breath. "I wanted to explain to you, I mean, I wanted to tell you about what happened in last night's game."

"Do you know what time it is?" Feeney demanded.

Williams glanced at his watch and, at the same time, felt a sinking, queasy, bottomless feeling in his stomach. "Why, it's nine o'clock, Chub."

"It may be nine o'clock in Montreal, young man," said Feeney loudly, "but in California it's still the middle of the night!"

Today, sitting on a stool in front of the sink in the umpires' room in Jarry Park in Montreal, his eyes avoiding an all too accurate mirror, the big black man splattered saliva and mud on the last baseball to be tossed into the cowhide bag. Sighing, he kneaded the mud into the ball with a silent fury, betrayed only by the grim set of his leathery lips.

"I'm telling you," he heard Wendelstedt in the next room, "there are no finer looking women in the world than those found right here in Montreal. You know how some women come to ballparks in other towns? In baggy pants and blue jeans, their hair blowing in a hundred different directions? Sometimes I look up in the stands and see these chicks munching on popcorn, smoking, their faces covered with rouge, and I say to myself, 'The monsters have invaded!' Later on I discover the truth. It's only ladies' day.

"Then I come to Montreal, which is probably where beautiful women were invented. I mean, they got furs on, fancy dresses, high-heeled shoes. When they go to the ballpark, they look sharp, the way women ought to look."

"So," said Harvey, "what's the point?"

"Harry don't ever talk to make a point," said Colosi, "Harry just talks."

"So I'm telling you, this happened to me last year," said Wendelstedt. "Are you listening to this, Art?" he queried, rising and walking slowly over to the door between the dressing room and the bathroom in his underpants.

Williams nodded, his back still turned.

"I'm working third base this particular night, see, and there's this broad, the most beautiful broad I've ever seen, sitting in the front box seat directly in line with the base. I'm tellin' ya, I've never seen anyone more gorgeous in my life. She's tall, and her long blonde hair, hair that's almost golden like the sun it's so shiny yellow, is swept into an absolutely meticulous bun. And that's not all," said Wendelstedt, shaking his head and lifting his eyes, "I swear, never in my life have I seen legs as long and curvaceous and smooth and white. Were I to give this chick a name, it would be Eve."

Wendelstedt paused for a deep breath to elongate suspense; he began to pace barefoot around the room. "This woman has also got the most appealing breasts I have ever seen. These were some tits, not too big, but luxurious, full and shaped perfectly. All I could think of when she leaned over the railing and I saw what I saw was cream puffs. Standing there, I wanted to bury my face in all that sweetness and goo for a month.

"You may well be sitting there and thinking I'm describing Miss America—or Miss Canada in this particular case," said Wendelstedt, "but if you'da seen her ass . . . 'Oh my God in heaven,' you'd say, 'better than Miss America, better even than Miss World.' I'm telling ya, this had to be Miss Universe, Miss Galaxy, Miss Solar System, she was so goddamn gorgeous. She was so beautiful that she was absolutely out of this world."

"Yeah, but Harry, hey Harry," said Colosi. "What did she look like?"

Harvey chuckled. Wendelstedt set his lips tight, made his face go red, and stared at Colosi momentarily before continuing. "The thing I remember about that night was the Expos were getting whipped something terrible. Something like ten to two after a few innings. A real massacre. And you know Montreal fans. They want to slit the throats of anybody scores a run against their team. But not this woman. She kept ogling me, staring at me, puckering up her lips at me as the game went on. And she let me see every part of her body and every morsel of clothes she was wearing. Which wasn't much. She got up and walked back and forth to the ladies' room, I'll betcha a hundred times, just so I could see her ass in that hiked-up black satin miniskirt. I'll tell ya, her ass swayed so much, I was getting seasick watching.

"I had a couple of pretty tough calls to make in that game, and they all happened to go against the Expos, but she didn't seem to mind. Sometimes you can stand around at third base three, four games in a row and nothing seems to happen. But on this night I was really getting the heat."

"Isn't that always the case?" asked Harvey. "Sometimes you go through a whole season without nothing to look at. Other times you get slam-bangers every time you stick your nose out on the field."

"In about the sixth inning," Wendelstedt momentarily raised his voice to regain the floor, "she took off her mink stole. That's right! She had on a silver mink stole, and the blouse she wore under that stole—or should I say the blouse she didn't wear under that stole—was virtually non-existent.

"Then, and I'm telling you, this is true, as sure as I'm standing here, she leaned her tits over the railing and started to call me. 'Vendelstedt, hey Vendelstedt,' " Wendelstedt mimicked in his finest imitation French accent. 'Cum 'ere, Vendelstedt. Cum 'ere.'

"Course I ain't about to stop the game to go talk to a chick— no matter what the chick looks like—but I'm telling you she was getting me so worked up I thought I was going to have a heart attack. Every time I went down the line with a foul ball I could feel myself—I couldn't stop myself—taking wider and wider circles along the sidelines near the railing so I could watch her more closely before returning to my position.

" 'Hey Vendelstedt, Vendelstedt, cum 'ere.' She wasn't yelling or anything like that, but speaking in this nice little, sexy French voice. I'm sure only a few people besides me could hear.

"I was going crazy," said Wendelstedt, sighing and lowering his voice to a more confidential tone. "My wanger was so hard that a line drive to the crotch woulda cracked it in half. It was so big and stretched out it was crawling up my stomach and halfway to my throat. If I woulda pissed, I could have hit the sky.

"So after the game," said Wendelstedt, raising his voice once again, "instead of going into the dugout, I walked halfway to the sidelines just to see what she would do. And she was still sitting there, waiting for me. I'm not kidding! Just sitting and waiting. I went closer and she motioned me over with her finger." He stuck out his forefinger and bent it five or six times.

" 'Vendelstedt, cum 'ere.' " Now Wendelstedt was whispering sexily and puckering his lips. " 'Ho Vendelstedt! Vendelstedt! Cum 'ere!' She was just cooing," said Wendelstedt. "I'm not kidding! And I kept coming closer and closer, and she started making these sexy signs with her lips like she wanted to tell me a secret, so I leaned my ear over till it was almost touching her lips. I could smell her perfume and I could feel the warmth of her skin. Ohhhhh boy," Wendelstedt moaned.

"Then she said," said Wendelstedt, "and her voice didn't change one little bit when she said it . . . 'Vendelstedt, oh, Vendelstedt, Vendelstedt. YOU COCKSUCKER! YOU EAT SHEET!'

"That's exactly what she told me," said Wendelstedt, throwing up his arms, feigning helplessness. "I'm telling you, there is no other umpire in the history of baseball that takes more abuse than me. That's exactly what she said. I'm telling you the God's truth."

Wendelstedt pulled his tight-fitting T-shirt up past his shoulders and dragged it over his head. He picked up a ballpoint pen from his suit jacket and carried the T-shirt and the pen into the bathroom, tightly closing the door of the stall. "How you doing, Art my boy?" he boomed.

"Just fine, Harry, just fine," Williams said, unable to match the joviality of his partner.

Williams went into the dressing room and sat down in the chair in front of his large black suitcase, staring absent-mindedly and still somewhat dejectedly at his neatly pressed blue uniform.

"What I want to know is," said Harvey, splattering a chunk of tobacco juice into a cardboard box by his chair, "would you rather take the clap home to your wife or leave with it after you've been with her? Tell me that, Nick."

"I'd rather take a black man fishing," said Colosi, winking secretly in Williams's direction.

"What the hell does that mean?"

"I like to use 'shiners' for bait."

"If I had it to do all over again," Wendelstedt's deep voice boomed from his stall in the bathroom, "I'd rather be a black umpire."

Wendelstedt waited, but Williams didn't much feel like making a reply.

"If I were a black umpire," said Wendelstedt, "then I wouldn't have to wash my hands after rubbing up the balls with mud."

"Sometimes," said Harvey, "when I'm working the plate and I look out at Art standing behind second base, I swear I can't tell where his uniform leaves off and his face and hands begin."

Williams managed to shrug his shoulders and smile weakly, then he sighed and began the long process of dressing and preparing for a game behind the plate. First he dug into his suitcase until he found the bottoms to a pair of long gray knit underwear. He held the underwear, its legs dangling in his lap, up to the light. This was the same underwear he had worn for his first major league plate assignment almost two years ago. He had, in fact, worn these same longjohns for each plate appearance since that time, but today he felt as if he were in need of a new good luck charm. Or no good luck charm. For some reason he thought it best to confront this plate job wholly on his own. He rolled the underwear into a loose ball, brought it back nearly to his face, then set shot it at the large wide mouth of the corrugated metal trash can. The underwear unrolled in the air and slid into the trash can, legs tiredly flapping like soggy, weathered streamers.

"Well, did you see that?" said Harvey. "It's about time."

"I never minded what the underwear looked like," said Colosi, "but he hasn't washed them since I've known him."

"If I did that," said Williams softly, "then the luck would have all been washed out."

"What you ought to do," said Harvey, "if you need a good luck charm, is drill a hole in your nose and insert a ring or a bone in it."

"I'll tell you what else he ought to do," Wendelstedt hollered. "I think he ought to get a haircut."

"Good idea," said Harvey, "I don't want no goddamn Afros on my crew."

New York: Giants' shortstop Chris Speier holds back Giants' manager Wes Westrum as he hears umpire Nick Colosi toss Speier out in the fifth inning in a game with the Mets at Shea Stadium. Westrum was then also thrown out for refusing to continue the game (7/6/74). World Wide Photos

Above: Philadelphia: Dodgers' pitcher Doug Rau tries to stretch a single into a double and is called out at second base by umpire Nick Colosi in a game with the Phillies (5/3/74). UPI Photos

Left: Rau argues with Colosi. UPI Photos

Right: Rau makes one last but futile appeal. UPI Photos

Left: New York: Reds' catcher Johnny Bench looks to umpire Doug Harvey for the call. Mets' catcher Jerry Grote (*left*) had tried to stretch it to home from second on a hit by Mets' pitcher John Matlack to short centerfield. Reds' centerfielder George Foster threw the ball to Bench in time for the out, ending the fourth inning at Shea Stadium (6/3/74). Wide World Photos

Bottom left: Houston: Umpire Doug Harvey, working both first and second, called Astros' Lee May out at second on a force and, still on his knee, called Astros' Bob Watson safe at first by inches. Expos' first baseman John Boccabella (21) and second baseman Ron Hunt protest the call, which broke up their double-play attempt. On his knees or not, Harvey's call held (6/13/72). Wide World Photos

Below: St. Louis: Umpire Harry Wendelstedt calls the play as Phillies' third baseman Don Money (16) scores when Cardinals' catcher Ted Simmons (23) takes a high throw too late (7/20/71). UPI Photos

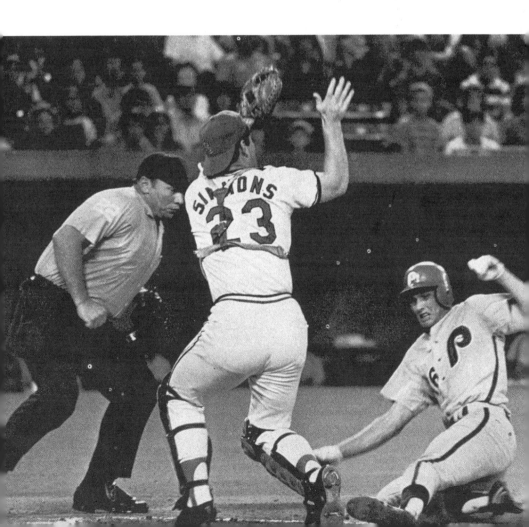

Top: Pittsburgh: Umpire Art Williams takes a close look as Cards' catcher Ted Simmons applies a late tag and Pirates' Al Oliver slides safely into home with the lead run in the seventh inning (9/19/74).   UPI Photos

Top right: San Diego: Umpire Art Williams is right on top of the play. Catcher Johnny Bench of the Reds makes a late tag as Padres' outfielder Bobby Tolan scores (5/23/74).   UPI Photos

Right: Houston: Giants' catcher Dave Rader (*on top*) and Astros' second baseman Tommy Helms collide as Helms comes across the plate. Rader lost the ball as Helms came in to score in the fourth inning of the game. Umpire Nick Colosi made the safe call (5/20/73).   UPI Photos

New York: Braves' Manager Clyde King has a pointed argument with plate umpire Nick Colosi. Catcher Vic Correll also criticized Colosi's calls, and both he and King were ejected from the game (9/1/74). Wide World Photos

"If Art got a haircut, we'd all be rich," said Colosi. "We could open up a Brillo factory with what he cut off."

With a deep breath Williams stifled a steely-eyed grimace, then turned to face Harvey and Colosi with a shy but satisfactory smile. This had only taken a quick second. With forty-two years' practice, he was a master at masking his irritation.

"Most of the time I laugh with Nick and Harry and Doug when they make jokes about my color or race because I think what they say is funny. I'm not so proud that I can't laugh at myself once in a while," Williams has said. "I laugh also because I trust them. There are other guys in this league—other umpires—who make racial comments and mean it. They believe that whites are different than blacks, better than blacks, but luckily, I'm in a crew with people who, I truly believe, feel that all men are equal.

"Sometimes I laugh when I don't think things are particularly funny," he says. "I think it's often better not to start trouble. I don't want people talking about me behind my back, saying I can't take a joke. Because I *can* take a joke, I can take a joke just as good, maybe better, than anybody.

"Now, up to this point, no one on this crew has ever gotten personal with me. If they do they'll be sorry for it, I can assure you of that.

"What I like about this crew is that we're all ribbing each other. I don't rib anybody, actually, but everybody is throwing jokes in all different directions. Nick is a greaser. Doug is an Indian squaw. Harry is the Nazi racist pig. I like that. It brings things out in the open and relaxes me. I get a real good feeling inside of me when all of us are laughing together.

"There are other umpire crews in this league," says Williams, "who aren't as close as us. They stay in separate hotels, eat dinners alone, and travel to the ballpark and from town to town individually. That's not right. Living with one another day after day you get to know how each man shines his shoes, what kind of clothes he wears, when he needs a haircut. It's like being in a family. It helps time pass. It's something like a security blanket to me, I guess."

Thinking of his days in the minor leagues, both as a player and an umpire, he could almost feel those mustard-soaked hot dogs and stale peanuts anchored permanently in the pit of his stomach; he remembered the embarrassment and shame of having his telephone service disconnected for lack of payment and, when it was paid at home, not having enough money in his pocket to make a long distance call to the family. Williams stared at his neatly-pressed blue uniform and his black, freshly polished shoes with the toes so shiny they looked like satin. He pictured the comfortable roll of five and ten dollar bills in his trouser pocket, and he savored the pleasure he would take tonight in calling home after the ballgame, the security of having credit cards and of having more than enough money in his checking account to cover his debts. I have earned these comforts, he said to himself. I have earned the authority of my position. I have earned the respect of other umpires and players. I like it when people give me special attention in hotels and in restaurants when they find out who I am. I like it when the little black boys wait for me outside of the ballpark, thrust a gritty, stubby pencil in my hand, and ask me to sign my name. I like it, I've earned it, I deserve it. God knows, I worked and prayed for this chance since 1953. Since long before that.

"Overhustle," says Art Williams, flashing a big, open-mouthed grin. "Although I'm sure other people have thought of it and used it, that's a word I've made up on my own. *"Overhustle,"* he says again, still smiling. "It perfectly describes my outlook on life, the way I conduct myself on the field, off the field, on the road, or at home.

"I don't want nobody to talk about me in this league, you see, because the way things are, with me the first and only black umpire, if they talk about me, they talk about my race. That's the way people are. I don't want nobody talking about me. That's the one thing I would hate, so I work real hard until I'm sure people know that I'm just one of the guys, 'cause that's exactly what I want to be.

"In everything I do, everywhere I go, in all of my life, I overhustle. That's the word. A ball's hit down the right field or left field line, or into center field, I run like the wind, faster than any umpire, 'cause I don't want anyone to be able to say I'm lazy, that blacks are lazy.

"When I'm supposed to meet somebody at six-thirty, I get there at six-twenty because I don't want anyone to say that I'm always late, that blacks are always late.

"When it comes to sharing a taxi fare, or picking up a tab in a restaurant, I always try to buy more than my share, two beers to everyone else's one, because I don't want anyone to say I'm cheap, or that blacks are cheap.

"I overhustle. I want to carry my load and I want everyone in the whole goddamn league, in the whole country, to know I'm doing it. That's what I want.

"Even when I'm home, I try to make an extra effort to carry double my load, to do things specifically to please my family. After a long road trip, I'm tired. I might have worked three or four double-headers in a row, or twenty games in twenty days in seven different cities, but I always try to remind myself that my wife has certain rights too. I want to sleep. Oh, sometimes I want to sleep so badly that while I'm sitting and watching television and talking to my kids, I dream about being asleep. . . . Then, after the kids go to bed, I take my wife out. She deserves a little fun, too, and it's my responsibility to do the best I can.

"You better believe I overhustle," says Art Williams, shaking his head and gesturing with his arms. He is smiling so openly that even the sternest of interrogators would want to smile with him. Then suddenly Williams's grin fades and his eyes become hard and stern.

"There are a lot of umpires in the minor leagues, and right up here in the majors, who are jealous of me because I'm black and have gotten a few breaks because of it. But they don't know, don't realize, that I've also lost out on many opportunities earlier in life for the same blackness. They don't understand, furthermore, that I can't help my color one way or another. I am what I am.

"I resent being called a 'token black' by reporters," he says. "I get that all the time. 'Don't you feel uncomfortable, or how does it feel to be the token black umpire in the major leagues?' they ask me.

" 'I'm not a token anything,' I tell them. 'I'm an umpire. It's pure and simple as that.'

"They smile and nod, but they never write my answer down. I guess my honesty doesn't have any news value."

Williams denies that black men in baseball are like gladiators performing for a white crowd. He believes that baseball is a game for white and black alike, wholeheartedly equal—as equal as unconscious prejudice will permit, that is.

"Sometimes I call a black player out on a close play and they look up at me, surprised. They are actually *surprised*," he says, shaking his head in astonishment, "and they say to me, 'Hey brother, you could have given me a break.'

"Well, I don't like that. They ain't doing me any good and they ain't doing my race any good. They are jeopardizing my authority, my position, and my job. On the field, I ain't nobody's brother. They're players and I'm an umpire, and it don't go no farther than that.

"In a way," says Williams, "umpires and black people have been lifted out of the same mold. We're both outcasts. We both find comfort and friendship only with our own kind.

"People don't understand that umpires as well as blacks have human feelings and normal functions. Most people don't think there's anything underneath our uniforms. We're just faces, masks, ghosts in blue. They don't understand that we eat and sleep, we feel pain and love, we shit and piss and fart like most everybody else. We're human beings. Black and white. In uniforms and street clothes. Flesh and blood and bone."

He unwrapped a fresh set of underwear, tossed the cellophane wrapping toward the corrugated metal can, then stood and dragged the elasticized cotton material up his muscular legs and over his athletic supporter. Although it was to be a warm and muggy night, Williams sat back down and pulled on a pair of knee-high woolen socks, then strapped on a pair of catcher's shin guards made of shiny blue heavy-duty plastic. Umpires wear such undergarments for a number of sensible reasons. First, the long underwear will not only soak up the heavy perspiration flowing freely under the heat-attracting blue uniforms, but will also prevent large quanities of dust from sweeping up their loosely-fitting pant legs. The socks and the underwear also help avoid potential chafing caused by the tightly drawn straps of the shin guards. In addition, the triple layer of material serves as a cushion in case an umpire is struck by a ball or bat, or is spiked behind the calf or around his relatively unprotected thigh.

Over the underwear, Williams pulled on his pants. He slipped into a pair of black, plain-toed oxfords, laced them tightly, and got to his feet. His shoes had half-inch, nail-like but dull-tipped spikes protruding from the soles and heels, similar to those on golf shoes. The shoes had an elongated, leather-wrapped steel tongue, which extended from the base of the toe and over the laces, and climbed up the bottom part of the ankle, meeting the lower portion of the shin guard. Most umpires purchase these shoes from retailers specializing in coal miner's gear.

He pulled his padded chest protector down from the top shelf of his cubbyhole, its heavy-duty plastic shoulder pads clattering, straps dangling, and paused for a second. "Shirts or jackets tonight, Chief?"

"Jackets."

Williams nodded, buckled his chest protector over his undershirt, slipped on a short-sleeved, light blue shirt over the protector, then pulled on his navy blue suit coat. Williams looked as if he were wearing a 1940s-style zoot suit.

Preparing for a game behind the plate, American League umpires dress themselves essentially the same way, except that the American League umpires use a larger, highly-inflated outside, or over-the-uniform, chest protector called a "balloon."

"Balloons are fairly easy to use," explains Doug Harvey. "There are two straps that go over your shoulders and slide down your arm, so when you relax, the balloon hangs loosely in front of you. This protector is light and provides a fair amount of mobility. There's a slot or indentation at the top of the protector. When calling strikes behind the plate you bend over as far as you can behind the catcher, lining the protector straight up and down, parallel to the catcher's back. Then you put your neck into that indentation and peer over the catcher's shoulder. It's basically an awkward position to get used to. It's almost like you're bending down, craning your neck upward, all the while holding a mattress up in front of you."

The balloon provides an umpire with much more protection than the National League protector against a wild pitch or sharply hit foul ball. It is not only longer, wider, and more thickly padded, but it can be lifted to protect the face or lowered to protect the upper thighs. On the other hand, it is fairly unwieldy and, to a certain extent, reduces an umpire's mobility.

Minor league umpires still have the option of using either the inside or outside protector. "I worked my first five years in the minors using the balloon," says Colosi. "I had been told some time before that the American League was interested in me, so naturally I tried to familiarize myself as thoroughly as possible with the way they liked to do things. All of a sudden, a year and a half before I made the majors, I discovered that the National League had purchased my contract, so I made a fast switch. Most young umpires will do that. They might use both the first couple of years —if they can afford to buy two chest protectors—but as soon as they receive any indication one particular league is more interested in them than the other, then they'll switch. Naturally, they'll do anything in their power to ingratiate themselves."

"What most people don't realize," says Doug Harvey, "is that the differences in the protectors significantly change the game. The National League umpire, with his inside protector, leans way over the catcher's shoulder. He can see the plate better and, consequently, call a much more accurate pitch.

"Because of the two different protectors, the strike zone is different from league to league. Because we're closer to the pitch in the National League, we'll call a low strike, maybe as much as an inch below the kneecap. We'll also go an inch or so below the pectorals on the chest."

Colosi nodded. "On the other hand, the American League umpire is standing further away from the pitch, behind the catcher rather than over him. He can see the high pitch good, but he can't see the low pitch too well. What happens is that the American League low strike might be as much as two or three or even four inches above the kneecap. An American League umpire could also call a high strike at the neck."

Says Harvey: "Which doesn't necessarily mean there is anything wrong with this. The strike zone may be a little different from league to league, but it's not any bigger or smaller in either league. The size of the strike zone is the same.

"I keep trying to tell Art Williams," Harvey continues, "that the most important thing for an umpire to remember is to maintain consistency. Consistency is the most important part of our job. As long as an umpire calls the same strike zone all the time in each league, then it doesn't matter too much if it's six inches higher or six inches lower. The batter can eventually adjust to it. As long as the batter knows where the strike zone is going to be, he'll be able to hit that ball.

"Of course," says Harvey, leaning forward and chawing rapidly, "we have what we call the 'twilight zone' in baseball. What I mean is, how accurate can we be? The rule book says we're supposed to call the strike at the knee. Does that mean the top of the knee or the bottom of the knee? Does that mean the top of the ball or the bottom of the ball? What happens if he misses the plate with a curve ball by a bare microscopic inch? If he's that close, we try to give the pitcher the benefit of the doubt. The idea in baseball is to try to open up that strike zone as much as possible and make the batter hit the ball. That's baseball. If we were 100 percent rigid, we'd average ten walks a game.

"Still," says Harvey, "an umpire's utmost consideration is consistency. If a pitcher's wild, if he's throwing the ball up and down and over and under the batter, the umpire won't give him the strike when a pitch just so happens to come an inch away from the corner of the plate. He's got to be able to get it there all of the time."

"Pitchers who invariably have trouble with their control," says Colosi, "are bitching at us all the time because we won't give them a break. We won't give them a break because they lack consistency. You give them a break on a couple of pitches and pretty soon they're fighting for a pitch nearly a foot off the plate."

"I've been having trouble with (Cardinal pitcher) Bob Gibson," Harvey explains, "since 1961 when I met him in the Puerto Rican League. Now, Gibson seems to think that the plate has four-inch corners. I told him, 'The home plate is seventeen inches wide. If I give you four-inch corners, that makes it twenty-five inches wide. That's not the way the game was written.'

"Gibson has been bitching about this to me for thirteen years, and he's getting more and more argumentative as he gets older—and less effective. Even his catcher one time, Ted Simmons, told him to 'fuck off.' Simmons makes his money as a hitter. He's smart. He knows that the bigger the strike zone the more difficult it's going to be for him to get on base. Why should we turn baseball into a pitcher's game?"

Says Colosi: "What makes me really mad is the reaction of the fans, or the players in the dugout, or the hypos in the press box. They think they can call the game as good as we can from where they are. Half the time, they're watching the catcher's glove. They don't understand that we couldn't give a shit less where the catcher catches the ball because we're watching how and where the ball crosses the plate. You take a pitcher with a good overhand fastball. The ball crosses the plate at the batter's knees, so we call it a strike. But the catcher receives the ball at the ankles, so to the fans or reporters it might look like a ball."

"Or how about a curve ball that breaks and hits the front corner of the plate?" asks Harvey. "By the time it reaches the catcher, it could be two feet outside, but in the meantime it nicked the plate and is consequently called a strike. It doesn't matter where the batter stands or where the catcher receives the ball. All I care about, all any umpire should care about, is where the ball crosses the plate. That's when the judgment is made."

Harvey lifted his rubber-soled oxfords onto a stool and began to tighten the laces. Looking in the mirror, Colosi carefully placed a blue, brimmed baseball cap on his head. Williams dragged his face mask and blue hat down slowly from the upper shelf. Harvey then looked at Colosi and Williams. "Where the hell is Harry?" he said.

Suddenly, Wendelstedt whooped, crashed through the toilet stall door, leaped in the air, twisted around and landed in the main room with a barefooted thud. He had shed his underwear, but stood in the middle of that room, staring sheepishly at his partners, and wearing a T-shirt on which he had drawn a large and elaborate swastika in blue ballpoint ink. Neatly lettered above the swastika were the words, "Super Kraut."

"Super Kraut!" he yelled, pounding his chest with his gigantic fist, then goose-stepping round and round the room. "Look! Up in the sky! It's a bird! It's a plane! It's Super Kraut! Super Kraut! Super Kraut!"

Harvey, Colosi, and Williams watched as the big man twirled

and paraded, bare-assed and barefooted, from one corner of the room to the other, again and again. They began to snicker and chuckle as Wendelstedt continued to perform, then finally they exploded in great gusts of laughter as Harry Wendelstedt, as straight-faced, apple-cheeked, and imperturbable as ever, put on his clothes, his light blue, short-sleeved shirt, his navy blue pants, and his suit jacket. He laced his black, ripple-soled oxfords and led his crew somberly out onto the field.

The players looked at the umpires strangely, then began winking at one another, but none would ever quite understand why these usually mean-jowled, grim-lipped men periodically chuckled and giggled, smiled, and suddenly guffawed through the game. Nor would the fans ever know, or even imagine, that one of the men on the field, wearing the blue suit of authority of that great and uniquely American game of baseball, was wearing a Nazi swastika over his heart, even though it was a joke.

Art Williams felt the fog and the weight above his eyes lift as he walked slowly out onto the field. He blinked his eyes and a delightful shiver of relief seemed to dance up his back. He accepted the lineups from both managers with an authoritative and enthusiastic nod, checked his digital ball-strike counter, and loaded up his pockets with five newly rubbed baseballs. He stood erect and respectful through the Canadian and American national anthems, staring up at the two flags flapping silently side by side.

With a great deal of satisfaction, as the dying music still reverberated in the dusty rafters of the ballpark, he turned to the visiting team's dugout, raised his arm up in a sharp, snapping manner, and yelled, "PLAY BALL!"

JULY 1974

STANDING OF
THE NATIONAL LEAGUE TEAMS

Eastern Division

	W.	L.	Pct.	G.B.
St. Louis	40	34	.541	—
Montreal	35	34	.507	2½
Philadelphia	38	37	.507	2½
Pittsburgh	32	40	.444	7
Chicago	31	41	.431	8
New York	30	44	.405	10

Western Division

	W.	L.	Pct.	G.B.
Los Angeles	52	24	.684	—
Cincinnati	44	31	.587	7½
Atlanta	42	35	.545	10½
Houston	38	39	.494	14½
San Francisco	34	45	.430	19½
San Diego	35	47	.427	20

Mounting
Problems

National League umpire Bruce Froemming had been particularly peeved by a recent article in the *New York Daily News* accusing unnamed major league umpires of carrying satchels to the ballpark to smuggle baseballs back to their homes or hotels after each game. The article, written by Dick Young, claimed that the New York Mets last year had ordered one of their employees to account for the number of balls hit into the stands. Young contended that the results of the report, sent to the league office, proved beyond a shadow of doubt that umpires were pocketing a half dozen or more baseballs per game for personal use. Their publicizing this report, one unnamed Met official stated, had caused the umpires to decide all close calls against the Mets in 1974. This was one way, the official continued, the umpires could get even. He concluded that he could name three games the Mets would have won, but for umpire prejudice.

Said Met Manager Yogi Berra, a few weeks later, after a bitterly disputed game: "This is the fourth time this year we've been robbed by umpires. I don't mind losing. I've done that many times in my career, but this is out and out robbery."

Froemming, a hot-blooded, fiery-eyed Dutchman, held his mounting anger until he and his crew of Ed Vargo (crew chief), Paul Runge, and Andy Olsen were scheduled to work again in New York. Having rubbed up the five dozen game baseballs provided by the Mets, Froemming returned them to the Mets's club-house with the following note: "Here's your five dozen baseballs. Count them. Bruce Froemming."

The Met ball boy showed the note to catcher Jerry Grote who read it slowly, nodded his head pensively—and snickered. "That article about the missing baseballs really must have hit home," he said.

A few innings later Grote neglected to catch or make any effort to block a pitch that had gotten away from pitcher Harry Parker; it narrowly missed Froemming's forehead. After the game, Froemming charged that Grote had deliberately let the pitch go by so that it would hit the umpire.

"Froemming doesn't know what he's talking about," said Met manager Yogi Berra. "Grote was crossed up on the pitch. He called for a curve, but Parker had trouble seeing the sign and threw a fastball."

"It happened earlier in the game, too," Grote defended himself, "but I was able to catch the ball that time."

"Bull," Froemming replied. "I tell you, he let it go on purpose. There were two keys to the play. First, Grote never moved his glove. Second, he never went out to the pitcher to tell him he crossed him up. This was a bush league stunt, strictly out of class D."

The situation concerning umpires' pilfering of baseballs has a basis of truth. Umpires do pocket baseballs now and again: they give them to the children of friends who are instrumental in helping them get along in a strange city more comfortably. They will offer a baseball to a policeman, a taxi driver, an especially helpful employee of their motel, or a relative who might serve them dinner or provide a pleasant evening. "After all," says Doug Harvey, "these people around the motel, the maids, waitresses, and desk clerks, are all part of our family. Away from home they're often all we have."

For umpires, the question has never been whether they do or do not take baseballs occasionally, but whether they abuse the privilege.

For the most part, they don't. There is no one more impartial, no one who works harder at being as scrupulously honest as the man in blue. What neither Dick Young's article nor the unnamed

Met official mentioned, what no person connected with the great game of baseball mentioned, was that players and managers take just as many baseballs as umpires, since they also meet people and make friends as they travel from town to town. It is part of the same pattern as all the office workers and executives who carry home office supplies for their personal use.

"What makes me so angry," says Doug Harvey, "is that the owners, players, and managers go through all sorts of contortions to cheat our asses off. They hose down base paths, tamper with bullpen mounds, back up their lying and cheating during a game by swearing in the name of Jesus Christ or on the graves of their mothers, yet they're ready and willing to crucify us at the slightest sign of weakness.

"As to the fact that our calls are going against the Mets or any other team because they've dared to cross us, this goes to show the remarkable ego these people have. Can you imagine? How could they think that I could care less about who wins or loses a ball game? I'm not getting a share of the profits from a winning team. I get paid the same amount and on the same day no matter who wins or loses. Do you think I would jeopardize my $25,000 a year salary for doing something I truly love just for the sake of token revenge? That's too preposterous to even consider.

"When we're right," says Harvey, smiling wryly, "nobody says a word. But when we're wrong, just the slightest bit wrong, the whole world knows it."

"If I gave five dollars for every call I've missed in my thirty-one years as an umpire in the major leagues, and I received five cents for every call I made right, I'd be a millionaire today," says former umpire Al Barlick. "Players can make twenty, thirty mistakes—errors—in one season and no one ever says anything. They make a particularly outstanding catch or hit a game-winning home run, and everybody pounds them on the back. But who cheers an umpire when he makes a good call, tell me that? But you just let an umpire make one mistake, and they're pegged for horseshit for life."

As the saying goes: an umpire is expected to be perfect at the start of his career and improve each day after that.

While their National League brothers were being condemned, the American League umpires, on the other hand, were having a relatively easy time of it. Until the evening of the Indian uprising in Cleveland. American League attendance figures were seriously sagging compared to the relative stability of the other league's drawing power: by the All Star break, the American League was half a million under 1973, while the National League was half a million over. So the club owners began coming up with a series of ideas to lure fans to the ballpark. The most popular and successful of these was beer night. In Cleveland, this meant that anyone who managed to find his way out of the woodwork or a reformatory to attend a ball game could drink as many twelve-ounce cups of beer as he could swallow at ten cents each. The results were devastating.

"We could have gotten killed out there very easily," said crew chief Nestor Chylak after the game in question. His hand was bleeding and his head was dirty and bruised. He had been hit on the head once by a chair and once by a beer bottle concealed in a paper sack. Chylak and his crew of Larry McCoy, Joe Brinkman, and Nick Bremigan, along with the entire Texas Ranger ballclub, had been attacked by many of the 25,194 beer-fogged fans. It had been two out in the bottom of the ninth inning just as the hometown Indians came from behind to rally for a 5-5 tie. But since the fans were unable to contain themselves, Chylak was forced to forfeit the game to the Rangers, 9–0. (When a game is forfeited like this, all runs for the team held responsible for the trouble are cancelled, and the winning team gets one point for each inning that has been played.)

Chylak, an eighteen-year major league veteran, said: "These people went beer mad. They turned into uncontrollable beasts. They could have killed somebody out there. Animals. Animals! Have I ever seen anything like it before? Yes, in a zoo."

The incident erupted when the fans started to harass Texas right fielder Jeff Burroughs. A few people came down onto the field and began pulling on his clothes, attempting to steal his hat and glove. Wielding bats, his Ranger teammates left the dugout to go to Burroughs's aid. Soon, members of both teams were on the field, battling hundreds of fans who poured out of the stands holding knives, throwing beer bottles and chairs, and setting off firecrackers.

The Cleveland club owners and management had control of the

beer and of the public address system so they could have at any time shut down their refreshment counters and requested that the fans control themselves. However, Indian General Manager Phil Seghi and Vice President Ted Bonda preferred to blame the umpires, rather than admit to any error in judgment on their own part.

"If the umpires had tried to keep all the players in the dugout and quell the Burroughs incident by itself," said Bonda, "I don't think this would have occurred. Besides, the umpires never warned the fans of the possibility that the game could be forfeited. The umpires were wrong."

"What the hell does Bonda expect an umpire to do?" asked Harry Wendelstedt, after reading an account of the riot in the newspaper. "They didn't have suits of armor on. How the hell can four men control 50 or 60 angry athletes and 25,000 drunken fans? I can't understand why, no matter what happens, no matter how clear the evidence is, the ball clubs are always willing to blame us and the fans are always ready to hurt and insult us."

Undoubtedly, umpires often deserve battle pay for the things they are forced to live through. In the recent past, umpires have been beaned by flying pop bottles, chased out of ballparks by hostile fans, assaulted by umbrella-swinging little old ladies, and showered with dirt and obscenities by players, fans, and managers. Only a decade ago, when the Chicago White Sox hosted a group of caddies on convention, the umpires were pelted with thousands of golf balls. A few years earlier, Ed Runge of the American League (whose son, Paul Runge, now works in the National League) was fire-bombed on the field after making a controversial decision.

"Last year," says umpire Billy Williams, "Ed Vargo's wife was getting a lot of threatening phone calls from some maniac every time Ed umpired a game involving a certain team. I'm telling you, that's frightening when those cruds—the goofballs, the crazy bastards who got nothing better to do—think umpires are supposed to be targets for any kind of deranged abuse.

"Couple of weeks ago, I'm sitting in the coffee shop of our hotel in Houston with some friends late at night, when a man came up and whispered in my ear, 'If the Astros lose tomorrow night, you'll be dead by morning.'

" 'What?' I looked at him like he was crazy. He *was* crazy. I didn't know what he was talking about for a minute. I was so shocked, nothing registered right. " 'Who are you?' I finally said.

" 'Pete Rose,' the man answered, " 'and you better listen to what I said, if you want to live.'

"Then he walked out. I woulda stopped him, but I couldn't gather myself together. That kind of stuff doesn't happen to you every day."

Despite these two instances which represent the worst extremes umpires encounter, Harry Wendelstedt feels that generally the fans' treatment of umpires has improved. "I think that people have a lot more to worry about than baseball these days, what with Watergate, inflation, and the Vietnamese and Middle East crises. Still, especially in New York and Philadelphia, you see the rowdiest and most ill-tempered fans in the history of baseball. In Philadelphia, you see the greatest, goriest fights in the history of street fighting right in the ballpark. The idea of retribution for losing has escalated to the point where kids now carry knives in their pockets where they used to carry jelly beans. Using these weapons, they obviously have a much lower regard for human life and for the idea of fair play."

"I had just finished working a game in Auburn in the New York-Penn (Pennsylvania) League," says ex-American League umpire Jake O'Donnell, now an American Basketball Association (ABA) official, "and I was on my way to the car. It had been a rough day. I ejected the home team's manager after an argument and the crowd wouldn't let me forget it. When the game was over, all I wanted to do was get to my car and get out of there. I reached the car, but I didn't go anywhere. All my tires were slashed. All I could think of was 'Helluva career you've chosen, Jake, helluva career.' "

Of course, any umpire asked to think back to his days and nights working minor league ball will grit his teeth and solemnly point out that nowhere else in America do baboons and wild hogs —deranged beyond rehabilitation—regularly collect in such large numbers each and every night.

"I was umpiring a game behind the plate one night," says George Hoffmann, eighty-two, a veteran minor league umpire. "You know, I was leaning real low over the catcher's shoulder, trying to concentrate above the noise of the crowd. And the people were really cheering. I didn't understand why, but I'll tell you, I had never heard them so happy in this particular town. Well, suddenly, I had a funny feeling. You know that kind of feeling you get when somebody is watching you or sneaking up close behind you? Just a feeling, a tickle, that's hard to explain. So I turned around. And there's this big black man, seemed to me he was ten feet tall, poised right behind me with his arm lifted up and a knife in his hand. I thought I had really had it that time. There was nothing else to do but run. I beat him by two steps and locked myself in the umpires' room until he went away. I musta waited two hours."

Hoffmann shook his head and laughed. Lines of memory and time zigzagged across his ruddy face.

"I got away 'most every time the fans were after me. I had a feeling that they really didn't want to catch me, they just liked chasing. One of the closest calls I had came early in my career in Class D ball when two rival towns, no more than twenty miles apart, were playing each other. It was definitely a grudge match. Anyway, the two managers got into a terrible fistfight during the course of the game and I ejected them both.

"Naturally, the fans had no other choice but to come after me. I mean, there was only two umpires, me and my partner, so we were much more vulnerable than anybody else. They waited for us outside the door to our dressing room, but we outsmarted them —at least we thought we did—by climbing out through the back window. Before we were spotted, we made it to the car and took off down the road.

"Unfortunately, there was only one road out of this area—we were in Pennsylvania—and either way we went we'd have to go through one of the two towns. Would you believe that they had roadblocks set up on the outskirts of both towns? They wouldn't let us in one town, so we turned around and went back—and they wouldn't let us in the other town. Oh, they would have let us in, all right, but they wouldn't have let us out alive. Well, we stayed on the road all night, continually driving back and forth for fear of stopping, falling asleep, and being ambushed. We waited until the next morning when they returned to their farms and went off to work. It was really frightening, though. I would have made book on the fact that my number was up. I kept trying to remember, all through that night, if I had purchased a grave site."

Says veteran Tom Gorman: "The toughest thing was being black in the minor leagues in the old days. I remember one time I was in Georgia—Gaymar, Georgia, I think it was—and Monte Irvin, one of the first black players in baseball, was playing on Leo Durocher's team. This was just at the beginning of Durocher's managing career. Irvin, of course, went on to be a star with the Giants and is now the public relations director for the major leagues.

"When I came out on the field before the game I saw the sheriff of the town sitting in the seat directly behind home plate. He was wearing a big, low-hanging six-shooter and a ten gallon hat. He said to me: 'Is that nigger going to play ball today?'

" 'I don't know,' I said.

" 'Well, if he steps up to that plate, I'll tell you what I'm going to do. I'm going to shoot him.'

" 'Sheriff, I want you to tell that to somebody else,' I said. Then I went and brought Leo over.

" 'If that nigger steps up to the plate tonight or any other night in this town,' the sheriff said, 'I'm going to shoot him.'

"Well, Leo didn't say anything. He just nodded reflectively, shuffled around a little bit, drawing designs in the dirt with the toe of his spikes, then walked away. I watched carefully, though, waiting for him to tell Irvin, but that old bastard never said a word to the kid. He was gonna let him play!

"Meanwhile, I was getting nervous. I was working behind the plate, you know? I didn't want to be in the line of fire. So I went over and I told Monte what the sheriff had said.

" 'Is that what he said?'

" 'I'm not kidding you, Monte.'

"Irvin nodded and went back into the dressing room, put on his street clothes and started walking back to his hotel. Durocher took off after him. They talked for a couple of seconds, then Leo turned around and tore into me.

" 'YOU TOLD HIM! YOU TOLD HIM!' Leo yelled. 'WHAT THE HELL DID YOU TELL HIM FOR? YOU WANT US TO LOSE THIS GAME?' "

There isn't an umpire in the major leagues today that doesn't have a couple of minor league stories on the tip of his tongue. Some have been exaggerated, but a good many are true. For umpires, working one's way into the major leagues often includes running a gauntlet made up of hostile players and fanatical fans. But, as many umpires have repeatedly found out—most recently Nestor Chylak and his crew in Cleveland—even reaching the major leagues, the fruition of their dreams, doesn't necessarily secure their safety. Even in the major leagues, insulting and abusing the umpire are integral parts of our national pastime.

The heat continued for Harvey, Wendelstedt, Colosi, and Williams as the 1974 baseball season plodded toward its midway point. In a four game series between Chicago and Pittsburgh held in Chicago, Harvey first took on the entire Pirate dugout in an argument involving a game-winning double by Bill Madlock which the Pirates claimed had been a foul ball. Wendelstedt then had his difficulties with the Pirates when he refused to call a third strike on Rick Monday. The Pirates contended that Monday had swung at the ball, and they appealed to third base umpire Doug Harvey, who ruled with Wendelstedt. This, the Pirates claimed, cost them still another game.

Thus, the Pirates left "the Windy City" for three games in St. Louis, breathing fire and resentment toward the men in blue, most of which was unjustified. The Pirates had been commiting an average of two errors a game, and they hadn't been hitting with regularity. They couldn't attribute their fifth place standing, nine and one half games behind the pack, to the umpires, although they tried when Harvey's crew showed up in St. Louis.

During the series, the Pirates lost three out of three games and eight out of eight arguments. The most disputed play came in the second inning of the second game of a Sunday doubleheader. With none out, Richie Hebner at second, and Paul Popovich at first, left fielder Lou Brock raced in, attempting to snatch Mike Ryan's fly ball. Hebner was so sure that it would fall in for a base hit that he kept running, not even pausing to see Doug Harvey's ruling on the play. Unfortunately for Hebner, however, Harvey ruled that Brock caught the ball. Brock threw to second and the Cardinals completed a double play. Eventually, they made a clean sweep of the double-header.

But bullpen coach Don Leppert was incensed and accused Harvey of loafing on the play: "If he (Harvey) was out there when he should have been, it would have been an easy call. The ball hit almost a foot in front of Brock."

In all, on that very tiring afternoon, Doug Harvey's crew ejected three members of the Pirate team and fined them a total of three hundred dollars for throwing batting helmets. Hebner was subsequently fined another two hundred fifty dollars by the league and even more money was taken from him by his own front office for not paying attention to the play. His mistake and subsequent outburst eventually reduced his bank account by nearly a thousand dollars.

Umpires' schedules are made up and forwarded to the crews two or three weeks in advance by Fred Fleig, secretary and second in command of the National League. Fleig, a graduate of Harvard Business School and a thirty-year veteran baseball administrator, tries to coordinate the travels of his umpiring crews so that they stay no more than four days in any one town or with any one team. He attempts to arrange that crews work each city and officiate games involving each team an equal number of times. Understandably, the distribution isn't perfect and when he can make exceptions to place umpires near their families, he will. Three of the four members of Tom Gorman's crew, for example, live in or near New York during the off season. Thus, Gorman's crew might work the Mets' home games more than any other crew in the league. Harvey's crew might be awarded an extra swing through the West Coast, since both Williams and Harvey live less than a few hours from Los Angeles and Harvey is quite close to San Diego.

Fleig, however, has been around long enough to know that a team, especially one that has been consistently losing since the beginning of the year, and a crew of umpires cannot sustain a peaceful relationship in ten straight games. (Prior to the Chicago series, Harvey and company had been in Pittsburgh for three games.)

"Umpires move around often, jumping from city to city," explains Doug Harvey. "Don't think we like to do this, living out of a suitcase and adjusting to a back-breaking bed every other day. But there are two good reasons why this is so important. First, we can't afford to get too involved with the problems of a ballteam or to become too cozy or casual with the players on the team. This can happen if you spend a long enough time with the same group of boys. Listen to a sportscaster or go up to the press box and talk to some of the writers. As reporters, they're supposed to be as objective as we are. But how can they, being with the same team and the same people nine months of the year? You spend ten, twelve games on their field with the same guys, you see them in the locker room, occasionally pass the time of day, and pretty soon your business relationship is eroded. They become casual, they think they can talk to you, reason with you, take advantage of your acquaintanceship. Being with a team that long is just no good.

"Secondly, if the team is losing, and you're there every time they drop a game, they're going to start to look for excuses. They'll make the connection all right, you can bet on it. And what happens if we do blow a play, the first or second game? It sometimes happens, you know. Well, they're going to be on you for the rest of your time together. It's expected. As it is, players never forget. They come up to you in August and ask about a pitch somebody threw in April. And we're expected to remember. They've got memories like elephants—for everything but their own mistakes. But if we get out of there in three days, the next time they see you, two, three weeks later, it's forgotten. But look here! When we stay with the Pirates ten days running there's going to be trouble. No way to avoid it. No way at all." He lifted up his shoulders, shrugged, and sighed.

It had not been a very invigorating or satisfying ten days for Doug Harvey. For that matter, it had not been a very good month or a very good season. It was the first time that any of the four men could remember umpires being under such continuous attack from all quarters. It was almost as if the whole structure of respect and regard for the importance and the integrity of the regulations and of the men who enforced them was crumbling.

Of course, as Doug Harvey pointed out, Richard M. Nixon's authority was also unravelling like a ragged shoelace under the onslaught of criticism from the press and the populace. But there was reason for the attacks on the President of the United States, there was reason for the pain inflicted upon him by the press, and reason for his fall from grace in the eyes of the people. But what had happened to the authority of the baseball umpire? What had caused the undermining of his position? What was happening to the great game of baseball when winning meant only dollar signs while losing was taken so personally that it was no longer accepted with grace, but occasioned open and furious hostility?

Such thoughts were in the umpires' minds on July 23 as they packed their bags and readied themselves for their trip home for the three-day All Star game break. In the privacy of their own rooms, each of the four men felt a shiver of foreboding edge its way up his back and prick his neck. Whatever had made the first four months of the season so difficult for them should pass in the heat of the pennant drive. Yet, each of the four, most especially Wendelstedt and Williams, would have to cope with much more serious and personal difficulties during the final two months of the baseball year.

AUGUST 1974

STANDING OF
THE NATIONAL LEAGUE TEAMS

Eastern Division

	W.	L.	Pct.	G.B.
Philadelphia	53	50	.515	—
St. Louis	53	50	.515	—
Pittsburgh	50	54	.481	3½
Montreal	49	53	.480	3½
New York	45	56	.446	7
Chicago	42	59	.416	10

Western Division

	W.	L.	Pct.	G.B.
Los Angeles	67	37	.644	—
Cincinnati	63	43	.594	5
Houston	55	50	.524	12½
Atlanta	54	51	.514	13½
San Francisco	48	58	.453	20
San Diego	44	62	.415	24

Don't
Let Anybody
Ever
Call You
Horseshit

Doug Harvey, Harry Wendelstedt, and Art Williams returned from their all too brief vacation a little bit healthier and a whole lot happier after spending three days with family and friends. Then they discovered that the National League had launched a major shake-up of umpiring crews to coincide with the All Star break. In the process, Nick Colosi had been snatched to beef up Tom Gorman's withering corps and had been replaced by a relative rookie, a man with only three years' experience in major league ball, Jerry Dale.

It was National League practice to switch umpire crews very late in the year, usually two or three weeks before the end of the season, especially during tight eastern and western division competition, so that the best four or eight umpires in the league could be collected in one or two crews to work the most significant games. This early reassignment, although unexpected, did not surprise either Doug Harvey or Harry Wendelstedt. National League President Chub Feeney had indicated his dissatisfaction with some of the umpires that year: he told a reporter in Pittsburgh during the All Star game that three of the twenty-four National League umpires were in danger of losing their jobs.

Although Feeney had mentioned no names, most of the reporters, players, coaches, and certainly the umpires had some pretty accurate ideas as to whom the President had in mind. Five-year-veteran Dave (Satch) Davidson, who, along with Colosi, had been assigned to join Tom Gorman, was in perhaps the most vulnerable position. Davidson, a product of the major league's Umpire Development Program, had been in trouble since first entering the National League, mostly because of his inability to coordinate his reflexes with his knowledge of the rule book. Although he usually knew the answers to the questions shot at him during disputed calls by players and managers, he often found himself flustered to inarticulateness under the heat and pressure of dissent. He seemed to wither under the excitement of close plays, sometimes changing his mind on a call, or flashing the hand sign for "out" while simultaneously yelling "safe!" Many umpires attributed Davidson's failings to an inability to maintain his concentration. He was the only umpire in the National League who reported to spring training season on a probationary contract. It was hoped that under the tutelage of Tom Gorman, twelve-year veteran Billy Williams, and Nick Colosi, Davidson would improve enough during the last third of the season to secure his position in the major leagues.

Jerry Dale was also in trouble. A native of Indiana now living in California, Dale taught junior high school during the winter months and had attained a masters degree from UCLA; his thesis had focused on the personality characteristics of major league umpires. Thirty-eight years old, gray-haired, stocky, and soft-spoken, Jerry Dale was not a favorite of many of the more fiery umpires in the league.

"I'm a loner," he said. "When I'm on an airplane I bury myself in a book. On the road, I don't stay in the same hotels with other umpires. I don't eat with them, drink with them, socialize with them very often. I'm a loner and I like it just that way."

Although Dale was considered a potentially skillful official, neither his quiet personality and his insistence upon a private existence, nor the fact that he would tolerate all kinds of abuse and criticism from coaches, managers, players on the field helped him as an umpire.

This latter problem also represented the ultimate danger for Art Williams, the third umpire Feeney had allegedly singled out. Much of the knowledge and many of the skills required for good major league umpiring could be learned through experience, practice, and study. But the most important, the essential quality demanded by the profession, was a spirit of unbending pride and insurmountable courage. Wendelstedt, Harvey, Froemming, Barlick, and many other umpires believed that an umpire was a man's man whose every bone and sinew, every bubble and breath of life should be a reflection and reinforcement of machismo. In short, that meant that on the field, you didn't take any shit from anyone.

Although Dale was experiencing other difficulties in adapting to the big leagues, the fact that he tolerated so much abuse was considered his primary problem. Art Williams's dilemma was even more complicated. Already a number of ballclubs had complained to the National League office about what they felt was his shoddy officiating. Fred Fleig, supervisor of umpires, in a meeting with Harvey, Wendelstedt, and Williams, had warned Williams that if he didn't show marked improvement during the last third of the season, his job would be in jeopardy.

Doug Harvey's patience was wearing thin. He just couldn't quite understand why the instructions and criticism he and Wendelstedt had offered throughout the season weren't reflected in the quality of Art Williams's work.

Both before and after Williams's disastrous confrontation with Expo Coach Walt Hriniak, they repeatedly told him that his fancy step-out call left him in an awkward position, off-balance to judge a follow-up play. But Williams seemed either unable or unwilling to control his footwork. Neither could Harvey understand why Williams seldom asked questions or sought advice to improve himself. "Certainly he doesn't believe he's umpiring up to major league standards," Harvey told Wendelstedt a few days after the All Star break. "It takes the best qualified umpire five years to learn to do a decent job in the major leagues, and Williams is far from the best in both ability and courage."

"In two years of major league umpiring," said Wendelstedt, "he's only ejected two men. And both this year. We're not in a contest to see how many people we can eject, I know that, but surely you can figure that something is terribly wrong with the way he's handling situations when every other umpire ejects anywhere from five to ten ballplayers each year. He's not immune to the heat, you know. He's got to learn to stand up for his rights."

Harvey nodded. "You're right, but I don't know what else to do. I want to help the kid."

Wendelstedt sighed and shrugged. He was not in very good spirits, mostly because he was missing his family again after having just been with them for three straight days and also because he had worn himself out during his vacation, splashing in the pool with his son, Harry Hunter, and Cheryl and eating, drinking, and visiting with his friends. It was a vacation after which he needed a vacation. He had tried to cram in a whole summer in less than half a week. "I'm giving up," he said. "I've taken Williams out for drinks and dinner and I've spent a lot of time talking to him, but I just can't do any more. I like him and I want to help, but he doesn't want my help. He won't respond. That's all there is to that."

"But he's going to lose his job."

"He won't lose his job," Wendelstedt shook his head. "The league is committed to having a black umpire."

"But Fleig said . . ."

"Fleig is a good guy. He's always done right by me, but this time, he's not saying what he means."

"Well, I'm going to keep trying," Harvey pledged.

"Not me," said Wendelstedt. "I'm too tired to go at it any more."

"Listen, Art," said Harvey that evening in the umpires' room in Busch Stadium in St. Louis. "You see Manny Sanguillen (Pirate catcher) complaining to me about a call I made out there tonight? You think I let him get away with it?"

Williams shook his head and looked up at Harvey. He had worked first base that evening and had a difficult time of it. Lou Brock, the Cardinal left fielder, who was attempting to break Maury Wills's record for most bases stolen in one season, had been very difficult to deal with. Brock had to get on base if he was going to add to his already impressive total of stolen bases, and so he fought for every close play with the fury and conviction of a man bent on destiny. That night Williams had been a constant target.

"You can't let people shit on you," said Wendelstedt. "You're an umpire. Don't you know what that means? We've got to control that game, we've got to rule those players. Otherwise, they're going to tramp all over us."

"Sanguillen was bitching about a call I made in the first inning," said Harvey. "Pitch after pitch, inning after inning, he's still bitching about that same call I made in that goddamn first inning."

"I can just picture him," Wendelstedt said, "that goddamn Sanguillen can drive you crazy. I can just picture him, looking up at you, smiling that goddamn gap-toothed smile of his and squealing, 'You mees that peetch! You mees that peetch! You no like me. You mees that peetch!' "

"You got it, Harry," said Williams, smiling.

"He's really something," said Wendelstedt.

"I stood up right in front of goddamn home plate, put my ass toward the pitcher and told him," said Harvey, 'Manny, let's get something straight right now. You didn't like that pitch I called, but I called it three innings ago, so right or wrong, good or bad, what's done is done. Now don't quote me history, Manny, I'm warning you right now. You've talked about that pitch for three innings and if you think I'm going to listen to you talk about that pitch for another three innings, you're fuckin' out of your mind. A crying catcher is like a bad tooth,' I told him, 'and if you don't get rid of a bad tooth it's going to hurt you more and more. I'm not here to pull the daisies, Manny, I'm here to work a game. Now, I'm tellin' you Manny, don't quote me history. Don't quote me history or I'll run your ass right out of the ballpark.' " Harvey turned to Williams, still sitting on his stool looking up at his crew chief. "You see what I mean, Art?"

"Sure," said Williams, "you gotta be tough like Harry." Williams smiled and winked over toward his partner.

Wendelstedt shrugged back at the black man, then lapsed into a weighty, almost painful silence. Considerably depressed, he just didn't feel like talking about umpiring anymore, to Williams or, for that matter, to anyone else right then. He sat there instead, silently thinking, unable to understand, yet understanding completely. He couldn't understand why the high standards necessary for superior accomplishment in his profession, a profession that required a man to be wholly honest and impartial for three to seven hours each day, a profession that demanded a demon's concentration, an artist's dedication, a clergyman's sense of propriety—were to be sacrificed or temporarily set aside for the sake of racial equality.

Logically, it didn't make sense. It didn't make sense to take a man who had spent only two and a half years of preparation in minor league ball and thrust him into the heartache and hell of major league competition, not when there were many more qualified people in the minor leagues, baking in the sun and breathing in the dust year after year, just waiting and praying for the opportunity which, through increased skill and everlasting patience, they had earned. What had ever happened to the great American concepts of fair play to all competitors and justice to all men, white or black or red or yellow?

For the American League to have purchased a Spanish-speaking umpire from the Mexican League last winter, a man who needed an interpreter to communicate in English, just so the league could boast a Latin American umpire, was unfair. For the National League to have rushed Art Williams through the minor league system was equally unfair. It was unfair to the ten or so umpires who had put in their time and paid their dues and were now ready to be tested in the majors. It was unfair to Art Williams, who had been put in the awkward position of trying to do a man's job with less than an adequate frame of reference. Because of his color, Wendelstedt knew, Art Williams might very well remain in the major leagues and eventually come to be an adequate umpire. But in the meantime, his mistakes undermined the efforts of umpires in both leagues. And if Art Williams failed to stick, what would this mean to other black umpires in the future? Surely, it couldn't have anything but a bad effect.

Wendelstedt knew that he would be accused of racism if he ever stated his views publicly, and he was honest enough with himself to know that deep down, evidence of prejudice and bigotry very well might be unearthed. Yet, he was convinced that his attitude and disappointment had nothing to do with the color of Art Williams's skin. It was the principle of the situation more than anything else, he thought, as he snapped open a cold can of beer and stared over at Harvey morosely.

Harvey, slumped like a sack of potatoes in a folding chair in front of his dressing cubicle, stared at Williams, shook his head, and sighed. He wondered whether it was worth continuing the discussion. He had tried so often this year to help Williams, repeatedly drilling him, attempting to transfer the knowledge that he, now a veteran, had learned. He was convinced that Williams had the physical tools to be a good umpire, but did he have the courage and the fortitude to hold up under the ever increasing pressure, especially in a season where, it seemed, none of the National League teams in the eastern division could win enough games to stumble far enough ahead to take a commanding lead? Right now, as they sat, their elbows resting on their knees, sweat dribbling down their cheeks and scarring the floor, only three and a half games separated the fourth place Pirates from the first place Philadelphia Phillies. In fact, only ten games separated the Phillies from the New York Mets in the back of the pack.

Doug Harvey stood, slipped the straps of his white chest protector down over his shoulders, and allowed the protector to thump to the floor. Grunting dejectedly, he picked it up and hung it on a hook in the wooden cubicle, then sat, stooped over, and began unlacing his shoes.

He was tired. In fact, he could never remember being as tired, as wrung out, as he felt right then. The game that night had gone almost four hours, twelve full innings, in windless, ninety degree heat, and Harvey's whole body throbbed. When he slipped off his shoes and socks, his feet were red and swollen, and when he tried to wiggle his toes to trigger the circulation, they only half-heartedly responded to his signal.

On their last trip to Houston before the All Star break, he had gone to see a specialist at the Texas Medical Center, where Dr. Denton Cooley had completed so many of those successful heart transplants. After a thorough examination the doctor had discovered that the bottoms of his feet were riddled with bone spurs. "These are something like knuckles," the doctor had explained, "that grow directly over a bruised or overused part of the bone. What happens is, these spurs must absorb and subsequently reject the entire weight of your body. It's damn painful."

"You're not telling me anything I don't know," Harvey said. "Sometimes I feel like I'm standing in a bed of hot coals or that there's a bonfire under my feet."

"Yes," the doctor nodded.

"I swear, doctor, I sleep twelve, fourteen, sometimes sixteen hours a day, and when I wake up, it's like I haven't been asleep for a week. Could these bone spurs be the cause of that?"

"I don't think so. I think the reaction you had to the penicillin from the dog bite was quite serious. It's obviously sapped your strength and will continue to do so for quite a long time. Recuperation is gradual. Slowly, you'll feel yourself gathering more energy. There's no telling how much longer it's going to take, but right now you'll just have to try to live through it."

"That's what the league doctor in San Francisco and my family doctor in San Diego told me."

"Judging from all the evidence, it's the only advice we can give."

Harvey had sunk his feet into molds of wet plaster of Paris that afternoon from which special insoles would subsequently be made for insertion in his shoes to alleviate some of the pressure on the spurs. He would pick them up on his next trip to Houston, two days hence.

Harvey looked across the dressing room. Williams, slowly chewing one of the sandwiches provided for the umpires after the game, was looking up at him expectantly. Dale had already stripped off his clothes and padded into the shower room and Harvey could hear the water spraying against the polished tile. Wendelstedt sat hunched on his stool in front of his cubicle, silently nursing a beer.

That Dale was certainly a strange case, Harvey thought. Dale did not travel with the umpires as they moved from town to town, nor did he participate in pre-game or post-game banter in the umpires' dressing room. Like a shadow, he moved in and out of their lives, doing his job, but doing little else to enhance the solidarity of the crew.

Yet, as with all conservative and understated people, Jerry Dale did have one flashy eccentricity known only to those who had seen the man with his pants down. He wore absolutely bizarre brief underwear, made of shiny black nylon with murals silk-screened in elaborate colors over the crotch. Dale had a red and blue and green and gold fighting cock, a purple and yellow crow, a gold and black tiger, and a red and amber jewel-studded gorilla, to name only a few of the works of art that adorned him.

"Look Art," said Harvey slowly, "umpires have been getting a lot of shit this season. The Pirates and the Mets especially have been throwing plenty at us, but let me tell you something son, you ain't seen the half of it. Up to this time, we been playing for peanuts here in the National League. None of the games were that important because there were plenty games remaining. None of the times at bat were that important for individual players because a guy could figure, if he was playing regular, that he'd be up another three hundred times. But now we're coming down to the wire, my boy, we're into the 'dog days' of the season, with double-headers up our ass in the hottest and most despicable month of the year. We got five months down and two months to go and the players and managers are starting to look more seriously into the future.

"And what do they see?" asked Harvey, pausing to raise a forefinger. "I'll tell ya what they see. They see, first of all, that any of the ten teams in this goddamn twelve-team division can ass-kick themselves into the playoffs. You got ten games separating all six teams in the eastern division and thirteen and a half games separating the first four teams in the west. You got the Dodgers five and a half games out in front of Cincinnati, but after last year, with Cincinnati down seven games with a month to go in the season and coming back to win in the last two weeks, the Dodgers ain't got it made. You know that well as I do.

"Come August, everybody's on fucking pins and needles 'cause the whole fucking season can be boiled down to the last six weeks. Everything's on the line. Most valuable player, batting title, Cy Young Award. You make a bad call at second base and maybe that deprives Lou Brock of stealing a hundred bases this year. What's he got now? Eighty? At the beginning of the season, he didn't know he had one chance in hell of breaking Wills's record, but now that he knows he's got a real shot, he's going to be fighting you every which way. No matter if you're right ninety-nine out of one hundred times, no matter if you're right one hundred out of one hundred times, he and everybody else is going to fight you for every questionable pitch and every close call. Right now, everything counts double.

"And how about the players having a bad season? They're going to be on the umpire's ass too. The good players, the steady ones that perform year after year, like Billy Williams of the Cubs, they won't hassle you. They know that if they're having a bad year, it's not the umpire's fault. They know the strike zone hasn't changed, *they've* changed, they've gotten older and maybe fucked up their swing. It's the goddamn younger players mostly, the marginal players, that are fighting for a job, the 'humpty dumpties' who don't know whether they'll be up here next year, they're the ones that's going to get you. They're going to argue their way to first base is what they're going to try to do, and if you keep taking the horseshit and abuse you been taking through this whole year, they're going to succeed. And you'll look like a chicken ass. To the players and the fans and the people in the league office, that's exactly what you'll look like. A goddamn, horseshit chicken ass!"

Harvey stood up and dropped his pants, his belt buckle clinking to the floor, and kicked them across the room. He pulled his T-shirt etched with a "straight arrow" over his head, then stepped out of his soggy long johns, brown with dust, and gray from repeated washings. He looked back over at Williams.

"Now you take a guy like Ralph Garr (Atlanta outfielder). Nice kid, doesn't cause any trouble. He's batting .360 and leading the whole goddamn league by thirty-five points. You'd think there'd be no reason in the world for him to bitch at me. But I had to eject him last week on that ground ball he tried to leg out to first base, didn't I? You see, he's starting to run scared. He's got the batting title in his pocket and the pressure to keep it there is tremendous."

"That was a tough play," said Williams.

"Horseshit tough play. He was out by half a step. He shoulda known it, but he wanted that goddamn base hit so bad he couldn't think straight."

"He sure was mad," said Williams.

"You talk about mad. I thought old Smokey Alston was going to beat your head in when you stopped that line shot by Jimmy Wynn. You can't go laughing at things like that."

"I was so embarrassed, Doug. I couldn't get out of the way. The ball just hit me and I felt terrible, 'cause there were men on base and it was sure to fall in for extra bases."

"I'm not faulting you for that," said Harvey. "That happens to all umpires once in a while, but what I'm saying is, you can't smile like a goddamn, horseshit Guinea. That was a serious thing for

Alston. With a couple of runs, he might have won that game. You can't do that, Art, embarrassed or not. These guys want to win too much."

Finishing his sandwich, Williams tossed his undershorts into a pile of dirty laundry in the middle of the floor and followed Harvey into the shower room. He eased under the shower backwards, so that the heat would first sooth the stiffness in the small of his back, then slowly stepped in so that the hard hot spray would climb up his neck and finally tumble over his head and chest. Stepping away from the water, he soaped himself thoroughly, white bubbles beading and popping on his brown smooth skin and pictured, as he washed, the layer of dust and sweat and worry accumulated during and after the game, swirling like a whirlpool down the gaping drain. Williams looked over at Doug Harvey as he washed. The man's eyes were closed, his head tilted back under the force of the water, his glittering silver hair plastered over his forehead and above his eyes.

Of all the men Art Williams had ever known, in baseball and in other walks of life, he thought Doug Harvey to be the finest. Never had he expected any man, most especially a white man, to take so much time and patience in helping him become what he most wanted to be: a major league umpire. Williams was never insulted or in any way distressed when Harvey criticized his performance on the field because he knew Doug Harvey wanted him to succeed. Harvey's willingness to give of his time and knowledge and to explain with impeccable patience any problem that might be confronting the young umpire was most appreciated. "I never mind telling you anything you want to know about officiating this game," Harvey often said. "I don't mind telling you anything once. But I never want to have to say it twice. Not ever."

And yet, what Art Williams couldn't understand, what he tried desperately to understand, was why he was being criticized so often and so intensely, not only by Harvey and Wendelstedt, but even by the league office in San Francisco. God knows he was trying to become a better umpire, trying harder and working more diligently than he ever thought possible. In his own mind he was convinced that he had made tremendous progress in the past two years, working with Harvey and Wendelstedt this year, and Harvey and veteran Shag Crawford the year before. He had attempted to copy the styles of Harvey and Crawford and was certain that a little of the best qualities of both men had rubbed off on him.

Art Williams could not understand what he was doing wrong. He was trying. Maybe he didn't do everything exactly the way they said, but they told him so many things, so often, that it was becoming increasingly difficult to work under the strain of criticism, and to fit together at one time all of the advice and directions they tried to cram into him. But he was trying. He was trying so hard to hustle and to concentrate and to do the right thing sometimes he felt as tight as a banjo string. Even tighter. Sometimes he felt he was so tight that the slightest bit of pressure, the slightest movement, a twitch, would pop him all apart.

"Yessir," said Harvey, stepping out of the shower and beginning to towel himself off. "A lot of guys with a quick mind and good reflexes can learn how to officiate adequately, but the real test is, can he handle situations of dissent? Can he control fifty athletes and thousands of fans and still maintain his cool enough to quote from the rule book and keep the game moving? Can he handle players, no matter what they're beefing about? Does he have the courage to take the criticism and abuse, to stand his ground and to thumb a guy out? That's the test of a good umpire.

"And I'll tell you something else," said Harvey. "Most people don't realize that the umpires are under as much pressure as the players—especially late in the season—maybe even more. We know that the futures of teams and individual players are often riding on our decisions. We know we gotta do right. I mean, look at us here in this dressing room. We're not arguing or anything like that, but let's face it, there's not as much kidding and fooling around as there used to be. We're tired from five months of a season, damn tired, and we're just now entering into the hardest part of the year. I'll tell you, it's tough and it's going to get tougher. And you gotta be ready, Art. If you know what's good for you, you gotta steel yourself, you just gotta be ready when the shit hits the fan."

Williams nodded, stepped out of the shower and walked into the dressing room. He saw that Dale was gone and that Wendelstedt had just undressed. They passed each other as the big man walked gravely into the shower room. "One of the hardest calls for me to get," Williams told Harvey, "is that swipe call. You know?

There's a ground ball to short, the ball is thrown wild, and the first baseman leaps, catches the ball, and swipes at the runner when he's crossing the bag."

Harvey sat down on a stool and began wiping his feet, toe after red, swollen, painful toe. If only he could be sure he was doing some good, if only he hadn't gone over these same points with Williams again and again, three, four, five times before . . . "You gotta watch the bag," he said, "that's first of all, and you gotta watch the runner, the fielder's glove, and the fielder's foot. But like I always tell you, if you're in the right position, in the slot, up on the balls of your feet, legs in tight, instantly ready to move, yet concentrating on exactly what's going on, you shouldn't have any trouble. It's only tough when you're loafing or out of position, or when you allow a fielder to get in front of you and block your vision of the play. That's the reason we want you to change that fancy footwork style of yours. Because once you make your call, you're out of position if a back-up call is necessary. You can't be sure each play is going to go like you first see it.

"Now I admit that umpires miss a call once in a while because we're human. We make mistakes. But there's no physical or practical reason for it. If we're in the right position, and we're completely concentrating, we should make every call right. An umpire has ears as well as eyes, you know, and if we're not completely sure of what we see, we should use our earpower to confirm our judgment. You should listen for the slap of the ball in the glove, and the thump of the runner's spike against the canvas. Now which came first? That's for your eyes to confirm. Or vice versa.

"Some base runners, I call them out, and they come up after the play and they say, 'Listen. I know as well as the umpires do whether I'm safe or out because I was right there with you. In fact, I was even closer. It happened to me! I felt the tag and I felt my foot touch the base.' "

Williams smiled and shook his head. "I get that lots of times, from honest players who really believe they're right."

"I'm not saying all ballplayers cheat," said Harvey, "but they don't understand the different factors that enter into each and every play. First off, a runner will feel his foot against the bag a minisecond before he hears the pop of the ball."

"Sound travels slower than contact," said Williams.

"Hell yes. The guys on the field hear the national anthem before the people in the stands, don't they? Sound travels slower. And how about when a player is sliding into a base?" said Harvey. "Let me ask you that?"

Williams shrugged. "What's the difference?"

"The most important thing there," said Harvey, "is that the runner's nerves are centered at his point of contact between the ground and his body. The rest of his body is somewhat numbed by the slide. His main thrust of concentration is on the pain or abrasion against the skin so he can never be sure exactly when his foot touches the bag. Consequently, he complains. But I can assure you, the player doesn't know, not for certain. There are far too many influencing factors."

Doug Harvey took a deep breath. With Williams around, he sometimes felt like a college professor babbling incessantly in front of a blackboard. Yet, in many ways, he had to admit that he liked the role he was attempting to play in Art Williams's development. He loved the game so much, took such pride in being the best, and worked so hard to maintain that position that he could, and would, go on talking about the intricacies and eccentricities of umpiring indefinitely—or at least as long as there was a moderately willing ear to listen. "Now you take instant replay," he said.

"You take instant replay," Wendelstedt said, his wet bare feet squeaking on the linoleum floor.

"Well," said Harvey, smiling broadly, "welcome back from the land of the dead. What got your ass so hot and quiet tonight?"

"I was just thinking," said Wendelstedt.

"As crew chief," said Harvey, "I demand to be the only umpire in this crew permitted to think."

"Well, it looks like you might get your wish," said Wendelstedt, casting a glance in Williams's direction.

Williams shrugged and began dressing, while Harvey continued. "They throw that instant replay up at us all the time, but how in the hell can a camera, no matter how powerful, be positioned at the best angle for each and every play? Why, you'd need a million cameras out on the field."

"And a million microphones," said Wendelstedt.

"You better believe it," said Harvey. "The sportswriters sit two tiers above us in the press box drinking beer and eating hot dogs and they think they can call pitches better than we do. Why, they can't even tell what kind of a pitch it is. Curve ball, fast ball, they haven't the slightest idea, yet you hear them on television second-guessing you all the time."

"I tell you what," said Wendelstedt, "if those goddamn cameras are so good, why don't they replace us? It'd be a lot cheaper and more sensible to use cameras instead of four live men."

"They've got a goddamn machine," said Harvey, "can call balls and strikes. I've seen it work before, but I ask you, can it call foul tips? Can it call obstructions? Let's face it, we're necessary evils. If you gave people a sensible way to replace us they would. But the owners and players and managers and even the fans have got to realize that we're irreplaceable. There ain't no machine that can do an umpire's job."

"Even if they did get a machine to replace us," said Wendelstedt, "you know what would happen to it? Why, the players would bust it to pieces every time it ruled against them. They'd clobber it with a bat."

"Ain't no machine can call a half-swing," said Harvey. "Far as I'm concerned, that's the hardest call for any umpire to make."

"The hardest call an umpire makes," said Wendelstedt, "is after he receives his new schedule and he has to call his wife to tell her he won't be home for four months."

"Couple years ago," said Harvey, "I bet Pirate manager Danny Murtaugh a keg of beer that a call I made was right. We were standing out near first base and he was bitching at me, said I had blown the play, so I made the proposition and he sent one of his coaches—I think it was Leppert—up to the press box to check out the replay. Well, Leppert gets back after a little while, he comes back and scrambles into the dugout, and he and Murtaugh start to talk. They talk for a whole goddamn inning, and Murtaugh looks mad as hell. At the end of the inning, Leppert came out, hanging his head like a goddamn sheep, he's so embarrassed. 'So?' I said.

" 'They didn't have the film of that play,' Leppert blurts out.

" 'Bullshit,' I told him, 'they film the whole game.'

" 'Well, they didn't have it,' Leppert tells me, then runs back to the dugout.

"Can you imagine that? Goddamn Murtaugh was too cheap to pay me the keg of beer!

"The managers and sportswriters can't stand it," continued Harvey, " 'cause the cameras are showing the fans that the umpires are right almost every time."

"Cameras," said Wendelstedt, shaking his head and hurling his wet towel down into the corner in disgust. "You show me a camera that can tell the difference between a brush-back pitch and a beanball. You show me a camera that can judge whether a guy is throwing a spitter, a fork ball, or a slip pitch."

"Far as I'm concerned," said Harvey, "the rule outlawing the spitter is useless anyway. The reason they outlawed the spitter in the first place was because it was too difficult to control, but these days, you got knuckle balls and fork balls that are just as hard to handle. A good forkball acts like a spitter. A spitter drops and a forkball drops the same way, then shoots out. That's the only difference."

"Of course, it depends on how you hold the ball," said Wendelstedt. "The further back in the fork of your hand, the more it's going to shoot out."

"It's a completely explosive pitch," said Harvey, "like (Pirate pitcher) Bruce Kison's slip pitch. He musta hit ten batters in 1974 with that pitch."

"Someday he's going to hurt somebody good," said Wendelstedt.

"He can't control it," said Harvey.

"Goddamn Kison can't control himself," said Wendelstedt. "He's the dumbest ballplayer in the major leagues. Why, I'll betcha they have to point him in the direction of the pitcher's mound at the beginning of every inning. Kison's so dumb, he's null and void. You see him on the street, he looks deranged."

"There's so much to learn," Harvey said, turning back to Williams. "That's the reason I keep saying, it takes anywhere from five to eight years to make a good major league umpire. I mean five to eight years in the major leagues before a guy can do a truly excellent job. You know what I mean, Art? The world wasn't made in a day. You gotta expect things to go wrong. You can't assume that you're nearly as good as we are. After all, we're established. We have respect."

Williams, sitting and quietly listening to the conversation was now dressed in a light blue suit with a muted plaid design and a brown turtleneck sweater. He sat on his stool in the corner of the room, his elbows resting on his knees and his chin cupped in his hand, trying as hard as he possibly could to absorb all of the information being indirectly transferred through Harvey and Wendelstedt. But there was so much, he thought to himself, so much to digest, so much to remember. And there was so little time. He wished he could take a course or read a book, but he knew he was past that stage. He had leapfrogged into the big leagues and now every scrap of knowledge he managed to consume was further insurance that he would remain there. Williams squinted so that his brows rolled over his eyes, looked up at Harvey, and nodded intensely.

"You remember that game in Pittsburgh?" Harvey said. "Lasted about five hours even though we had to call it in the eighth inning 'count of rain. You were working the plate, Art, and I know we had to stop the game a couple times because of the weather, but still I calculate that you cost us at least twenty unnecessary minutes out on the field. Simply because you insisted on wiping the ball dry every time it hit the ground. You wiped it dry, then threw it to the pitcher and he rubbed it up with his hands. What I keep trying to tell you is that, for the fans' sake, if not our own, you gotta keep that game moving. We got five dozen balls and a ball boy with a towel. If there's any reason you think the ball's no good, you throw out a new one. That saves us ten, twenty seconds, maybe more, for each batter.

"The other thing is, I notice you like to watch those foul balls hit back into the stands. I know it's interesting to see if one of the fans catches it or not, but that's not an umpire's concern. He's not there to enjoy the game, he's there to officiate it. If someone hits a ball back foul, throw out a new one immediately. The pitcher ought to have a new ball before the old one reaches the stands. We gotta keep this game moving. Baseball is long enough as it is."

"I can see that," said Williams, still nodding, "it only makes sense."

"There's so much to learn," Harvey said again. "People think we go to school for a few weeks, spend a couple years in the minor leagues, and an umpire is ready for the big time. That's not even near the truth."

"And how about catchers?" said Wendelstedt. "You gotta know how to adjust to each and every catcher behind the plate. You gotta know, for example, that a guy like Manny Sanguillen is fidgety, moving around all the time. If you don't know that beforehand so that you can easily adjust to it, he's going to block you out of a couple of calls in the first few innings of every game."

"And McCarver (of the Cardinals)," said Harvey. "He's getting old now and he can't stoop down as far as he used to. So you have got to learn to call the game sometimes standing sort of halfway beside him, rather than behind. If you can't train your eye to do that, to adjust under any and all circumstances, then you'll lack all consistency."

"Grote goes down real low," said Williams.

"Yeah, and he's also moving the ball in his glove all the time back to the strike zone."

"Just like a little leaguer," said Wendelstedt. "Some catchers don't understand that when they keep moving the ball back into the center of the strike zone, they're costing the pitchers, because on any close pitch, with the catcher trying to hide the ball, the umpire has got to assume that it was bad. I'll bet Grote costs a pitcher ten strikes a game."

Harvey pulled on a pair of white, patent leather boots and zipped them up the side. He stood and began buttoning his sweater. "Seems all we do in this game is dress and undress," he said.

"Boy, I'll tell you, there's a hell of a lot to learn, and all we're trying to do is teach you, Art," said Wendelstedt.

"I know that," said Williams, standing up to face Harvey.

"Long about this time in the season," said Harvey, "players start telling me about how red-assed I've become. Well, that's right. I *am* red-assed. I'm as mean as a grizzly, as ferocious as a lion. And it's the goddamn players who are making me that way.

"I'm telling you here and now, Art, and Harry is my witness, black as you are, that if you expect to keep your job next season, then you better become red-assed right away. That's the only way you're going to survive this fucking tight race for the playoffs. And if you aren't red-assed, if you let the ballplayers shit all over you during a game, then you're making it tough for the other umpires, not only in this crew, but all over the league. Goddamn players find out they can throw horseshit at you, then they figure they can throw horseshit at all other umpires. Makes our job ten times, twenty times more difficult." Harvey paused to yell and lift a fist. "You see what I mean? You see what I mean, don't you, goddamn it?"

Williams, his hands in his pockets, his head bowed as he studied the squares of tile on the floor, nodded almost imperceptibly.

"There's one thing I'm trying to drill into you, one thing you got to remember," said Harvey loudly, stepping close enough to Williams to touch him. "What I'm going to say now is the most important thing I have ever tried to tell you. This is the key to being a good umpire. This is what separates the men from the boys. This is what makes a man's man out of a mortal man.

"Now listen to me, Art," said Harvey, spreading his arms and raising his voice as if he were delivering a sermon on a Sunday morning pulpit. "Art, I tell you now like I was your father, I talk to you with the warmth of a brother, so you listen to me closely and you listen good 'cause here it is: Don't let anybody ever call you horseshit. That's the rule one of umpiring. Don't let anybody ever call you horseshit, Art. Anybody calls you horseshit, you throw his ass the hell out of the game.

"As red-assed as I become during August and September, I tell those goddamn players, 'Don't you ever call me horseshit. Don't call me horseshit,' I tell them," Harvey quivered. " 'Goddamn it, don't call me horseshit. You can say I made a horseshit call. That's all right.' " He paused and raised the palms of his hands, then continued expounding. " 'I can call you a horseshit player. That's all right, too. But I'm telling you right now, I don't want anybody calling me something I wouldn't call them. And that's horseshit,' " said Harvey, his wet silver hair reflecting under the bare lightbulb.

"I tell those goddamn players," said Harvey " 'I don't want you to call all umpires horseshit either. If you say all umpires are horseshit, then you're calling *me* horseshit. You do that and I'm going to throw your horseshit ass out of the game.'

"I'm telling you right now, Art, and I'm telling you true, that if there's anything you cannot do in this great game of baseball, it is to allow a player, coach, or manager to call you horseshit. That you simply must not do.

"The way I figure it," said Harvey, "the way you gotta figure it," he pointed at Williams, "is that ballplayers arguing with you are trying to steal food out of our children's mouths."

Williams looked up quickly.

"That's what I said," Harvey nodded, "now you listen to me, son, 'cause I'm telling you straight. A ballplayer arguing with you is trying to steal food out of the mouth of your children, they're trying to repossess your home and throw your family to the dogs.

"You gotta understand that the only reason a ballplayer argues with you is because he's trying to make himself look good. And the only way he's going to make himself look good under those circumstances is to make you look like horseshit.

"You look like horseshit too many times," said Harvey, "and it gets back to the league office. And when the league office begins to think that you look like horseshit, the next thing you know, you're out of a job. Now, you tell me that that player bitching at you, calling you horseshit right out in front of twenty million people, isn't endangering the health and education and care of your children. Why, they're trying to sabotage your future, they're trying to ruin your whole life, they're trying to lift you out of baseball and set you down in the unemployment lines.

"All because you stood there," said Harvey, his voice rising and falling in a singsong, "and took it like a sop-faced chicken ass while they called you horseshit. An umpire can't allow anybody to call him horseshit. You can't call a good umpire horseshit even once."

Harvey concluded with a deep breath and a flourish, dragging the soles of his boots as he moved quickly across the room to the door. Both Williams and Harvey walked briskly outside without another word.

Harry Wendelstedt, still hunching naked on his stool, waited until he could hear the door thump closed decisively. Then he sighed. For a while he sat there on the cold, wooden stool studying his bare feet and the corns and callouses on the tops of his toes, listening to the echoes in the hollow room and then the ever-increasing roar of silence.

Much later Wendelstedt awoke in bed, kicked his blankets and pillows to the floor, then opened his eyes. The whole room was spinning. The walls seemed to be whirling around his head as if he had been dropped into the center of a great whirlpool.

Harry Wendelstedt stood on the Astroturf in Houston, Texas, two days later at the opening game of a three-game series with Cincinnati, listening to the national anthem. Standing with his hat over his heart, watching the scoreboard flash the words to a relatively disinterested audience, Wendelstedt felt the ground move out from under him. The whole world seemed to simultaneously tilt in a thousand different directions. He remembered crashing to the ground.

"I felt them grabbing my feet and my head and rolling me over onto a canvas stretcher," he said many days after. "I felt them lifting me up. I felt light, like a balloon drifting with the clouds, but I couldn't get my bearings. I tried opening and closing my eyes. Each time I opened my eyes I saw the stadium swirling around me. Each time I closed my eyes I had this sensation of falling, plunging with incredible speed down through a seam in the earth."

He was shoveled into a station wagon ambulance which sped over the field, off the Astroturf, down a concrete ramp, across the parking lot, and into traffic. At some point along that highway the driver flipped the siren on, but only much later did Wendelstedt realize that the noise he was hearing was coming from the dome on the roof of the vehicle in which he was traveling, rather than from the screeching inside his head.

Dog
Days

The doctors diagnosed Wendelstedt's sudden sickness as an inner ear infection caused by water leaking into the inside of the ear. A fungus had begun to grow, which, when developed enough, tended to totally disrupt the victim's equilibrium. Thus, in a stationary or prone position, Wendelstedt could converse easily, judge distances, and maintain a satisfactory sense of balance. In trying to stand up, however, he would be overwhelmed by nausea and dizziness, almost as if the floor were being swept right out from under him. The treatment? Drugs and a long, drawn-out sentence of bed rest.

Although the former part of the treatment turned Wendelstedt into, as he put it, a perpetual zombie, the latter part also affected the other three members of his umpiring crew. Harry Wendelstedt languished in a lonely bed for one week in a Houston Hospital and then, in much more comfortable surroundings, for two and a half additional weeks at his home in Daytona Beach, Florida. That left Doug Harvey, Art Williams, and Jerry Dale with the awesome task of umpiring major league baseball through the dog days of the season with a crew short one man. This was especially hard on crew chief Doug Harvey.

Harvey received his new arch supports, designed to alleviate the pressure of his body weight on the bone spurs, and thankfully, the pain he had come to expect in his feet, which then welled up into his calves after only a few innings of each game, quickly diminished.

And yet, as the doctor in Houston had predicted, the supports did little to improve the state of weariness in which he lived. Doug Harvey was wrung out, like a sponge squeezed dry. It seemed as if fate or fortune had planned to allow him no edge, for each time he sensed some improvement in his physical condition, something always happened to make up for it. Three or four times through the season he had felt his strength and stamina returning only to be set back by a fourteen- or sixteen-inning, five-hour game behind the plate or an eight-hour, rain-delayed double-header. Now, with Harry Wendelstedt ill and out for an indefinite time, Harvey, burdened with two of the weaker umpires in the league, had to work a three-man umpiring system, which often meant calling a game behind the plate every other day, as well as doing double duty on the base paths—covering a foul line, one half of the outfield, and the diamond—during the grimiest, hottest, and most difficult month of the year.

To complicate matters, that same evening that Harry Wendelstedt found himself swimming with dizziness, crew chief Chris Pelekoudas, following a line-shot foul ball down the first base line in Philadelphia's Veterans' Stadium, suddenly stumbled and fell. He pulled himself up onto one knee and began choking, his mouth open wide and sucking in the moist summer air. He couldn't seem to catch his breath and he felt his limbs stiffening up, so much so that he, too, needed the aid of a stretcher and was taken from the field in an ambulance. Initially diagnosed as a stroke, Pelekoudas was actually suffering from severe hypertension, a malady that also required bed rest for cure.

Thus, within an hour, one twelfth of the National League's umpiring corps had been struck down.

The unfortunate coincidence of losing two umpires in the same league at the same time points up one of the biggest weaknesses in the major leagues' umpiring setup. With all its money and power and talk of future expansion (both leagues had recently decided to add two additional teams within the next three years), neither the National nor American League had been willing to, nor were capable of, establishing a reasonable back-up system for their officials. Baseball's illogical tradition of treating the umpires like machinery rather than men extends past the fans and players and into management. Major league administrators, led by their well-dressed front man Bowie Kuhn, can't seem to cope with the idea that umpires can become seriously ill, or that they could require a leave of absence to come to the aid of a family member. There is absolutely no well-conceived contingency plan for such an eventuality.

In case of emergency, both leagues own the contracts of a few minor league umpires who, like ballplayers, are available for call-up to the major leagues on twenty-four-hour notice. Jim Quick, twenty-five, and Eric Gregg, twenty-one, both of the Pacific Coast AAA League are owned by the National League, but the very fact that the league has only two reserve umpires and that neither of them had, up to that point, ever worked a day of major league ball, further illustrates the weakness of the system. To plunge an inexperienced and predictably frightened umpire into the heat of a pennant race is like throwing a child into a swimming pool and hoping he will immediately learn enough not to drown. And of the two minor league umpires under contract to the National League, Gregg, a twenty-one-year-old black, was anything but ready for the major leagues. Consequently, Quick joined Pelekoudas's crew in California two days after the Philadelphia series, but Harvey's crew received little help.

Harvey, Williams, and Dale limped through the four games in Houston without Wendelstedt, then worked two games in Atlanta. Next they went to Pittsburgh for two games with the Cardinals and three with the Cubs. For the St. Louis series, the National League sent Andy Olsen to Pittsburgh to work the fourth man's position, since his crew had received an unusual schedule that included two days off. But then, after two games, Olsen was sent back to New York, leaving Harvey, Williams, and Dale to work a single game Saturday and a Sunday double-header in 94 degree heat and in pollution hovering near the danger zone. Harvey and crew received Monday off, moved to Philadelphia for three games, on to New York for three more, and back to Philadelphia for four additional contests. When Pelekoudas returned to work and Harvey and company were dragging themselves into Montreal for six straight games, the National League finally submitted and dispatched Jim Quick to join them.

In the end they worked nineteen games as a three-man unit, and six games with a totally inexperienced umpire. In all, they were confronted with twenty-seven games in twenty-seven days, at a period when they were undoubtedly way below their average level of efficiency. Eleven of the games in which the three-man system was utilized involved teams in a tight race for a pennant.

It makes little sense to put men through such physical and mental hardship. It makes little sense to jeopardize the seasons and careers of those players and teams for whom the three men umpired, just to save a few dollars. The solution to replacing umpires temporarily out of action is simple: an alternate suggestion has been advanced by a number of umpires, including Harvey and Wendelstedt.

"What we need is more major league umpires," they say, "young kids up from the minors. They would be here sort of on an internship basis, learning, yet participating simultaneously in the game. When someone is ill or when an umpire is unavoidably called away from his crew, one of these guys can jump in and take over. When all the umpires are healthy, these 'substitutes' can alternate around the league. After all, umpires are lonely . . . why not send them home a couple of days a month? Sometimes umpires work when they're not feeling too well—so why not use one of these alternate umpires to allow a veteran a few days' rest?"

This idea would offer young umpires some needed major league experience, so that they would be much more qualified to officiate effectively during the more important parts of the season. National League officials would also gain by having the opportunity to study prospective umpires and assess their potential for continued major league ball. At this point, the league's evaluation of young officials is based on their work and effectiveness in the minor leagues and during major league spring training. But managers and coaches of any major league ball club attest to the fact that minor league sensations are as plentiful as mice in a meadow. Big-time ball is the only realistic proving ground for players and, therefore, for umpires.

Such a system would have helped Art Williams tremendously, for he could have been worked into the major league umpiring network gradually, rather than be thrust into it as he was. The system would have made it possible for Doug Harvey to regain his strength so that, in the latter half of the season, he would have been strong enough to work up to his maximum potential.

Most major league umpires feel that such suggestions are totally unrealistic, not because such a plan is a bad one, but because neither league would be willing to invest the time and money necessary to operate this system. Only in the past few years have umpires made significant advances in salary, medical, and retirement benefits, and the leaders of the Major League Umpires Association feel that they have more financial objectives to lobby for first.

"Think of it this way," says Harry Wendelstedt. "Ten years ago a guy entering major league ball as an umpire was paid seventy-five hundred dollars. That's at a time when the average middle class family was making ten thousand dollars a year. We couldn't go any further as far as advancement—after all, we were in the major leagues, and crew chiefs don't get any more money than anyone else—yet we were twenty-five hundred dollars below the middle class average. We were offered no dental coverage and we paid our own Blue Cross and Blue Shield. We had no job security. Now at least there's a tenure system after five years of major league ball. But before we went on strike during the 1971 playoff games, we had nothing. Baseball's bigwigs could fuck us over with one fell swoop of the pen.

"Why, our pension only totaled two hundred dollars a year for each year of major league service. That meant that a guy who might have as much as forty years in baseball, but only ten years in the major leagues before retirement—and we can't wait for sixty-five until we retire, we gotta go at fifty-five—ends up with a grand total of twenty-four hundred dollars a year. And he's been at the top of his profession for ten years!

"We've made some important progress since then, I admit. Great medical benefits, a halfway decent retirement program that pays an umpire five hundred dollars for each year of major league ball. Umpires now start in the major leagues at $15,500 and a twenty year major league veteran can make more than $30,000; we get $11,000 to work a World Series and about half that amount if we're selected for the playoffs. But still, that's pretty pitiful for a person who has worked maybe twenty, thirty years and advanced to the pinnacle of his profession. We're talking about a person who has to make his mark in the world—at least in a financial sense, before he hits fifty-five. Compare what we make to the $200,000 salaries of players. Compare it with the average run-of-the-mill player who makes anywhere from $35,000 to $50,000 a year. You better believe that if we're going to do any striking or lobbying, it's going to be on behalf of our pocketbooks right now. Our request for increased pension benefits has been tabled until next year to see what effect the energy crisis has on attendance figures, but we won't hold still when we meet around a conference table this winter. Already, some of the guys who just recently retired have been forced to take part-time jobs.

"Out of a sense of pure practicality," Wendelstedt continued, "the league should provide those alternate umpires. With umpires who are well and rested, baseball could be a better game.

"But improving the game doesn't seem to concern the administrators and owners of baseball teams," Wendelstedt frowned. "All they want to do is win—at anybody's expense. To make bundles of money and to win. That seems to be their only clear-cut objective."

Harry Wendelstedt made that statement and others like it near the beginning of the 1974 baseball year, but in his bed in his home in Daytona Beach, Florida, recuperating from an inner ear infection, spending a good part of his days mulling over the plight of the umpire—a constant preoccupation—he would have undoubtedly added more fire and bitterness and profanity to his words. Umpires' tongues seem to loosen near the end of the season, their patience wears thinner, their tolerance for criticism and their ability to control tempers grow brittle. The pressure of the final month of the season seems to sap an umpire's self-control. Like flint scraped against a rock, the sparks fly. Harry Wendelstedt was to discover this unfortunate truth upon his return to umpiring, when he would rendezvous with his crew in California during the first few days of September.

SEPTEMBER 1974

STANDING OF
THE NATIONAL LEAGUE TEAMS

Eastern Division

	W.	L.	Pct.	G.B.
Pittsburgh	69	62	.527	—
St. Louis	68	65	.511	2
Philadelphia	64	67	.489	5
Montreal	60	69	.465	8
New York	59	71	.454	9½
Chicago	54	75	.419	14

Western Division

	W.	L.	Pct.	G.B.
Los Angeles	83	48	.634	—
Cincinnati	80	52	.606	3½
Atlanta	73	60	.549	11
Houston	68	63	.519	15
San Francisco	60	73	.451	24
San Diego	50	83	.376	34

Nice
Guys
Finish
Last

It was in San Diego, on a breezy Thursday night three days after Wendelstedt had rejoined the crew, still somewhat sluggish and groggy from his twenty-seven-day menu of medicine, that the bare threads of ego and anger finally snapped.

"What the hell is wrong with him?" Wendelstedt asked Harvey as they met halfway down the third base line between innings. "I think he's losing his marbles. He's in a fog."

Harvey shook his head and sighed. Both men were becoming increasingly impatient with their partner's lack of attentiveness to the more sophisticated aspects of umpiring. Wendelstedt had almost exploded the evening before when the Cardinals had sent in their top reliever, Al Hrabosky, to work the final two innings and protect a slim one run lead. At some point in his career Hrabosky had acquired the irritating and time-consuming habit of stepping off the mound and talking to himself, sort of psyching himself up between each and every pitch. Certainly there was no rule prohibiting such tactics—as long as the pitcher consumes no more than twenty seconds from the time he receives the ball until he delivers it. This eliminates the possibility of a pitcher being able to delay the game indefinitely—a ruse often employed during poor weather conditions with one team hopelessly behind. The second base umpire is charged with the responsibility of carrying a stopwatch, timing the pitcher when he becomes suspect, and calling an automatic ball after the full twenty seconds between pitches have lapsed. (When no one is on base. The rule is suspended with base runners.)

Although, in their own minds, Wendelstedt and Harvey had counted anywhere from thirty to thirty-five seconds between some pitches, Williams hadn't even pulled out the stopwatch until Wendelstedt trotted over from first base to remind him. Even then, he didn't seem to be paying enough attention to cite an infraction.

"Damn," Williams had said after the game, "I just forgot. I had my hand in my pocket, my fingers over the watch, I knew exactly what Hrabosky was doing, but I forgot to time him. I can't explain it."

"But I reminded you," Wendelstedt said. "I went right over and told you. Don't you remember?"

"And I pulled the watch out after that. He went to about eighteen and a half seconds and then he threw. He never hit twenty as I timed him."

"I counted thirty," said Harvey.

"I counted thirty and then started over again," said Wendelstedt.

"Now wait a minute," Williams said. "I'm telling you I had the watch on him the last part of the last inning and he never went over eighteen and a half. I'm telling you."

"Well, he did before that," said Harvey.

"I didn't have the watch on him before that."

"That's what we're trying to impress upon you," said Wendelstedt, "the fact that you didn't do what you were supposed to."

"I can't understand it," said Williams, shaking his head, "I just plain old forgot."

Now, a day later, Harry Wendelstedt pounded his fist against his chest protector and scowled. He never once considered that he was being overly sensitive to Art Williams's mistakes or far too harsh toward the young umpire's inadequacies. To Wendelstedt, an umpire was a perfectly functioning piece of human machinery. Although Wendelstedt granted that a physical breakdown was indeed possible in an umpire's intricate system, a mental malfunction, in his narrow point of view, was decidedly not. "Greif (San Diego pitcher) is balking," he said.

"He's starting and stopping," Harvey nodded. "He's walking into his stretch, then pulling himself out of it and starting over again."

"He's done that about five times."

"It's a clear balk," Harvey said, "but Art's not calling it."

"Well, he's on first base. If we call it for him, it would discredit our whole crew. It's his call."

"The only thing to do is wait and see if the Cardinals notice. If they start to bitch, we gotta call it."

"I hate to play that way," said Wendelstedt.

"It's not right," Harvey agreed, "but I can't see what else there is to do."

Wendelstedt trotted back down the third base line, the spikes of his heavy golf shoes perforating the turf; he assumed his position, crouched low above the stooping catcher. He was angry and embarrassed—not necessarily angry at Art Williams as much as at the frustration of the situation, at his total inability to assert any influence over Williams or, without Williams's help, to assume command of the game. He was embarrassed for himself and for Al Barlick and Bruce Froemming and Doug Harvey, for all other umpires who try so desperately hard to do the right thing, to be part of a well-oiled unit, to officiate a perfect game. "How could *he* be a part of *me?*" Wendelstedt asked himself again and again, as he watched pitch after pitch pop into the catcher's glove or crack against a bat: "How could *he* be a part of *me?*"

"I knowed it was a balk," said Art Williams, in answer to Wendelstedt's first query after the game.

Wendelstedt spread his heavy arms, shrugged those mountainous shoulders, and looked over toward Harvey in exasperation. Dale, who had stripped down quickly, padded into the shower room without a word.

"If you knew it was a balk, then why didn't you call it?" asked Harvey. "With Harry at third and me behind the plate, we can't see it as clearly as you. You're the guy at first base that's supposed to call the play."

"We could have called it," said Wendelstedt. "We both suspected it. At least I did. But you're the only man in a position to be sure."

"If me or Harry woulda called it, then the Padres woulda wanted to know why the hell you didn't see it. It was your call to make."

"I should have called it," said Williams, shaking his head, peering down at the floor.

"What I can't understand," said Harvey, "is why you didn't call it, if you knew it was a balk."

"My heart beats wrong when I see something like that," said Wendelstedt, turning toward Williams. "I get a quick and unusual feeling in my heart even before a pitcher does it. A good umpire has to have that sixth sense."

"I knowed he did it as soon as it happened," said Williams.

"Then why in the hell didn't you call it? I keep asking you," said Harvey. He slammed his hat down onto the floor and kicked it across the room.

"I don't know. I couldn't think. It was too late when I realized..."

"You couldn't think!" Wendelstedt, still standing in the middle of the floor with his arms outstretched, shouted. "I can't believe it." He looked at Harvey.

"You said you saw it four or five times," said Harvey.

"He coulda done it a hundred times as far as we know," Wendelstedt shouted. "The Cardinals are fighting for a pennant. You gotta be fair to them."

"Why didn't you call it?" Harvey demanded.

"I . . . I . . . I don't know," the black man stammered. "I knowed it was a balk, I knowed it right away, but . . ."

"You knowed it! You knowed it!" Wendelstedt ranted. "That's no fucking excuse for a good umpire. I'm telling you, you're in big trouble. Even the boss (Fred Fleig) told you that three days ago in San Francisco, you're in big trouble. What'd he say? What'd he say the first day I got back and we all got together for that big meeting?"

Williams stared morosely at the floor without speaking. He looked like a big sack. He hardly moved.

"He said you better listen to Harry and Doug, didn't he? He said you better listen to what they tell you or your fucking job is down the drain, didn't he? He said you better fucking shape up or ship out. That's what he said. Now what the hell are you trying to pull three days later?"

"If you knew it was a balk, you should have nailed his ass!" shouted Harvey. "An umpire can't sit through a game with his hand on his crotch. What have I been trying to tell you this whole goddamn season?"

Williams slammed his fist to his knee. "I knowed I shoulda called it right away. I just can't understand what happened. I went blank."

"Went blank," Wendelstedt repeated dully. "Of all the horse-shit."

"A good umpire is not supposed to go blank," said Harvey. "An umpire has got to maintain his concentration through every second of each goddamn game. An umpire who loses his concentration is a horseshit umpire. He's not doing his job."

"No man lets his mind go blank," said Wendelstedt. "No *real* man."

"Horseshit," said Harvey, shaking his head again and again. "That's really horseshit."

"We might as well throw the fucking rule book out the window for this crew," said Wendelstedt.

"I can't explain it," said Williams softly, hiding his eyes and studying the floor. "I just went blank. I try so hard all the time, but for an instant, I can't quite understand it, I went blank."

"You're going to blank yourself out of this game," said Wendelstedt. "You let the players ignore the rules. That means they're shitting on you, and that makes you a gutless human being for letting them do it. I'm telling you, you're in big trouble. Even *you* won't be able to hold a job if you keep this up another year. If you don't listen to us and do what we say, you'll be a burden to every crew you ever work with for your entire life." He ripped off his jacket and hurled it onto his trunk, then quickly began pulling off the rest of his clothes—pants, shirt, socks, underwear, throwing them savagely on top. Breathlessly he turned to Williams, who sat, masking his eyes with his hand, still studying the floor.

"Maybe you think we're trying to embarrass you or shame you," he said, "but that's not true. What we want most from this world is what you want most from this world. And that's to be a good umpire. To men like us, there's nothing more difficult or more important than that."

His voice trailed off. There was nothing more to say, and nothing more for Wendelstedt, Harvey, and Williams to do but shed the rest of their clothes and drown their anger and embarrassment under the scalding hot spray of shower water. Dale was already gone when the other three men dripping-wet, white towels hanging from waists and shoulders, emerged and moved across the quiet room. Their backs to one another, they rubbed themselves dry, dressed quickly, and left the room and the ballpark without as much as a sign of either forgiveness or farewell. They would let it pass. It had happened before, and it had passed. And it would happen again. And it would pass. So too would each game pass and each week pass. Even the season would pass, sometime and somehow.

Wendelstedt rolled all the windows down in his rented car as he sped alone back to the hotel. The cold wind soothed his hot cheeks and dulled the thumping pain which seemed to start above his brow and encompass the entire back of his head. Before leaving his home in Florida to join the crew on the coast, the doctors had warned him about allowing himself to get too upset. They had also warned him about drinking and over-exertion and had advised him to continue to sleep as much as possible.

But Harry Wendelstedt wasn't tired; he was angry. He pulled a cold can of beer from the side pocket of his suit jacket, snapped the top and drank it down furiously as he drove with one hand. He wasn't hungry, but thirsty. He lifted a second cold can from his side pocket and drank that too, then crushed both empty cans with his gigantic right hand and flipped them over into the back seat. By the time he stopped the car in front of his room at the Mission Valley Inn he was feeling better, a little better, but far from good.

Wendelstedt knew that Ed Vargo's crew of Bruce Froemming, Andy Olsen, and Paul Runge had already arrived at Mission Valley to officiate the Padres' series with the Giants the following day. He phoned Froemming, snatched a bottle of J & B Scotch from his suitcase and headed for his friend's room.

If Harry Wendelstedt reminded some people of a German

baker, then Bruce Froemming was surely, unmistakably a Dutch brewmaster. A small man with brownish-blond hair cut in straight bangs across his forehead and heavy round features, Froemming had a rusty, raspy voice and an infectious laugh that erupted like a machine gun. In contrast, Andy Olsen is gangling, lanky, and bony, with distinctively chiseled features, a long broad nose, a jutting chin, and shiny black hair combed back without a part. Olsen had a bright and winning smile, and when he smiled, which was often, he looked more like a farmer from the midwestern corn belt than an umpire with seven years service in the major leagues.

They sat for a while, talking quietly, Wendelstedt sipping from a cup full of Scotch and Froemming and Olsen drinking steadily from water glasses filled to the brim with ice and German brandy. Froemming opened the bottle of brandy a few minutes after Wendelstedt arrived, but within an hour the bottle was only half full, and within two and a half hours it was completely empty. Wendelstedt had entered the room with a half bottle of J & B which, during the course of the evening, he fully drained.

"I tell ya, Bruce," Wendelstedt said, slouching down amongst the cushions of the padded arm chair and shaking his head, "I'm trying and Harvey's trying, but neither of us know what the hell to do any more. He's just not listening to us. You tell him something and he says he knows it already. But when he gets out on the goddamn field, he's not doing his job."

"It's not right," said Froemming.

"Of course it's not right."

"I mean it's not right that a goddamn guy gets his job because of his color. Especially when he's a horseshit umpire."

"Especially," said Wendelstedt, "when there's a bunch of kids down in the minors who deserve to be up here, who're *screaming* to be up here, they want it so bad."

"It's not right," said Froemming, who was sitting in a straight-backed chair in front of a blond wood desk.

Lying on the bed, his head propped behind a mound of pillows, Olsen could see one side of Froemming's face, round and full and slightly rosy, while the other side, ostensibly hidden from him, was reflected in the mirror above the desk. "Maybe he's just scared," said Olsen. "Maybe he wants to do the right thing, but gets so scared he can't perform."

"Yeah, and maybe I'm a racist," said Wendelstedt, lifting his drink and clinking the ice in his cup.

"Well maybe you are," said Olsen, "I don't know. All I'm saying is, maybe you guys have scared him so much he can't do a decent job."

"Horseshit," said Froemming.

"A good umpire can't be scared," Wendelstedt said loudly. "An umpire has got to be a man, and a man, a real man, is never scared. He faces up to his fucking responsibilities." Wendelstedt shook his head and sighed. "I told him tonight he was a gutless human being. I told him he's letting the players shit all over him."

"You did!" Olsen asked, surprised.

"And what'd he say," said Froemming.

" 'I knowed I should have called a balk! I knowed it! I knowed it!' "

"Goddamn," said Froemming. "It ain't right, Harry. It ain't right. A man's color has nothing to do with how good he can umpire. You tell me it's right, Harry, with all those poor guys down waiting in the minors. I spent thirteen fucking years in the minors, I know." Froemming waved his arm and shook his head. He reached over, yanked the bottle from his desk, filled his glass, and drank deeply.

"I told you I didn't think it was right, Bruce. I don't agree with it. Maybe someday he'll make a good umpire, but he's just not ready yet."

"You're goddamn right, it's not right!"

"Maybe I *am* a racist, like Andy says."

"I didn't say that, Harry, I said *maybe* you're a racist. I don't know."

"The trouble with you, Andy," said Wendelstedt, "is that you're too fucking nice. You're always willing to give somebody the benefit of the doubt. You can't look at the bad side of people, you're always looking for the good side."

"So what if I do?"

" 'Cause when people talk about you Andy, players or coaches

or managers or anybody, you know what they say? They say
you're a nice guy."

"So? So?" Olsen leaned forward in the bed toward Wendelstedt.
"What the hell's wrong with that?"

"Do they ever say you're a good umpire? Do they ever say
you're a man who don't take shit from anybody? No, they say
you're a goddamn nice guy. What fuckin' umpire wants to be
known as a nice guy? Goddamn players, they think you're a nice
guy, they'll shit all over you, that's why."

Said Froemming: "Some writer told me he's been taking a poll
on umpires in the press box. He said every fucking sportscaster
and reporter he talked to thought I was a son of a bitch. Now to
me, that's a compliment." Froemming ran a set of stubby fingers
through his dark blond hair. "We're umpires, Andy," he said,
"we're not supposed to be nice guys. We're supposed to be honest
and fair and totally impartial, and there's no way in the world we
can be nice guys and do that."

Froemming stood up, grabbed the neck of the bottle and poured
more brandy into his half-full glass. "What about Harvey," he
said, "what about Doug Harvey? He talks to players more than
anybody else out on the field."

"Well, that don't make him a bad umpire," said Olsen. "You
can't take that away from him."

"I admit the fucking guy can umpire. I'm not saying anything against that. He's the one exception as far as that goes.
But how the fuck does he get his goddamn top rating in the
player poll of umpires? By sucking in, that's how. He gets on
the field . . ." Froemming walked across the room and waved
his arms, " 'Hey Joe! Hi Bill! How's your wife? How's your
kids? How's your mother in Fort Worth?' Well, screw that.
The goddamn player poll of umpires is a popularity contest.
What the hell do they know about umpires? They watch the
game, they watch the other players, they're never watching
you. There's only two ways players can judge umpires. When
the calls go for them, they say a guy is a good umpire. When
the calls go against them, they say he's horseshit. Harvey got
on top of that poll because he ingratiates himself out on the
field."

"Harvey's first on the National League's manager-general manager poll of umpires they take at the end of the season. He was first last year," said Olsen.

"Horseshit," said Wendelstedt. "What the hell do managers and general managers know about umpires?"

"I'm just telling you what we all know to be true," said Olsen.

"You're such a goddamn nice guy, Andy, it's sickening," said Wendelstedt. "If somebody murdered your best friend, you'd want to take the murderer to a psychiatrist."

Olsen slammed his glass down on the night table, splashing liquor and scattering ice cubes on the bed and raised up his arm. "I would not, Harry. Goddamn it! You're getting me mad. I would not!"

"Harvey's first on the manager-general manager poll because he ingratiates himself," said Froemming, "that's why. He gets into town every year and calls up the manager or general manager of the ballclub and takes the guy to lunch. His wife is president of the Madres—the women's booster organization for the San Diego Padres. What do you think of a goddamn umpire who lets his wife do that? You know as well as I do, Andy, we're not supposed to be taking sides."

Wendelstedt filled his cup to the brim with Scotch, drank half of it down, then shook his head. It had been months since he had been able to pour out his pent-up anger and the gnawing frustrations of his work on friendly, willing ears. "Doug Harvey's my friend," he said, "and I'll never say anything behind his back that I wouldn't tell him, or haven't already told him to his face."

"He's a suck-in," Froemming mumbled.

"Now wait a minute, you don't understand about Doug. Doug Harvey wants to be the best umpire in the world. He's obsessed with that idea—and he's going to play all the angles to get himself and keep himself at that point year after year. You gotta understand, he wants it that bad. He's not trying to screw us. He just wants to be known as the best umpire in baseball."

"Sure he's first on the goddamn player poll of umpires," said Froemming, who began to parade around the room in his stocking feet, waving. " 'Well, hello John Bench, how's your wife and family? How you hitting the curve ball, Johnny old buddy, old pal?'

" 'Oh well, I guess that pitch was a little too low,' " Froemming mimicked, gliding the little finger of his right hand over his eyebrow and puckering up his lips. " 'Well yessir, nossir . . .'

"FUCK HIM!" Froemming suddenly yelled, jumping up and down. "FUCK THAT SUCK-IN BASTARD. WHAT'S HE EXPECT US TO DO? TAKE A PUBLIC RELATIONS COURSE? I'M AN UMPIRE! I'M A MAN! I'M NO SUCK-IN GLAD-HANDER!"

"Now Bruce," Olsen said, laughing, "don't get so upset. It isn't that serious."

Wendelstedt shook his head and turned to Froemming. "Can you imagine this? Listen to that guy. That Andy is so nice, he'd give the benefit of the doubt to a rat."

"He's so nice, he'd let somebody shoot his mother in the ass with a cannon," said Froemming.

"He's so nice," said Wendelstedt, "if somebody shit on his head, he'd say, 'Pardon me, sir, but did you mean to do that?' "

Now Olsen stood up, whirled around, and kicked the table. "I would not! I would not, goddamn it!" he yelled.

Wendelstedt waved him down. "Andy, you're the nicest guy in the world."

"I AM NOT! I AM NOT! I'M AN UMPIRE!"

"Andy's baseball's Joan of Arc," Froemming did a little dancing two-step. "Everybody loves Andy Olsen," Froemming said.

"Even his worst enemy," said Wendelstedt.

Olsen, his shiny black hair now tumbling over his eyes, again jumped from the bed, this time sticking up his fists. "THEY DO NOT! THEY DO NOT, GODDAMN IT. I'M AN UMPIRE! I'M AN UMPIRE! I'M AN UMPIRE, GODDAMN IT," he cried, stomping his foot.

Froemming suddenly leaned forward and began to cackle. His laughter sputtered into the room, then erupted. Listening to Froemming, Wendelstedt leaned back and began to pound the side of his chair. First he choked, then he giggled, and finally, he emitted an ear-piercing howl. "*Wooooeeee, wooooeeeee,*" he heard himself yelling. He saw Froemming point his finger at him and kick the desk with his foot. He saw Olsen explode in a spray of spit, roll on the bed, and heard him start hooting. The three men hooted and cackled and shrieked, pounded their fists and rolled on the floor for what seemed like hours, till Wendelstedt felt he could no longer continue to breathe. Then for a while they drank silently and somberly, periodically erupting into shivers of laughter, until finally they steadied one another enough to calm themselves down.

"Well, shit," said Froemming after a while, smiling and giggling.

"That was really something," said Wendelstedt.

"You guys," Oslen grinned wryly and shook his head. "Always putting somebody on."

"That's because you're so nice."

"Now come on, Harry," Olsen shouted.

"OK. OK."

"Seriously, Andy," said Froemming, drawing himself up in his chair and tipping his glass to his lips. "You have to admit that it doesn't pay to be nice in this business. It just doesn't pay. The players take advantage of you, the league takes advantage of you, the owners and managers take advantage of you. Wherever you go in baseball, umpires are always on the bottom of the heap."

"Andy," said Froemming, shaking his head and waving emphatically over at Wendelstedt. "Harry, Andy, I love baseball. You know I do. It's the greatest fucking game in the world and umpiring is the greatest goddamn profession that ever lived. I've dedicated my life to it, and I'd do it all over again if I got the chance. But Jesus Christ, Harry, Jesus Christ, Andy, the umpires are getting screwed in every goddamn different direction."

"You ain't telling me anything I don't know," said Wendelstedt.

"It's such a goddamn shame," said Froemming. "Sure, the minor league umpire's salaries are higher than ten years ago, but so is the cost of living. Umpires, good kids, are getting five thousand dollars a year for seven months work, work away from their family, work with no rewards, for just a bare chance at a major league future. Five years ago I got forty dollars a day to work major league spring training. That forty dollars included expenses and travel and everything else. And do you know what those poor kids are getting now?"

"Sure I know," said Wendelstedt.

"That same fucking forty dollars, that's what," said Froemming.

"Well," said Olsen. "Times are bad right now. Money's tight."

"Listen to that," said Froemming, grinning.

"Andy, you're so fucking nice," said Wendelstedt, "you suck."

Perhaps if there had been time between that late night of bitterness with Olsen and Froemming after the game in San Diego and the subsequent contest between the Pirates and the Dodgers in Los Angeles on that fateful Friday, the following day, . . . Perhaps if there had been an off day for travel allowing Wendelstedt, still withdrawing from three weeks of drugs, to gather some badly needed sleep, . . . Perhaps if the Pirates hadn't been so tight, having just hopped over the Cardinals and assumed undisputed possession of first place in the eastern division of the National League, . . . Perhaps if it weren't for all these factors, then the final and most wicked confrontation between a still-fuming Harry Wendelstedt and the usually placid Art Williams would have never come to pass. But it did.

"YOU LIAR!" shouted Harry Wendelstedt, his hands resting on his hips above the big bulky pockets of his blue jacket.

"YOU COCKSUCKER," he bellowed, his lips curled with scorn, his cheeks red with rage.

"YOU BLACK MOTHERFUCKER. YOU BLACK MOTHERFUCKER!"

Heaving up his shoulders, the big black man turned to Wendelstedt, regarding him with quiet, gray eyes.

"That's what he called you," said Wendelstedt. "Half the players on the field heard it, and so did we. You let (Pirate third baseman) Richie Hebner call you that right to your face and you didn't do a fucking thing about it. What are you going to say now?

Are you going to deny it? I saw you mumbling at the son of a bitch. You should have run his ass."

"He didn't," said Williams, quietly, his soft voice edged with steel.

"Jesus Christ! Jesus Christ! You can't allow that," said Harvey. "YOU'RE UNDERMINING OUR AUTHORITY! YOU'RE MAKING US SITTING DUCKS FOR ANY GODDAMN PLAYER WHO WANTS TO COME ALONG AND TAKE POTSHOTS AT US."

"We're umpires," said Harvey. "How many times have we told you what that means?"

"WE'RE UMPIRES! UMPIRES! SYMBOLS OF LAW AND ORDER!"

"You gotta be red-assed," said Harvey. "You can't afford to let them call you horseshit. You can't afford to give them a break. We're not supposed to be merciful. We're the backbone and the lifeblood of baseball. Can't you see that? Can't you see it? Can't you see it? We're the conscience and the integrity of the entire game."

"YOU'RE A HORSESHIT UMPIRE. YOU'RE INCONSISTENT. YOU'RE FORGETFUL. YOU'RE SO FUCKING PROUD, YOU WON'T ADMIT TO A FUCKING MISTAKE."

"You've got it wrong," said Williams, in a soft but steady voice. "He didn't call me anything like that."

"We heard him," said Harvey. "Everybody in that infield and half the players on the bench heard him."

"YOU'RE GUTLESS. YOU'RE A GUTLESS SON OF A BITCH. YOU DON'T HAVE A FUCKING GUT IN YOUR BODY!"

Art Williams stepped forward and looked Harry Wendelstedt unblinkingly in the eye. "Now that's just enough," he said quietly. "That's just plenty."

"Now wait a minute," said Harvey. "We don't want any of *that* kind of trouble."

"NO," yelled Wendelstedt, pushing Harvey out of the way. "I WANT HIM TO GET MAD. GET MAD! GET MAD! I WANT YOU TO GET MAD! A GOOD UMPIRE HAS GOTTA BE MAD! YOU NEED A FIRE UP YOUR ASS!

YOU COCKSUCKER! YOU BLACK MOTHERFUCKER!"

Wendelstedt tapped his chin with the tip of his forefinger. "HIT ME, YOU BLACK MOTHERFUCKER, HIT ME, HIT ME, HIT ME!"

Art Williams shifted his weight. His skin seemed momentarily to turn purple, yet when he spoke, his countenance and his voice seemed completely controlled. The words came slowly, evenly, rigidly . . .

"He didn't . . . call me what you said he did . . . and I'm trying as hard as I can . . . to do the right thing. Now I don't want . . . to hear anything more . . . about it. I'm warning you . . . I don't want to hear anything more . . . right now."

The two men watched each other for a few brief seconds that ticked like eternity on the clock on the wall.

"OK, Art," Wendelstedt said quietly, letting out the tension in one breath. "Never again. I just care, you know?"

"I know," said Williams.

"I care what happens to you, and I care what happens to us—to umpires."

"I know," Williams said. "I do the best I can. I have a lot to learn."

"We don't say these things to embarrass you, Art," said Harvey.

"I know," said Williams.

"We want you to do right," said Harvey. "We want everything right. We're umpires . . . umpires." He shrugged his shoulders and dropped his eyes to his hands.

Umpire. Umpire. Doug Harvey had always wanted to be an umpire. *Umpire.* The sound of the word and the realization that he had made it provided continuous joy. Doug Harvey could never recall wanting to do anything else or be anything other than an umpire. He remembered the topaz ring he bought for himself with his savings on the day after his high school graduation and the vow he made never to remove that ring until it could be replaced by another given to him on the occasion of umpiring a world series. He had wanted to be an umpire that far back in time; from the moment he ventured into adolescence, he had that goal in mind. He trained himself to sleep during the day and to wake up as if he were working a night game. He might take a walk, then would rest in the afternoon; he might watch TV to kill some time but always took care not to stay out too late. Working for the El Centro baseball team, Class C California League, after high school, he had been a flag raiser, a bat boy, an iceman, and a ticket-taker. He had never done anything for any length of time that wasn't associated with baseball. Baseball was his only world and he believed that umpiring was his God-given slot in life. Irrevocably. He had reached the pinnacle of his life. He was not just a man—he was an umpire—which required something more of a man. And he was not just an umpire, but a major league umpire—the best goddamn umpire in the world. Doug Harvey could ask nothing more than that.

Harvey looked up at Wendelstedt and Williams, still uncomfortably watching each other, and said: "Not many more games to go."

Williams looked at Harvey, then moved back across the room. "Yeah, the season will be over soon," he said.

"Those Pirates are really something special," said Harvey.

" 'Specially stupid," said Williams. "Particularly Hebner and (pitcher Ken) Brett."

"Hebner and Brett are quarter-wits," Wendelstedt said.

"Quarter-wits?"

"Put them both together and all you've got is a half-wit."

Harvey and Williams smiled, then quietly chuckled.

Wendelstedt shrugged, threw off his jacket, and sat down wearily in a chair. It was so frustrating to him, so painfully, terribly frustrating . . . losing control. Harry Wendelstedt truly believed that an umpire symbolized all that was right and decent about this country.

There is no better judge of what is right and wrong than an umpire. There is no man more honest and impartial than an umpire. An umpire is a rock. On the field, he is unaffected by pleas for mercy, unaffected by heartbreak, by desire, by criticism, by danger. His entire being, 100 percent of himself is focused on the variances of a tiny white ball moving at anywhere from eighty-five to one hundred miles per hour over or around an eighteen inch slab of rubber approximately two hundred times in each three hour period. The ball was the all and the everything in baseball, the nucleus of an umpire's universe, the cornerstone of his life.

Harry Wendelstedt loved his four-year-old son Harry Hunter, and his wife Cheryl, but for the period of time he spent out on the field, the woman and the child were nothing more than distant mirages on a desert of memories. That was how much umpiring meant to him. How or when he had fully embraced this feeling and belief he didn't really know. Nor did he know why—except that he realized that the game and the man were no longer separate entities, that once he stepped into that blue uniform he was no longer a man to whom the real world had any relation. He was an umpire and, as such, he was larger than life.

No
More
Players'
Dirty
Looks

The 1974 baseball season inched its way through the final three weeks of the year.

The National League, seemingly convinced that Harvey and Wendelstedt were the dynamic duo of umpiredom, mercilessly dispatched the crew to city after city in which the tight and tension-filled battles for the playoff race were being fought. Beginning on September 12, and stretching through twenty-one days, all the way down to the dwindling innings of the year, the crew officiated eighteen games involving the Cardinals, Pirates, Dodgers, or Reds. Certainly it is no secret, since now it is indelibly printed in our memories and on the pages of baseball history that the Dodgers withstood a stubborn but ill-fated charge by a partially anemic Cincinnati team and captured the western division title. And the Pirates, immersed in a season-long exercise of braggadocio and buffoonery, somehow survived the National League East by winning the final game of a rather pitiful year.

But the pressure took its toll.

In the umpires' dressing room, before and after each and every game, Jerry Dale began announcing numbers. Without as much as clearing his throat for introduction, with nothing as articulate as a sigh in explanation, Dale would suddenly shout . . .

"Twenty-four."

"Eighteen."

"Twelve."

. . . and it was to take Harvey, Wendelstedt, and Williams more than a little while before they came to realize that Dale was actually counting off the games separating him from the end of the campaign.

No more baseballs, no more bats.
No more players' dirty hats.

Dale was in his fourth season as a major league umpire. Under the agreement constituted in 1971 by the Major League Umpires Association and the National and American Leagues, Dale, were he permitted to work just one major league game during the 1975 baseball season, would be granted tenure and thus be virtually assured of permanent security in his position. Under normal circumstances Dale might be in much more serious trouble than he really was, but there were as many as three retirements expected at the end of the season: Chris Pelekoudas, fifty-five; Shag Crawford, fifty-five; Tom Gorman, fifty-four. The league seemed to be in no position, as witnessed by the dearth of available mid-season replacements, to deal with three openings, let alone four—or even five, if Satch Davidson were dropped. Davidson, incidentally, had tenure, and it had become apparent that the National League would be pitched into court if it tried to relieve him.

Unfortunately, Dale was not a very good umpire. Not only did he lack the backbone to stand up against the fury and belligerence of players and coaches, but he was particularly weak behind the plate—especially when calling pitches against left-handed batters. Both Harvey and Wendelstedt recognized Dale's problem soon after he joined the crew. He had somehow developed the habit of ducking his head away from the plate and around the catcher's shoulder, thus losing sight of the pitch for an instant or viewing the ball as it crossed the plate from an entirely different angle. Such a tactic resulted in a number of bad calls and in a very low level of consistency.

Dale had also been having a tough time on the bases. He missed a very simple call in Houston one night in mid-September that cost Cincinnati a run and perhaps the game. It had prompted tens of thousands of people in Cincinnati who had seen the replay on television to endorse a petition condemning him for incompetence.

Obviously, the pressure of officiating the most important games in two tight divisional contests was adversely affecting Jerry Dale. Previously Dale had been, either by design or by choice, placed with some of the weaker crews in the league for the final month of the season. Most of the games he had officiated in September, consequently, were of no major importance except, perhaps, in individual instances of player accomplishment.

Now he was feeling the heat, so much so that his penchant for privacy seemed to edge into a state bordering paranoia. It increased to the point where he began registering in hotels under the assumed name of Palmer.

Once in New York, on the last day in September, Harvey, Wendelstedt, and Williams, swaying on a clanging subway headed toward Shea Stadium, watched Dale climb aboard the same car, glance in both directions, then slip stealthily into a seat.

"Hey, Phantom! Hey, Palmer the Phantom!" Wendelstedt called. "C'mon over here!"

Dale turned and regarded his fellow crew members for a long time, without even a sign of recognition. Finally, as if his memory had just jarred him, he nodded almost imperceptibly, lifted up the collar of his trenchcoat around his neck, then turned away.

For Jerry Dale, it had been a long, tough year.

It had been a long, tough year for Doug Harvey, too, but as the grueling innings and rain-delayed double-headers followed one after another toward a final outcome, he could at last begin to see and feel the re-emergence of his physical and emotional health. The special insoles he had acquired in Houston had alleviated much of the pain in his legs, and the high protein diet with which he had been experimenting seemed to be firming him up. No longer was his belly bloated and his face puffed as it had been since his reaction to penicillin earlier in the year. The promises made by the many doctors he had consulted that his strength would gradually return were finally bearing fruit. He still spent an inordinate amount of time sleeping, but now, when he awoke, he felt rested and was able to maintain a good deal of strength through the balance of the day. This was a welcome turnabout, especially since he had been recently selected to work the World Series.

"Selected" is a rather inaccurate way of describing the process that leads to National and American League umpires' appearances in World Series competition, however. Throughout baseball history, up until an agreement was reached with baseball's bigwigs and the Major League Umpires Association, umpires were indeed "selected" to work All Star and postseason championships on the basis of their year-to-year accomplishments. As the playoffs and World Series continued to grow more financially rewarding, however, it became evident that the best or most popular umpires in the league were making far more money than the average, run-of-the-mill official. It hardly seems possible that this could have gone unnoticed for as long as twenty-five years, but the leaders of the Major League Umpires Association waited until 1971 before petitioning for and receiving permission from both the American and National League to establish a new system. Now each official, once receiving tenure, would be automatically placed in rotation from the All Star game to the playoffs and on to the World Series. Although Doug Harvey, Tom Gorman, and Andy Olsen, the three National League representatives, most definitely deserved the opportunity of working a World Series, the rotation system also made possible many inequities. Which is how Satch Davidson was "selected" to help officiate the 1974 National League playoffs.

Not only did Doug Harvey begin to shape up during the last few weeks of the season, but so too did Doug Harvey's problem pupil, Art Williams. Something had happened—something good —although Harvey was unable to pinpoint the reason. Perhaps it had been triggered by that bitter confrontation between Williams and Wendelstedt in Los Angeles, Harvey mused. Perhaps Williams had at last come to his senses and realized the vulnerability of his position. Perhaps the information planted throughout the season by Harvey and Wendelstedt had finally traveled from Williams's ears, toward his brain and recognition had dawned. Whatever. Williams was not only bearing up under the pressure and tension of a major league pennant race, but was actually umpiring with crisp and thorough efficiency.

"He's showin' me something," Doug Harvey told Wendelstedt as they sat side by side on the swaying subway train clattering toward Shea Stadium. It was Sunday afternoon, September 30, the last time this year the four men would work together. Williams and Dale were being shipped to San Francisco to officiate two meaningless games with San Diego, while Harvey and Wendelstedt were joining Tom Gorman and Billy Williams for

Cincinnati's last-chance showdown with Atlanta.

"I mean to tell ya," Wendelstedt said, eyeing Williams, who had found a seat across the aisle, "he's come alive in the past few weeks. I never would have believed it. I told him yesterday that the series we worked in St. Louis with the Pirates were his best four games of the year."

"Can you imagine?" asked Harvey. "Here we are down to the wire . . ."

"I thought he'd buckle," said Wendelstedt. "I thought he'd fall all apart, but just the opposite has happened. He seems to have discovered the meaning of the word *courage.* You know, Doug, he might have found himself."

"I hope so," mumbled Harvey, shifting in his cushionless seat.

"What?" Wendelstedt cupped his hand over his ear.

"I said 'I hope so,' " Harvey elevated his voice over the train's rattle.

Wendelstedt nodded, crossed his legs, and leaned back. "I do too," he answered quietly. Then he sighed.

So the season was just about over, he thought. Two more games and the fire would be out, the heat would be off, and he could pack up his poor old body, still hung over with a residue of dopiness, and carry it home. With longing and pleasure he thought of his four-year-old son Harry Hunter riding around in the backyard of their new home on his tricycle, then splashing in the water after an ill-fated, Evel Knievel-like attempt at hurtling the pool. Wendelstedt smiled silently and giggled.

Harry Wendelstedt had never before felt the loneliness of family separation as keenly as he had through the end of this particular summer. The truth of that had hit him abruptly only twelve hours earlier when he had awakened suddenly, glanced at the discouraging emptiness of the four blank walls of his room, leapt out of bed, threw on some clothes, and literally hurled himself out of his room, swooped down the elevator, through the lobby, and out into the night like a bat.

And then he stopped.

Standing on the cold, windy, gray sidewalk, glancing hopefully for recognition at each and every hurrying passerby, Harry Wendelstedt realized he had nowhere to go. Nothing to do, no one to talk to, nowhere to go.

He walked into the nearest bar, ordered, and drank one, two ... five, six quick ones, then stumbled back to his hotel. The watch on his wrist told him not more than an hour had passed when he returned to his empty room. He cradled the telephone receiver between his cheek and shoulder, recited ten numbers to an operator who connected him with his wife in Florida for the third time that evening. And only after a long and erratic conversation with Cheryl and his groggy, bewildered son, had he been able to muffle the remainder of the night in sleep.

Wendelstedt sighed, glancing across the aisle at the rushing darkness of the tunnel through a smeared and grimy window.

Art Williams, slumped and seemingly dozing, half opened his eyes and silently watched his partners. With much satisfaction he had overheard a good deal of what they had said about him, but as sly as he was, he would never let on. He would wait for them to come to him and tell him. Maybe they would and maybe they wouldn't, but in any case, he would remain silent. Although he wasn't at all surprised.

"I just knew—I know—I'm not as bad an umpire as they were claiming," Art Williams said. "I knew if I just kept my mouth shut and worked to the best of my ability, they'd have to admit, they'd be forced to admit that I was doing a decent job. I know it, and Fred Fleig knows it, too, and when we talk together privately he tells me to cool it, not to complain, not to make waves, just cool it. So I do.

"I know all about the jealousy and all about the prejudice among many of my fellow umpires in the league. How couldn't I know about it? I feel it, I see it, I hear it. Some umpires tell me to my face that I'm horseshit and other umpires tell players. Then the players tell me. There were, in fact, three umpires in the National League who refused to work with me this year. Don't you think it hurts me when I find these things out? But what can I do about it? *Prejudice,*" he says heavily, "prejudice against me, against my race exists. It's a fact of life."

Williams, hunching forward, resting his elbows on his knees, cupping his chin in his large ebony hands, thought back.

He was sitting in the living room of his home, his arm resting loosely on Shirley's warm, soft shoulders, watching the films of a game he had umpired. Another umpire had joined the network commentator. Together, they criticized the way in which Williams officiated and his very jerky and "ineffective" style.

Williams leaped up, grabbed his shoe, and hurled it at the screen. Shirley shrieked, watching the slivers of glass falling at her feet.

"That umpire, a National League umpire, spent fifteen minutes on national television telling the world how bad I was," said Williams. "I sat there in my living room, holding my wife's hand, nervously fumbling with her shoulder. *I took that shit until I couldn't take it any more.* If I hadn't thrown that shoe, I would have exploded. I would have probably been able to control myself if other umpires were around. But in front of my wife? I was embarrassed. I was enraged.

"It isn't as if I didn't expect this. Emmett Ashford warned me that I would be resented and berated up here. He was speaking from experience. They resented him because he clowned. That's the way he umpired. The fans liked it and he didn't do anything wrong. It was the way he was."

Williams remembers one time, standing in front of home plate last year before the start of a game, listening to the other three umpires talking.

"Well, I've got six years in the minor leagues and six years in the majors," the first umpire said.

"I've got eleven years in the major leagues and eight years in the minors," the second umpire said.

"I've got seventeen years in the major leagues and five years in the minors," the third umpire said.

"How many years you got in the game altogether, Art?"

How to tell the difference between being put on, which is acceptable, and put down, which is not? How to know when you are being too sensitive? How to know when you are not being sensitive enough? Such questions had plagued Williams through the entire season. He was a trooper plodding through a minefield, a skater gliding over uncharted ice.

"I try to make everybody think that I don't care what they say about me," says Williams, "because, goddamn it, I know I can't be as bad an umpire as they claim. I know I'm not. I just can't be. Certainly I don't have as much experience as I should, and I have a lot to learn—especially behind the plate—although I've gotten pretty good around the bases this year. But all in all, I gotta be better than some of the older umpires in the game who are so confident and cocky that they hardly move for a play. I gotta be better than those guys. I gotta be better than them.

"So what I do, whenever I can, what I do, is cool it. I cool it. I don't make waves. I don't let these things bother me. I funnel it through one ear and pour it out the other. Because I'm an umpire. I can't afford to think about criticism. I can't afford to worry about hate."

"How many years have you got in this game altogether, Art?" the question was repeated.

Art Williams turned his back on his fellow crew members, stooped, and flicked the dust off home plate with the bristles of his whisk broom. Then he sighed and straightened up, glancing first at the pea-green outfield, then at the turd-brown infield, spotted with four squares of sparkling white. He peered into the dugouts crammed with fidgety and apprehensive players, dolls of different colors in identical costumes, then looked through the artificial glow of the lights into the stands. Here were the people. Here was his life. Here was what the whole game, the whole country, the entire world was all about. He turned back around, lowered his eyes, transforming a faint glimmer of hope and satisfaction that had momentarily crept onto his face into that characteristically hard-assed umpire's frown.

"PLAY BALL!" he yelled.

OCTOBER 4 1974

FINAL STANDING OF TEAMS

Eastern Division

	W.	L.	Pct.	G.B.
Pittsburgh	88	74	.543	—
St. Louis	86	75	.534	1½
Philadelphia	80	82	.494	8
Montreal	79	82	.491	8½
New York	71	91	.438	17
Chicago	66	96	.407	22

Western Division

	W.	L.	Pct.	G.B.
Los Angeles	102	60	.630	—
Cincinnati	98	64	.605	4
Atlanta	88	74	.543	14
Houston	81	81	.500	21
San Francisco	72	90	.444	30
San Diego	60	102	.370	42

Author's Note: Adventures of a Horse Blanket

My first book was about motorcycles, detailing my experiences tripping back and forth across the United States on a two-wheeled machine. I never needed a suit, a tie, an Arrow shirt for such adventures and, consequently, when I entered the world of umpires and baseball, my wardrobe consisted of a number of pairs of Levis, some of which fit tight, and others that fit much tighter. I had four denim jackets, one with the sleeves cut to the shoulders, another at the elbows, a third with frayed cuffs, and a fourth with a skull and crossbones sewn jauntily on the back. For more formal occasions, I had a burgundy leather suit, with silver-studded shoulders, zippered sleeves, and pegged pants with an embroidered seat.

The umpires, however, very traditional men, wore suits with straight-leg pants, small cuffs, low-heeled oxfords or loafers, and white shirts with narrow ties. I soon discovered that to umpires there were only two kinds of men in this world: denim-clad dirtballs and respectable, red-blooded, well-dressed, good old-fashioned, downhome American boys. So I set out to change my image and embellish my wardrobe so that I would fit in.

I purchased a green silk shirt, a pair of black loafers, two pair of linen pants, one yellow, one navy, and a wide blue tie with embroidered white horses. The pièce de résistance was a Pierre Cardin jacket, a sharp plaid of blues, greens, yellows, and reds over an off-white background, styled like a corset so that my shoulders looked broad, my waist thin. The jacket cost $165. With the exception of my burgundy leather suit, that figure represented more than double the worth of my entire wardrobe, collected with great care over my first thirty years. I wore sunglasses with this outfit as well, so that I would look like a movie star, or failing that, so that I wouldn't be easily recognized by my motorcycle friends.

Proud and beaming, I opened the door of the umpires' dressing room at Shea Stadium one evening early in May and paused dramatically, my arms outstretched, cavalier-like, so that Wendelstedt, Harvey, Colosi, and Williams could see me in all my splendor in the proper light. Then I walked inside. I walked all the way across the room, twirled around nonchalantly, then sat down near the coffeepot, unbuttoned my jacket, and crossed my linen legs, awaiting their praise. I was half expecting applause.

Wendelstedt blew up his cheeks as round and red as a circus balloon. He looked at me and then at Harvey. Flaring his nostrils belligerently, Harvey looked at Wendelstedt; then he looked at me.

"He's wearing a fucking horse blanket," Harvey shook his head and said.

Wendelstedt sneered: "This is the first time I have ever seen a patchwork kike."

My worth increased significantly in the umpires' eyes when they discovered that I was Jewish. ("Hey Abie! A nice Jewish boy!") With Art Williams and me around, the umpires could vary their routine, intermingling their never-ending barrage of racial slurs with some pretty awful ethnic insults. When Harvey and Wendelstedt didn't call me Horse Blanket, they would refer to me as The Pittsburgh Piker, The Galloping Yid, or Roger the Rabbi. Wendelstedt had this song he would sing to the tune of Tennessee Ernie Ford's, "Sixteen Tons." It began a number of ways:

> Six million Jews and what do you get?
> Twelve million shoes and deeper in debt.
>
> or
>
> Some folks say a man is made out of mud.
> A Jew is made out of other folks' blood.

I'm sure that their forty-seven dollars and fifty cents per diem has a lot to do with it, but to a man, umpires are the most generous people I have ever met. At first I tried to pay my share of bar and restaurant bills, taxi fares, and porters' tips, but invariably they would grapple for the check. I joined in this grappling, but never fought hard. In fact, it got to the point where I stopped even trying to pay for anything. I would eat, drink, and be merry; I was just along for the ride. Once in a while, maybe two or three times a month, Wendelstedt would feign indignation and say: "You goddamn lazy miser Jew, why don't you pay for something?" And I would.

Moderation is a word for which Harry Wendelstedt has no use. He doesn't eat or drink, but rather inhales food and liquor. I remember once going into the hotel bar with him in Chicago, ordering a drink, then excusing myself to go to the men's room. When I returned he had already gone through two more Scotches. That made three drinks lined up on the bar in front of my stool. After-dinner snacks for Harry Wendelstedt often included a quart of soup, a half pound of roast beef, a triple decker hot pastrami sandwich, a dozen pickles, six bottles of beer, a few orders of french fries, and half a blueberry pie.

A good deal of the information gathered for this book came from Harry Wendelstedt, as we drank and talked and staggered from bar to everlasting bar each night. He had unquenchable energy. I once believed myself a pretty good hand with a beer bottle, but there is no way in the world to keep up with Harry Wendelstedt when he gets started. It was important to me to maintain a semblance of sobriety so that he, as my subject, would still feel that we were having a lucid conversation, so that he would tell me things. I devised as many ways as possible to bluff my way through drink after drink. For example, I began drinking whatever poison he would be drinking that night, and when he went to the bathroom or over to another table to visit somebody, I would pour half of my measure into his. I tried to sit near potted plants and would periodically and somewhat shamefully water the roots with bourbon. Sometimes I would take a big sip of my drink, move quickly to the john, and spit the mouthful into the sink. He must have suspected that I had some kind of terrible bladder infection because I spent an enormous amount of time in bar bathrooms dousing my face with water, or hiding in a stall, jotting down a few notes. A writer's notebook makes many people uncomfortable, so I kept mine hidden most of the time, whipping it out only when my penchant for accuracy might impress my subject.

I sat through that frantic conversation between Froemming, Wendelstedt, and Olsen in the second to last chapter, pretending I was drunk and asleep. Once I got up and staggered outside, leaving the door slightly and unnoticeably ajar, and sat down on the curb to record my notes.

"What about that fucking writer?" Froemming asked. "Can you trust him to tell the truth?"

"The Horse Blanket? I don't trust him completely. I don't trust any man, for that matter," I heard Wendelstedt saying. "Except for umpires. And only some umpires. Not all."

"You can get into a lot of trouble, telling him these things," said Olsen.

"Andy," said Wendelstedt, "those fuckers in the league are going to crucify me. I know it. I live in Florida and nine chances out of ten when they see this book, they'll send my ass to spring training in Arizona. Fleig, Feeney, Bowie Kuhn, they're going to get me. I'm not going to get a day off next season. They'll be sending me all over the fucking country doing exhibition games, but I'll tell ya, I don't give a shit. It's about time people find out what umpires go through."

When every bar and private club had closed from one end of the city to another, and the dawn was beginning to glow, we would stop somewhere and have breakfast. Then Wendelstedt would return to his hotel room and sleep through the rest of the day while I, in my room, would confront my typewriter with my notes. At ten thirty I would meet Harvey for breakfast. At noon, I would attempt to catch a few hours' sleep. I could always count on seeing each of the umpires at certain places at the exact same time. Like Harvey, who never misses ten-thirty breakfast. Umpires thrive on schedules and rely on certain habits the way Linus needs his blanket. That's their way of passing through all of that dull and deadly time.

There came the day at Shea Stadium, the second to last game of the season, when Harvey, Wendelstedt, Williams (and perhaps even Dale) shared a moment of closeness.

Unbeknownst to Met management, National League umpires had been feeding and caring for two kittens in the umpires' room. Responsibility for the kittens was passed on to each crew moving into New York through the final days of the year. The kittens were gray and fuzzy; caterpillar-like, they crawled and wriggled, clawing at tables, towels and clothes, and Harvey, Wendelstedt, Williams and Dale were watching them closely. They danced from Wendelstedt's arms to Dale's legs to Williams's lap to Harvey's shoulder, pausing briefly to be fondled by each new set of hands.

At first, the umps weren't actually laughing, but their faces glowed with pleasure. Simultaneously, unconsciously, they moved closer together, each man lightly touching another so that the kittens had an unbroken chain of arms and laps and shoulders to travel. The four men giggled, grinned, then finally they started laughing, increasing the pace, bouncing the kittens back and forth from man to man.

Suddenly they stopped. Without looking at each other, they realized they were touching, and that real men, good, old-fashioned, down-home, American men, weren't supposed to touch, that it was wrong to touch. And then, on the same abbreviated beat, they parted, sidling back to their own corners and cubbyholes, assuming their practiced impersonal detachment. But I felt it for a split second and I'm sure they felt it, too, a brief spiritual and physical intimacy.

I remember. I did not feel isolated or abandoned. From the start it was clear that I was not a part—could never be an *integral* part —of their world of balls, bats, tobacco juice and sun-baked dust. A stranger, I had been welcomed into their world, tolerated politely, permitted to observe and record, but never to share.

I was a horse blanket amoung four men in blue.

November 26, 1974
Pittsburgh, Pennsylvania

LEE GUTKIND, founder and editor of the popular journal *Creative Nonfiction*, has performed as a clown, scrubbed with heart and liver transplant surgeons, wandered the country on a motorcycle, and experienced psychotherapy with a distressed family—all as research for eight books and numerous profiles and essays. His award-winning *Many Sleepless Nights*, an inside chronicle of the world of organ transplantation, has been reprinted in Italian, Korean, and Japanese editions, while his most recent nonfiction book, *An Unspoken Art*, a Book-of-the-Month-Club selection, was selected by the New York Public Library for the 1998 Books for the Teen Age Awards. Former director of the writing program at the University of Pittsburgh and currently a professor of English there, Gutkind is also the director of the Mid-Atlantic Creative Nonfiction Writers' Conference at Goucher College in Baltimore.